the Unofficial Guide™ to Divorce

Sharon Naylor

WILEY

Wiley Publishing, Inc.

Published by Wiley Publishing, Inc., Hoboken, NJ

No part of this publication may be reproduced, stored in a retrieval system or transmitted in any form or by any means, electronic, mechanical, photocopying, recording, scanning or otherwise, except as permitted under Sections 107 or 108 of the 1976 United States Copyright Act, without either the prior written permission of the Publisher, or authorization through payment of the appropriate per-copy fee to the Copyright Clearance Center, 222 Rosewood Drive, Danvers, MA 01923, (978) 750-8400, fax (978) 646-8700. Requests to the Publisher for permission should be addressed to the Legal Department, Wiley Publishing, Inc., 10475 Crosspoint Blvd., Indianapolis, IN 46256, (317) 572-3447, fax (317) 572-4447, E-Mail: permcoordinator@wiley.com.

Trademarks: Wiley, the Wiley Publishing logo, and related trade dress are trademarks or registered trademarks of John Wiley & Sons, Inc. and/or its affiliates in the United States and other countries and may not be used without written permission. All other trademarks are the property of their respective owners. Wiley Publishing, Inc., is not associated with any product or vendor mentioned in this book.

For general information on our other products and services or to obtain technical support please contact our Customer Care Department within the U.S. at 800-762-2974, outside the U.S. at 317-572-3993 or fax 317-572-4002.

Wiley also publishes its books in a variety of electronic formats. Some content that appears in print may not be available in electronic books.

Library of Congress Cataloging-in-Publication Data:

ISBN: 0-02-862455-6

Manufactured in the United States of America

10 9 8 7 6 5

First edition

*This book is dedicated to my own divorce support system:
Joanne Blahitka, Andrew Blahitka, Karen Beyke, Steve
Blahitka, Leanne Rossi, Peanut, Greg Beyke, Madison
Beyke, Kevin Beyke, Susan Cefolo McDermott, Jill
Althouse Wood, Pamela Bishop, Susan DeLong, Laura
Schmidt, Tara Bruno, Dr. Donna Cantalupo, Elizabeth
Frost Knappman, Ed Knappman, Jessica Hartshorn,
Karen Mynatt, Joanne, Dr. David F. Romano, Laura
Romano, Dr. Sam Locatelli and his wonderful staff,
Erin, Colleen, Heather, Johanne, Annajean, Chris, Brett
Levine, Susan and Vic Gonnelli, Millie Somers, Annie
and Nick Fagone, and the Patanella Family.
My thanks and love to my wonderful friends and brothers
Mark Tolentino, Brian Perillo, Tony Bassolino,
Rob Briscoe, and Mike Patanella.
A very special thank you to Ron Farrington, the most
genuine, caring, and understanding friend I could ever
hope for. Thank you for always being there for me, and
for teaching me how to trust again.
And, especially, to Savvie.*

Acknowledgments

The author would like to thank the following people for their invaluable assistance during the writing of this book: Brett Levine, Dr. Paula Bortnichak, Karen Beyke, Jennifer Farthing, Ed Knappman, Elizabeth Frost Knappman, Chris Adamec, Lynn O'Shaughnessy, Dr. Gary Berman, Dr. Sam Locatelli, Dr. David F. Romano, Dr. Donna Cantalupo, the American Bar Association, the National Center for Health Statistics, the U.S. Census Bureau, the Internal Revenue Service, the National Organization for Women, Jersey Battered Women's Services, Inc., Divorce Care, and the many, many recently divorced and divorcing people who spoke to me about their experiences.

Contents

The *Unofficial Guide* Reader's Bill of Rights

We Give You More Than the Official Line

Welcome to the *Unofficial Guide* series of Lifestyles titles—books that deliver critical, unbiased information that other books can't or won't reveal—*the inside scoop*. Our goal is to provide you with the *most accessible, useful* information and advice possible. The recommendations we offer in these pages are not influenced by the corporate line of any organization or industry; we give you the hard facts, whether those institutions like them or not. If something is ill-advised or will cause a loss of time and/or money, we'll give you ample warning. And if it is a worthwhile option, we'll let you know that, too.

Armed and Ready

Our hand-picked authors confidently and critically report on a wide range of topics that matter to smart readers like you. Our authors are passionate about their subjects, but have distanced themselves enough from them to help you be armed and protected and help you make educated decisions as you go through your process. It is our intent that, from having read this book, you will avoid the pitfalls everyone else falls into and get it right the first time.

Don't be fooled by cheap imitations; this is the genuine article *Unofficial Guide* series from Wiley Publishing, Inc. You may be familiar with our proven track record of the travel *Unofficial Guides,* which have more than three million copies in print. Each year thousands of travelers—new and old—are armed with a brand new, fully updated edition of the flagship *Unofficial Guide to Walt Disney World,* by Bob Sehlinger. It is our intention here to provide you with the same level of objective authority that Mr. Sehlinger does in his brainchild.

The Unofficial Panel of Experts

Every work in the Lifestyle *Unofficial Guides* is intensively inspected by a team of three top professionals in their fields. These experts review the manuscript for factual accuracy, comprehensiveness, and an insider's determination as to whether the manuscript fulfills the credo in this Reader's Bill of Rights. In other words, our Panel ensures that you are, in fact, getting "the inside scoop."

Our Pledge

The authors, the editorial staff, and the Unofficial Panel of Experts assembled for *Unofficial Guides* are determined to lay out the most valuable alternatives available for our readers. This dictum means that our writers must be explicit, prescriptive, and above all, direct. We strive to be thorough and complete, but our goal is not necessarily to have the "most" or "all" of the information on a topic; this is not, after all, an encyclopedia. Our objective is to help you narrow down your options to the best of what is available, unbiased by affiliation with any industry or organization.

In each *Unofficial Guide* we give you:

- Comprehensive coverage of necessary and vital information
- Authoritative, rigidly fact-checked data
- The most up-to-date insights into trends
- Savvy, sophisticated writing that's also readable
- Sensible, applicable facts and secrets that only an insider knows

Special Features

Every book in our series offers the following six special sidebars in the margins that were devised to help you get things done cheaply, efficiently, and smartly.

1. "Timesaver"—tips and shortcuts that save you time.

2. "Moneysaver"—tips and shortcuts that save you money.

3. "Watch Out!"—more serious cautions and warnings.

4. "Bright Idea"—general tips and shortcuts to help you find an easier or smarter way to do something.

5. "Quote"—statements from real people that are intended to be prescriptive and valuable to you.

6. "Unofficially ..."—an insider's fact or anecdote.

We also recognize your need to have quick information at your fingertips, and have thus provided the following comprehensive sections at the back of the book:

1. **Glossary:** Definitions of complicated terminology and jargon.

2. **Resource Guide:** Lists of relevant agencies, associations, institutions, web sites, etc.

3. **Recommended Reading List:** Suggested titles that can help you get more in-depth information on related topics.

4. **Important Documents:** "Official" pieces of information you need to refer to, such as government forms.

5. **Important Statistics:** Facts and numbers presented at-a-glance for easy reference.

6. **Index.**

Letters, Comments, and Questions from Readers

We strive to continually improve the *Unofficial* series, and input from our readers is a valuable way for us to do that.

Many of those who have used the *Unofficial Guide* travel books write to the authors to ask questions, make comments, or share their own discoveries and lessons. For lifestyle *Unofficial Guides,* we would also appreciate all such correspondence, both positive and critical, and we will make best efforts to incorporate appropriate readers' feedback and comments in revised editions of this work.

How to write to us:
Unofficial Guides
Attention: Reader's Comments
Wiley Publishing, Inc.
111 River Street
Hoboken, NJ 07030

The *Unofficial Guide* Panel of Experts

The *Unofficial Guide* editorial team recognizes that you've purchased this book with the expectation of getting the most authoritative, carefully inspected information currently available. Toward that end, on each and every title in this series, we have selected a minimum of three "official" experts comprising the "Unofficial Panel" who painstakingly review the manuscripts to ensure factual accuracy of all data; inclusion of the most up-to-date and relevant information; and that, from an insider's perspective, the authors have armed you with all the necessary facts you need—but the institutions don't want you to know.

For *The Unofficial Guide to Divorce*, we are proud to introduce the following panel of experts:

Brett Levine Mr. Levine is the managing attorney of the law firm of Levine and Levine in Florham Park, New Jersey. The firm specializes in family law and handles contested cases as well as divorce mediation. Mr. Levine conducts seminars and teaches courses pertaining to family law matters. He is appointed by the court to serve as a settlement panelist to assist other attorneys and their clients resolve contested divorce issues. He received his JD from George Washington University and his B.A., with honors, from Muhlenberg College.

Karen Marie Beyke   Ms. Beyke is a professor of International Business Law at Kennesaw State University in Georgia, and frequently lectures on the subject of family law and wills. She received her JD from Golden Gate University School of Law in San Francisco and is licensed to practice law in both California and Georgia. In addition to her teaching position, she currently works for the State Court of Cobb County, Georgia.

Paula McFadden Bortnichak, M.D.   Dr. Bortnichak received her medical degree from the University of Pennsylvania. She trained in Psychiatry and Forensic Psychiatry at Yale University. Dr. Bortnichak practices Forensic and Corporate Psychiatry in Sparta, New Jersey, where she lives with her husband and two teenage sons. She is a member of the American Academy of Psychiatry and the Law, the Academy of Occupational and Organizational Psychiatry, and the National Association of Medical Communicators.

Sara Dulaney Gilbert, M.D.   Dr. Gilbert is the author of 25 self-help and useful-service books, including *The Complete Idiot's Guide to Single Parenting, How to Live With a Single Parent* (for teenagers), and *Trouble at Home*. Sara Dulaney Gilbert has become a specialist in helping readers of all ages find their way through career changes, personal development stages, and major life events. She has also written articles on family matters and legal issues. In addition to professional familiarity with divorce and its impact, she has personal experience too: Raised by a divorced single mother, she is the divorced mother of a now-grown son. She has also worked extensively in the field of higher education and lifelong learning, and holds a Masters degree from the Graduate School of Education at New York University.

Introduction

I f you've picked up this book, then chances are pretty good that all is not roses and sunshine in your marriage. Perhaps you're separated and considering divorce. Perhaps you're shaking with anger at recent revelations about your partner's post-work activities. Or, perhaps you've had it with your partner's insensitivity and you're not going to take it anymore. Whatever the reason, if you're about to enter into divorce proceedings, you could do yourself (and your children, if you have them) no greater favor than to arm yourself with the expert advice provided in this book.

According to the U.S. Census Bureau, 50 percent of all marriages end in divorce. This year alone, 2.5 million people in this country will be involved in divorce proceedings. You are not alone.

What's in this Book?

The Unofficial Guide to Divorce provides you with the most useful and up-to-date advice on the big divorce issues, such as securing fair alimony and child support payments, discovering your spouse's hidden assets, setting up child custody and visitation, and succeeding at trial. It also provides you with valuable financial advice—not only for use during the heated money issues that crop up during negotiations, but for your future financial health. You also learn tips for stress relief and inside information on a range of special circumstances.

Within these pages, you'll find expert advice from highly esteemed divorce lawyers, family therapists, financial counselors, and medical specialists. These professionals will share with you the ins and outs of every step in the process. They're providing you with the inside scoop on the divorce process from start to finish, drawing on their own discoveries and expertise to keep you from making costly and devastating mistakes.

With the information provided, you'll learn the inside secrets to forming agreements and other legal documents. You'll also learn how to keep your head together in this stressful time so you can make those important decisions and stay on your toes at all times.

Divorce is the second-highest-ranking cause of stress after death of a loved one. But even though the emotional toll of divorce is so great, it is very important for you and for your family that you remain strong throughout the process. Your whole life has been shaken by this turn of events in your life. You're understandably experiencing a wide range of emotions, but whatever your state, you'll have to function optimally to make smart decisions. The best thing you can do is learn from the experts, avoiding costly trial and error, and get yourself through this as quickly, painlessly, and efficiently as possible. For this reason we've consulted medical specialists who have contributed advice that will help you deal with your emotions and with the very large issue of self-esteem and personal identity.

Here's a general rundown of the easy-access sections of this book:

- Preparation: Options to divorce; making key decisions; choosing an attorney; pre-filing to-dos.

- Process: The initial filing; the discovery process; what happens in court; and reaching resolution.

- Legal Issues: Division of assets; alimony; and custody.

- Coping: Surviving the ordeal; dealing with your emotions; dealing with your ex; dealing with children; and where to go for help.

- Sticky Situations: Handling spouse and family discord; problem solving tips; and dealing with special circumstances.

- Post-Divorce Financial Issues: Handling the legal, financial, and insurance issues that will arise from your divorce.

In addition to all this information, you'll find a great deal of helpful information in the back of the book. Turn there if you need to consult the glossary, resource guides (including where to go on the Internet), sample documents, and checklists, all of which have been included to help make getting through this process easier. Use these appendixes to track down helpful resources provided in your state, to look up information on legislation that helps your case, to find support groups, divorce hotlines, recommended websites, and books for further reading—everything you need to help yourself out in the many areas of the divorce process.

Throughout the book, we're going to encourage you to keep it civil—as best you can—because through civility and fair play, you're more likely to create a workable divorce settlement in as short a time as possible. Saving time, money, and frustration is the key here.

How this Book Is Different

This is not a "How I Survived My Divorce" tome. Such books may be inspiring to those who need proof that this whole terrible ordeal can be gotten through, but such books can't address all the issues you may find yourself facing because every divorce is different. This book is also not just a cut-and-dried discussion of technical terms that require you to have an advanced law degree. We're not going to talk over your head, nor are we going to scare you with lurid horror stories of non-custodial parents swiping children away to Mexico, homeless divorcees, and a life of welfare and food stamps for the jilted spouse. While we've all heard divorce-court "horror stories," the point of this book is that, with proper care and knowledge on your side, you can make this life-changing event a constructive one.

Right now you should be concentrating on figuring out just what you need to make your divorce an event that leads you toward a better future for yourself and your children. This will require that you understand the very real processes of the judicial system, and that you learn the best way to use that system to your best advantage. This book offers you that knowledge—the inside scoop on what's going on in the world of divorce law.

In addition to providing you with instruction as to the smartest steps to take at each stage of your divorce, we also encourage you to develop a sense of acceptance and optimism about your life. As a recent divorcee myself, I can assure you that the day will come when you can indeed see your life in positive terms again—and there are definite steps you can take to make that day come faster.

How to Use this Book

The book is broken down by parts: legal, financial, emotional, and so on. You can use the index to find out where you are in the process. As you go through the book, highlight helpful points that apply to you and your family and make notes in the margins. Use the worksheets provided to help analyze your situation and make a new plan for your life. Jot down the questions you want to ask your lawyer or your therapist. One piece of advice we'll give you right now: During this stressful period, it's best to leave nothing to memory.

In addition, we strongly suggest you get yourself a big spiral notebook, and use it to record any of your questions, notes, appointments, and reminders. Vow to write all of your divorce information in that notebook, so that you're never looking for the cocktail napkin on which you wrote down the number of that child advocate.

Think of this book as a wise and trusted friend who has been through it all before you. All of the experts we've consulted are the tops in their fields, and their advice—gleaned from the sum of their expertise and their inside knowledge of the legal system—is sure to be of great value to you. Best of all, they're not charging you their regular hourly rates!

How to Be a Savvy Consumer

What does being a consumer have to do with divorce? Everything. Think about what being a "good consumer" means. It means shopping around for the highest quality at the best price, making the most of your money. This is as true when you shop around for a lawyer or a marriage counselor as it would be if you were shopping around for a car.

The rules of smart shopping include analyzing your options for their advantages, assessing disadvantages, checking past performance and reliability, and making smart money choices. You should research the credentials of your legal and financial advisors at least as carefully as you would look up a new car's ratings in *Consumer Reports*. To check the credentials of the professionals you'll be consulting during the course of your divorce, you should consult your state's bar association and the professional associations of your financial advisor and/or therapist. Read on and we'll tell you how.

You can actually save money by spending a little bit more on your representation. Just as buying a cheap car can cost you more money in the long run when the car breaks down, hiring a cheap lawyer will cost you more in the long run when you have to find new representation or return to court over and over to adapt your settlement. But smart consumerism goes beyond researching professional credentials and checking prices. In order to make the most of your investment in your advisors' services, you should cooperate fully, answering all questions and delivering all requested materials and information in order to help your lawyer, therapist or financial planner to do his or her job to maximum capacity. You can get the most mileage out of your paid partnerships by being a good client.

The experts—and people who've been through the divorce process themselves—agree on the following list of savvy decision-making ideas:

- Research your options. There's no such thing as too much research, when you think of how important the outcome of this process is to you. So commit your time to the process. Since time is a commodity, think of it as investing in your future.

- Ask questions. There is no such thing as a dumb question; it's only dumb not to ask for clarification if you're confused. Remember: Your lawyer, therapist, etc., has heard every question and every comment possible. They know you're not an expert in their field, and they expect you to speak up if you're getting overwhelmed.

- Invest your time in finding the best representation possible. It makes all the difference in the world, so don't just flip open the Yellow Pages, close your eyes and point a finger to the page. The first rule of smart consumerism is choosing the highest quality "model" available.

Once you've got your professional team in place, there's still more you can do to make your divorce run as smoothly as possible:

- Take your time. Don't act on impulse or let your emotions rule your decisions.

- Don't worry about making waves. You have to do what's right for you. The easy path is not always the best path.

- Be organized and on time, so you don't waste money backtracking or re-doing finished business.

- Be realistic about what you want and deserve in your divorce agreement.

- Make sure you understand all fees, and that you keep your own careful track of what you owe. Don't just accept a bill for services if you aren't sure what it is that you're paying for.

- Be open to advice from experts, but think for yourself. If something your advisor tells you to do seems unethical or unfair, follow your gut instinct. Remember, this is your case.

- Keep in mind: Winning is not the ultimate goal. It's securing what you rightly need to go on.

- Be *proactive!* Learn about the rules and the paperwork, every term applicable. Don't just sign what's put before you.

How to Keep Your Sanity During the Process

As mentioned earlier, divorce is the second biggest cause of stress that you are likely to face in your lifetime. Only the death of a loved one ranks higher. Divorce hits you hard on every level: emotionally, financially, physically, and socially. You may feel like your entire world has been shaken up, like you've been torn in half. And you're not alone in these feelings—just look at what some recent veterans of the divorce process have to say:

Jake: "I was so out of it in the initial phase of filing for divorce that I didn't even know what my assets were. My lawyer had to ask me if I had a car."

Lila: "I was not very quick on the uptake when my ex-husband was leaving home. I very foolishly let him take some valuables from our home that I had to fight him in court to get back later."

Bryan: "It cost me a lot of money to change and add things to my initial divorce complaint paperwork that I was too numb to remember in the first place. It wound up adding a few thousand dollars to my bill."

So you see, you can't let the stress make you take to your bed, zombie-like or allow yourself to be eaten up by the fear, insecurity, guilt, and anger that is the natural damage caused by divorce. After all, what good does that do you? What do you gain by lying in bed with the shades drawn, scarfing your way through a box of Mallomars and watching sad movies (or worse . . . your wedding video!). Allowing yourself to sink into despair or depression is only going to hurt your abilities to protect yourself and your children in the settling of the divorce case.

To get through this process, you're going to have to find a way to calm your nerves, keep your wits about you, and think straight. This is when having a good support system is extremely valuable—not one of our divorced experts made it through his or her own situation without the help of family, friends, and support groups. All of them emphasize—and we'll cover this in greater detail in the "Coping" section—that you have to recognize your value as an individual, not just as part of a married couple, and you have to look at this whole experience as a new beginning, not a devastating ending.

You owe it to yourself to tackle this project for your own well-being and your children's well-being. Done well, it can be the dawn of a new era in your life, one in which you are in control of your own happiness and well-being.

And now, get ready to learn everything you need to know to make it through your divorce successfully. With *The Unofficial Guide to Divorce* on your side, you've gained an advantage.

Get the Lowdown on Preparation

PART I

GET THE SCOOP ON...
Preparing for the split ▪ Marital counseling,
separation, postponement ▪
Soul searching ▪ Changing your mind

Is Divorce Your Only Option?

The foundation of any marriage is the human connection—the bond that is formed between two people who have chosen to share their love and their lives. There are many ways in which you and your spouse connect—physically, mentally, emotionally, spiritually, and functionally. But if you reach the point where you feel you're losing—or have lost—that human connection—that's where trouble arises in a marriage. Your communication may be gone; the joy of spending time together has diminished. Perhaps your sex life is suffering. It was the very concept of connection that bound you together, and it is the breaking of this connection that tears you apart.

The breakdown of a relationship can happen for all sorts of reasons, and in the heat of an angry argument or during a period of high stress it is easy to leap to the conclusion that divorce is the answer. And it may well be true—but before you start filing your divorce complaint it's important to look at the big picture. Have you thought this through? Do all of your problems, all the things that have gotten on your nerves over the years, all your spouse's wrong-doings, add up to the end of your marriage? Take the time to consider what you really want and need before you enter into the grueling process of divorce. In this chapter you'll learn about resources and options available to couples who want to make certain that they have tried all avenues before giving up on a marriage.

Deciding to decide

Watch Out!
When you consider the possibility of ending your marriage, you face the realities of divorce for the first time. Perhaps the specter of such a reality will be enough to give you both some perspective on your troubles. Maybe you'll discover a shred of hope that your problems can be solved, thereby avoiding the dissolution of your marriage.

Only you can decide if divorce is your best, or only, option right now. Of course, you may wish to seek the aid of counselors, clergy, friends, and family when making this decision, but before you begin the divorce process, you should be fully comfortable that this is the right decision for you.

Except on very rare occasions, a court will easily grant you a divorce, if you decide that this is what you want. It is important to understand that it is not the court's job, nor your lawyer's, to decide *whether or not* you should seek a divorce. Instead, your lawyer's job is to make you aware of all the legal consequences of your divorce and to help guide you through the process. And the court's job is to make certain that all legal requirements are met before officially granting the divorce. A good divorce lawyer may provide you with moral support, but he or she will focus chiefly on the legal protections you require to best raise your children, or to support yourself after the divorce is final. Your lawyer can tell you that, in her experience, your reasons for divorce are valid and meet the requirements of the law; however, the final decision is very personal and should not be made solely upon the basis of legal considerations.

There *are* options to divorce

In the extreme cases of abuse or adultery, your best option is, of course, to simply end the connection. These are special cases and need to be handled carefully—particularly situations in which violence or abuse has occurred. In Part 5 you'll learn about some of the special concerns raised by domestic violence, and you'll find some important tips and advice on how to make certain that you and any children you may have are protected. In less drastic situations—where the problems have more to do with a couple growing apart or losing sight of what once bound them together—the sign of a mature relationship, and of mature individuals within the relationship, is a willingness to put some effort into evaluating the problems and trying to save the partnership. So, even if right now you're pretty sure that divorce is the only way to go, it may still be a good idea to give some of your other options a little thought. You have several to choose from, including marital counseling, separation, and postponement. Some couples try each option. They recognize the value of their marriage and of keeping their family intact, and they really do want to work out their problems. In such cases, and especially if there are children in the marriage, the first step is to explore the possibility of working together to reconcile your differences—in short, it's time to give marital counseling a try.

Bright Idea
Focus at this time on pure communication. Really work to discover the root of your problems and to understand why that fundamental connection between you and your spouse has been weakened or severed.

Marital counseling

As mentioned, the human connection between partners is the very heart of a marriage. When it breaks down, couples might need help to reconnect. Often, the first step in achieving this is to turn to counseling. You might choose a psychiatrist, a psychologist, or a religious counselor who has been trained to guide you through the basic steps of communication. But, particularly if you have not yet initiated action for a divorce, you'll have to take the initiative yourself. Although a court might demand that you and your spouse attend parenting- or family-type counseling in divorce cases involving children, no court will force you or your partner to go to pre-divorce marital counseling. When it comes to going to counseling to work out the problems of your marriage, it's up to you to get it done.

What's going on here?

If you've never gone to counseling or therapy before, you may be curious as to just what you'll be facing in marital counseling. It need not be intimidating, if you know the reasons why things are done—so here's the general flow of events. On your first visit to the qualified and licensed therapist of your choice you will be asked some basic questions about your situation—after all, the therapist doesn't know you or the circumstances that led to your marital problems. The counselor needs to get a general idea of what he or she is dealing with in order to give you the best level of help.

If, on the strength of your first meeting, your therapist can determine that you and your spouse are not actively fighting, that rather, the two of you simply agree that there are areas of strain and uncertainty in your marriage, the therapist can assume that counseling sessions will be good-natured and without conflict. You come to the sessions as two people who care about each other who have discovered that you need a third-party opinion and a nudge in the right direction. In such cases the

Watch Out!
Once divorce papers are filed, the court typically only considers the legal requirements, and rarely takes into account prior attempts to reconcile. In other words, from a legal standpoint there is really no right or wrong party, and the private decision to attempt pre-divorce marital counseling generally will not affect a later decision by the court.

therapist will develop a counseling approach that best suits these circumstances. On the other hand, if you and your spouse are at each other's throats, or if there are big issues of anger and hurt feelings within the marriage, your therapist will no doubt have to adopt a different approach, one that will effectively address your areas of conflict, and help you to discover ways to resolve them.

Your therapist's questions may surprise you— some of them may seem to have little or nothing to do with your immediate problems. But there is a reason for all these questions. For example, your therapist may ask you questions about how you and your spouse met: Did you have a whirlwind courtship? That might mean you didn't know each other fully before you decided to get married. Did you marry because you had to, or because you wanted to? Your answer may disclose sources of hostility you never acknowledged before. The counselor may also ask about how well the two of you communicated during the earlier stages of your marriage. Maybe some of today's issues were always present, but were ignored when you were in the first blush of romance. In addition, the counselor may want to know about your relationship with your in-laws. If this relationship is troubled, maybe it's setting up conflicts of loyalty for you or your spouse.

Many people get frustrated with these kinds of questions. They want to get right to the heart of their present problems, so to speak, and they don't see the point in talking about their first date. Indeed, it is hard for a couple to stick with it while the therapist gathers this important background information. But your therapist knows that the couple you are now has evolved from the couple you

Moneysaver
For your therapist, background data about your parents' marriage, your dating relationship, and the like is crucial to understanding the foundations of your marriage. Cut down on the time spent on this by writing a basic outline of your history as a couple before you go to counseling. Such a list can shave two to four sessions off your total, which can save you several hundred dollars.

were then, and the problems you have now evolved from the kinds of problems you may have had then.

Patterns, patterns

Early in her marital counseling sessions, my friend Linda was surprised when the therapist asked about one of her old boyfriends, Pete. She'd been with him for six years before they broke up, after which time she eventually met and married her current husband. When Linda talked about the relationship with her old boyfriend, the therapist discovered that Linda had been very dependent on Pete, which led Pete to feel smothered and, in turn, caused Linda and Pete to break up. It's no surprise, then, that Linda's husband was currently complaining of feeling smothered as well. This revelation gave the therapist a starting point—an issue that Linda and her husband could now begin to address.

We all develop our styles of relating from the patterns we've seen, or followed, in the past. This fact, which a good therapist well knows, is something that counseling helps us to discover for ourselves. For example, your notions of what marriage should be like are very much colored by the example of marriage you grew up with. If your parents had an unhappy marriage and you grew up with fighting and verbal abuse in your home, you might be likely to repeat those patterns within your own marriage. Just as likely, you may be unwilling to have a healthy argument with your spouse because you never saw an argument between your parents turn out constructively. Understanding the role models that shaped your individual expectations of marriage can help your counselor either debunk or support the lessons you've learned through the examples within your life.

> 66
> Marriage is a system. Think of it as a machine, with you and your spouse as main working pieces of that machine. If one piece is 'broken' or not functioning right, the machine doesn't work as it should. . . . Just as you'd bring a broken machine to a repair shop, you're bringing your broken marriage to a counselor.
> —Dr. Paula Bortnichak, family therapist
> 99

You will also be asked personal questions—questions about how you perceive yourself and your place in the world as an individual. At the very core of counseling is the notion that two people come into a marriage with their own individual identities. These identities may be fairly well-adjusted or they may be insecure. By helping you deal with the pasts, beliefs, personal fears, and values held by you and your spouse, the counselor can work with you to see how the pieces fit together now, and how you can make them fit together better in the future.

It may take a few sessions, but once the necessary background information has been gathered, you and your spouse will work with the counselor to identify what is and isn't working in your marriage. This work may be done in one or more of several different ways. You may be asked to fill out detailed questionnaires. You may be given essays to write, or you might be asked to write letters to your partner. You may be given specific topics to discuss, or you may be given the floor to bring up whatever topics are most important to you at the moment. You might even be given exercises to do at home—scripts you can use to foster better communication within your home environment.

The techniques your therapist gives you may take a little time before they start to work. Don't get discouraged, however—remember, your counselor is not a magician. And, since we all generally try to be on our best behavior in front of strangers, you may not be presenting your counselor a clear view of your communication and fighting styles—at least, not at the beginning. So your therapist may not hit on the most effective techniques to recommend right away. Be prepared for the fact that it is probably going to

Timesaver
You may have seen the relationship experts on *Oprah* telling people to listen to what their spouse says, and then calmly repeat back 'I hear what you're saying . . . You're saying you don't feel appreciated.' Such exercises work for some, but they may not work for you. If a prescribed exercise is not bringing about change, call your therapist and work out another method.

take some time for you and your spouse to become comfortable enough within therapy to open up naturally. The time invested is worth it, however—after awhile you'll begin to find it easier to communicate, and thus to constructively address your problems.

When only one will go

What happens, though, when you want counseling, but your spouse refuses to go? This happens often, but before you give up on the counseling option, find out why your spouse is refusing. Here are some of the most common reasons for lack of cooperation:

- **Denial:** Your spouse thinks the problems aren't that major.
- **Defeatism:** Your spouse thinks it's too late to fix the problems.
- **Avoidance:** Your spouse is afraid to face up to what he or she is doing wrong, or is afraid that an honest discussion of problems will cause you pain.
- **Control issues:** Your spouse doesn't want an outside authority figure to tell him or her what to do. This attitude may also spring from a lack of respect for the mental health industry.
- **Economic issues:** Your spouse may be reluctant to pay for counseling.

You can't force someone to go into counseling if they don't want to—it just defeats the whole purpose. But you *can* be careful not to over-analyze your spouse's decision. You *can* stay open to other means of working on your marriage. And even if your partner won't go, you might choose to enter into counseling alone. If you do, you might at least be able to figure out what can be done on your end to help solve your marital problems. There is a danger

Watch Out!
Conflict over a spouse's refusal to go to counseling often becomes the breaking point in a marriage. One spouse interprets a partner's unwillingness to pursue this particular method as a cut-and-dry refusal to work on the marriage at all. But this may not be so. Keep things in perspective, and remember that counseling is just one way to resolve your problems.

in this, however—for while individual counseling can give you insights into your own behavior and feelings, it can't address the problems of the entire "machine." After all, the counselor is only getting your side of the story, and can't, therefore, directly help you to work on how you and your spouse interact. If your partner won't agree to work with you in counseling, then maybe you should look at your other options.

Separation

Sometimes two people get *too* close to their problems, or begin to take one another for granted. In such cases, a little distance and time spent apart might be all the two of you need to cool off and gain perspective. A short period of separation may allow the swiftly building pressure time to decrease, and a little time apart also gives both of you time to think more clearly. It puts you in your separate corners, removing you from the fray. There are two aspects to separation, however, that you should be very clear about: the personal decision to separate, and "legal separation."

Absence makes the heart grow fonder.

You *can* look at separation as a kind of "trial" divorce. During a separation, both parties have an opportunity to see what life without the other would be like. For many people, a separation comes as a relief; for others it's extremely unsettling. They miss being at home, being with their children—maybe they even miss their spouse. The old saying, "Be careful what you wish for, you just might get it" sometimes comes to haunt people during a separation, making them realize that the initial decision to live apart may have been ill-advised. These are the instances in which a temporary separation can actually help avoid getting a divorce.

On the other hand, some people use separation as a convenient escape from the responsibilities of marriage, one that even gives them permission to have relationships with other people. In such cases, separation no longer becomes a means of cooling down and getting better prepared to work on the marriage. It becomes an excuse to party.

As we've seen, separation can mean different things to different people. It's even common for some couples to shuttle back and forth between living apart and getting back together again, never really making a full commitment one way or another. For such couples, separation and reconciliation becomes a way of life.

An informal agreement to separate is very different from a "legal separation." In an informal separation, one party in the marriage may simply pack up and move out on his or her own. A legal separation involves court action. But, no matter what your reason to separate—whether it's because you and your spouse simply need a time to cool off and gain perspective or because you see this as a first step to making a more final split—you must still deal with all the practical issues that will arise once you decide to live apart. You have to make decisions about visitation with your children, payment of support and/or monthly expenses, division of assets (such as bank accounts and automobiles), payment of debt, and the division of future income. To protect your interests, you have to know where you stand not only for the time you're separated, but also in the event that you ultimately *do* get divorced.

The separation agreement

Regardless of the legal status of your separation, all resolutions or agreements arrived at by you and your spouse should be in writing and signed by both

Unofficially . . .
Some states recognize the status of "legal separation"—in which a couple separates but neither party pursues a divorce—but many states do not. Although the couple may be physically living apart, these states continue to characterize the parties as married, with the same rights and obligations they had when they were still living together.

of you. This agreement, typically known as a Settlement or Separation Agreement, will serve as the law of your separation and may eventually be used as the basis for a final divorce agreement.

A written agreement protects you, because unless you can prove to the court that your spouse did not meet his or her agreed-upon obligations, your agreements cannot be enforced. No matter how amicable you and your spouse may be at the time you separate, this may change. Without a written and signed agreement, the two of you may find yourself fighting over issues that could have been resolved as part of a fair and equitable contract. The wording of the agreement, like other official documents, can be a little formal, but don't let the "legalese" frighten you—your lawyer can take you step by step through the form, and the document will protect your interests.

Although you and your spouse no longer live together, you generally cannot financially abandon each other. For example, where alimony or child support would be applicable in the event of a divorce, this type of support should also be paid during a separation.

Similarly, the spouse who moves out still has an obligation to share in the household expenses, and each of you typically shares in the financial obligations incurred by the other. If you separate, especially in a state that does not recognize a legal separation, it is important to understand how you and your spouse plan to divide your income, assets, and liabilities—including those that arise after your separation. For example, your spouse may incur substantial credit card bills or acquire an increase in income after you separate. The two of you should address these types of issues, if possible, prior to or

> 66
> When my husband first suggested that we separate, I thought he needed a little time to get his head together and think. . . . It turns out that he just wanted a bachelor pad, and his girlfriend decorated it for him. When I called him on it, when I told him that we were still married and that we did not have an open marriage as far as I was concerned, he said 'But we were on a break.'
> —Katie, recently divorced
> 99

in conjunction with the separation. A separation agreement will allow you to petition the court for relief in the event that your spouse fails to abide by its terms. Without a written agreement, you will be hard-pressed to enforce what you believed to be an understanding between you and your spouse. For example, should your spouse refuse to contribute toward agreed-upon mortgage payments as set out in your agreement, you may turn to the court for enforcement. Be aware that even when a separation begins amicably, circumstances can change. It is therefore best to anticipate, and forestall, potential problems by having the terms of your separation spelled out in writing.

You've got work to do

You'll need to lay some ground rules, so that the terms of your separation are consistent with both your needs and the needs of your spouse. By all means, get legal advice (turn to Chapter 4 for information on how to find and hire an attorney), and draw up an official agreement on the following issues:

- Who gets custody of the children, and how is visitation to be handled?

- Who gets what personal belongings?

- How will you handle paying the mortgage, household expenses, and debts—and especially, meeting the kids' financial needs?

- What about insurance?

- What about contact between the two of you, post-separation?

- What'll you do with the mail?

This last one may strike many people as being a bit trivial, but it often becomes a real hot spot for separated couples. What happens to mail that comes in both your names? How about bills addressed to both of you? The post office may not forward third-class mail (including magazines or journals)—what should you do with those? You will want to make arrangements with your partner to have important items set aside for some sort of regularly scheduled pick up.

Reality check

Separation is never an easy time, but it can be used as a constructive tool in deciding where your marriage is going to go in the future. The time you spend apart can show how much you really want to be together. On the other hand, separation can teach you both that you really are much happier without each other. For some, that's a liberating realization, one that makes the divorce process easier to begin and endure, and so the separation has served a useful purpose. For other people, who enter into the separation thinking it is only temporary, it can come as an unexpected, and unwanted, surprise.

Is this the end?

So, you've tried counseling, and maybe even took a breather in the form of a separation, and things still aren't working out. If all efforts to re-connect with your partner are unsuccessful, it's probably time to consider the option of divorce. Don't rush yourself on this, however. This is a highly emotional decision, a huge life change that will affect everyone in your lives. Take it one step at a time. It may be best to begin with exploring the issue thoroughly—both privately and with your spouse.

The following questionnaire is designed to help you determine whether divorce is the right choice for you. The questions are intended to get you

66
. . . I really didn't miss him. I didn't miss the things he expected of me, I didn't miss his taking me for granted, his bad habits, his verbal abuse, his unwillingness to help me out around the house. His being gone for a while was enough to convince me that I'd be much happier alone.
—Kerin, recently divorced
99

thinking about what you truly want. Remember, however, that you are not the only one who may have questions about the state of your marriage. And your spouse may answer these questions differently than you. Be prepared to probe deeply, and honestly, and recognize that this is something that the two of you have a stake in.

Watch Out!
It's only natural to feel a little bitter right about now. But keep in mind that nothing is ever just black and white. While you may be angry at your spouse, he or she *does* still have some good qualities. Be willing to see the gray areas, and try to stay objective while assessing your marriage.

The answers to these questions—asked of yourself *and* of your spouse—will help clarify whether divorce is truly the best route to take. If nothing else, they will help to bring you to a deeper understanding of yourself and your needs. But, again, keep in mind that only you can make the ultimate decision that divorce is the best thing for your situation. And there are other considerations to keep in mind. Divorce will have an effect on many aspects of your life.

Because marriage—and divorce—is a two-way street, you really should check with your spouse. How does he or she feel about the issues raised by the questions in the following questionnaire? Communication is important—even in divorce. But before you bound in on your spouse with a list of soul-searching questions in hand, keep the following few ground rules in mind to keep the discussion amicable:

- Watch your timing. Don't confront your spouse when he or she is tired or stressed.

- Make an appointment with your spouse to talk. It may be as simple as "Do you have a few minutes after dinner? I have some important things to discuss with you."

- Minimize distractions. Wait until the kids go to bed. Turn off the television and turn off the phone.

PERSONAL QUESTIONS TO ASK YOURSELF AND YOUR SPOUSE:

1. How am I doing in my life? Am I content within myself?

2. What are the roles and tasks that I consider important in my life? How does my marriage affect these roles, and how would divorce affect them?

3. What gives me satisfaction? Marriage? Job? Caring for kids? Friendships?

4. Where do I want to be right now? In one year? In five years?

5. Are the conditions and needs of my marriage holding me back from what I need? Would divorce move me closer to, or further away from, fulfilling those needs?

6. Are the problems in the marriage fixable, or are they beyond my control?

7. Is there an outside influence that is affecting our marriage that can be eliminated?

8. Can I openly share my frustrations with my partner? If not, why not?

9. Can I forgive my partner for what I perceive to be his or her wrong-doings?

- Pick a neutral location. You might want to get out of the house for this and talk over dinner.

- Really listen to what your partner says; keep an open mind and don't interrupt.

Because this conversation may be the first time you or your spouse has openly admitted to dissatisfaction in your marriage, there is an inherent risk that the responses you receive may come as a shock. But it's generally better to be completely honest now than to let resentments and anger simmer below the surface. By beginning the discussion of divorce in this way, you minimize the possibility of resentments and confrontation further down the road.

Changing your mind

We've said it before—the decision to divorce is a highly emotional one, and one that will affect your whole future. But take things one step at a time. It's always possible to put the brakes on, even after you've begun the process of a separation or divorce. If necessary, you always have the option of postponement.

Maybe you need a bit of time and reflection to make the right choice. Or, if you or your partner are going through some rough life events (a family member might be ill, or there's been a death in the family, or one of you has just lost a job), maybe the stress arising from these outside events is all that is causing your current marital distress. Such ups and downs of life may coincide with a time of marital discord, and the resulting turmoil may be all-consuming. If this is true, dealing with your marriage may just have to wait until you're both a little more coherent, a little less emotional, and a little better able to think clearly.

If you're going to put off making a final decision right now, you'll still have to deal with the underlying issues of unhappiness in your marriage. Since you'll be getting back together, you'll need to find a way to coexist. Here are some tips to make this possible:

1. Don't pretend there are no problems. Deal with issues in a constructive and communicative way.

2. Have a definite length of time for the postponement. Don't leave things hanging indefinitely.

3. Notify your counselor or lawyer of this development so they know what they're working with and what your status is.

4. Notify your friends and family that you're postponing your decision. Even well-meaning friends and relatives, if uninformed, can escalate tensions between the two of you and push you out of postponement into finalization.

5. Notify your children of the postponement. They have a right to know what's going on.

6. Use this time to think, to measure the depth of your problems, or to see the good in your spouse and in your marriage. This thinking, of course, may deepen your commitment to divorce, but it is honest consideration, a mature handling of the realities of your partnership.

Bright Idea
The decision to end your marriage should never be made in the midst of a larger tragedy or upheaval in the family. Couples with larger problems in their lives often transfer their emotions, fears, and frustrations onto their partner. If you're dealing with a family crisis, put off decisions about your marriage until the smoke has cleared.

Even if the divorce process has already begun, if it doesn't feel right, you still have choices. Don't despair. People do cancel their divorce proceedings. The gravity of the process is sometimes enough to convince them that their problems are not insurmountable. Just talk to your lawyer. If your case has reached the filing stage, your lawyers will contact the judge and inform the court of the new situation. Depending on where you live, you may have to fill out forms stating your reconciliation for the record, but otherwise you'll be free to go home and work on your marriage.

Watch Out!
Keep in mind that although you may change your mind after filing divorce papers—especially if you did it as a threat or an impulsive act—your spouse may not have a similar change of heart. If you find yourself in this situation, your only recourse is to talk to your spouse and perhaps get counseling for the two of you.

Of course, a fair amount of counseling is always going to be recommended to help patch up the damage that may have occurred during the divorce—perhaps your lawyers can recommend a good marital counselor. What's important to know is that the process can be stopped, if necessary, right up until the final court date.

Looking ahead

It happens, however, that no matter how hard a couple tries, they still find that they can't work things out and a divorce becomes the only answer to their problems. If this is true for you, then read on. In upcoming chapters you will learn that a divorce does not have to be destructive—in fact, it can be the beginning of a new and better life for yourself, your spouse, and your children. In the next chapter you'll learn just what it takes to set up a "successful" divorce—one in which you can avoid destructive behaviors and confrontations. Then you'll learn what you need to do to get your affairs in order so that you can protect your interests, what to look for in an attorney, and how to effectively participate in your own divorce.

Just the facts

- The decision to divorce is one that will affect all aspects of your life—it should never be taken lightly.

- Consider marital counseling if you're not yet certain that divorce is the answer.

- A separation, wisely used, provides the opportunity to cool off for a while and gain some perspective on your marriage.

- At every stage of the divorce process you have the option to slow down—divorces can be postponed or even canceled.

GET THE SCOOP ON...
Breaking the news ▪ Setting priorities
and goals ▪ The elements of
a successful divorce

Chapter 2

Setting Up a Successful Divorce: The First Steps

A successful divorce—it seems like a contradiction in terms, doesn't it? How can a divorce be successful? But if you look at the process as a constructive act rather than a grim ending, the idea of "success" begins to make sense. Divorce is, after all, an organized process designed to provide a fair resolution to your marital problems and to ensure a fair level of support and security for yourself and your children. A successful divorce, then, is one that reaches an equitable agreement that protects the interests of all parties involved.

You might not be ready to think about your divorce in a businesslike way right now. Chances are, you're still reeling from the shock of this new situation in your life. The idea of treating it like a calm, cool, business dealing might be a bit too much to ask of you at this time. However, you'll soon start to see that although working toward a successful divorce takes many steps, in the end it really can be

a constructive process. In this chapter you will learn
how to make your divorce a positive life change.

You have to start somewhere

Once you decide that divorce is the only way to go,
your first step in the process is to ask yourself some
key questions. What do you want out of this divorce?
What's most important to you? The answers to these
questions will create the foundation of your divorce.
Before you even think of calling a lawyer, do a bit of
thinking first. Organize your thoughts so that when
you do speak to a lawyer you have something concrete to present. In the following sections, we'll discuss some of the issues you'll want to consider.

Establish your priorities

Start by getting your priorities in check. If you have
children, your most important decisions will be
determining what's best for them. Throughout the
entire divorce process, they should always be your
main concern. Ask yourself these questions: Who
will the children be better off with? How much child
support should be established to adequately provide
for them? What kind of custody agreement would
best suit their needs? If you make your decisions
with the children's well-being in mind, then your
priorities will fall into line.

If you do not have children, then your main concern should be to secure a fair settlement for yourself—one that will allow you to conduct your new
life with some sense of security. You'll need enough
money to live on, you'll need a place to live, and
you'll need adequate means by which to support
yourself. As you'll see throughout this book, divorce
settlements are intended to provide both of the
divorcing parties with the means for self-reliance

and financial survival, post-divorce. The court attempts to shape its decisions based on considerations of fairness and true need. So forget about all those media stories of spectacular settlements—a successful divorce is *not* about "winning."

What you want to avoid is an unrealistic expectation—either positive or negative—of what is owed to you for your contributions to the marriage. At the outset of a divorce, it is common for many divorcing partners to fear that their personal contribution to the marriage will be devalued. There is, for example, no dollar value attached to running a home. How, then, do you fairly determine a proper settlement? We'll discuss these issues in greater depth in Chapters 7 and 8, but until then here are a few steps you can take to get a sense of where you stand. Perhaps the best place to start is to make a simple list like the one provided below.

Sample contributions list:

1. I paid half of his law school tuition.

2. I helped him study for the bar.

3. I'm the president of his firm's Wives' Club.

4. I maintain his wardrobe by bringing his suits to the cleaners.

5. I prepare dinner parties for his bosses and partners.

6. I take care of all of the household accounts: paying the bills, arranging for maintenance and repairs, and keeping the house presentable when clients come over.

Believe it or not, you should also take into consideration what is fair for your ex. At this point in your life bitterness or anger may be running strong,

Watch Out!
Do not allow your initial assessments to be colored by the presence of an "I'll get you" mentality.

but your best-made decisions, now and later, will be realistic ones. Remember, the goal here is to create a *successful* divorce, so fairness should be your watchword at all times.

Begin with a plan

Bright Idea
Just as you created a list to assess your own contributions to your marriage, make a separate one outlining your spouse's. Be objective and honest. Seeing this list on paper will help you acknowledge your partner's true contributions, and that will help you accept that he or she is deserving of some consideration in the divorce settlement.

Having the right priorities from the outset will help you create a fair and realistic list of goals, so you can decide what you want out of the divorce. It's never too early to get organized. Making a list is always a good way to keep yourself on track. The following questions will help you draw up a complete list of your goals, and it is this list that will help you and your lawyer create your divorce agreement:

1. Do you want full custody of the kids, or would you consider joint custody?

2. Do you want to keep the house?

3. Do you require alimony from your spouse? What amount?

4. What other financial assistance do you think you'll need? Child support? Continued insurance coverage for the kids? Help paying school tuition?

5. Which physical assets do you want to keep and which are you willing to let go to your spouse?

6. Which financial assets (IRAs, stocks, other investments) do you want?

7. Will you maintain a share of a jointly owned business? If so, how do you want to handle working together after the divorce?

Take your time in putting this list together—put some real thought into it. It's what your lawyer will work with when he or she starts to build your case. Lawyers look for basic elements within the divorce:

Will they be dealing with child custody issues? Alimony issues? Are there business dealings that have to be divided?

But as we've tried to emphasize from the start, marriage—and divorce—is ultimately about the connection between people. When you first think about divorce, your focus is on you and your spouse, but there are many other people who will be affected by the actions you are about to take. In the next section, we'll be looking at how to deal with them.

Breaking the news

Now that you've explored the issues and decided that divorce is the right thing for you to do, it's time to consider all the other people whose lives will be touched—this is, after all, not just between you and your spouse. Children, especially, deserve to know what's going on, but others may need to be told as well. How you handle telling them will have a major impact on the "successfulness" of your divorce.

Telling the kids

While breaking the news of divorce to children is never a pleasant task, there are ways that you and your spouse can present the news of your impending split in a comforting and supportive way. Keep the following tips in mind:

1. Before you approach your children, you and your spouse should privately discuss what you are going to say, how you are going to say it, and how you will handle the children's reactions. Having a script will make the process much easier than going in unprepared.

2. Before you speak to the children, it is a good idea to already have some of the details of the divorce worked out, particularly those that

Moneysaver
If you take the time to create a list of goals *before* you visit your lawyer, you will not have to pay for the time your lawyer would otherwise spend recording your thoughts in his or her office. Better to do it on your own time, beforehand, so you're ready with a workable outline.

directly relate to the children. For instance, you might be able to quell the children's fears about where they'll live if you can tell them right away that you'll both be sharing custody, or that they'll be spending weekends at Dad's new place from now on.

3. Tell the children together, if possible. This lets them know that you have made this decision together, that you've thought it out fully, and that you're both committed to the decision. This simple shared act makes it clear to them that you are serious about the divorce and may help them avoid feelings of divided loyalties.

4. Do not assume that your child knows the reasons for the divorce. He or she may not have witnessed any of your arguments. It's important to spell out the fact that you cannot get along anymore—especially because children are likely to assume that the divorce is their fault.

5. Expect interruptions, and allow the child to ask questions as they arise.

6. You and your spouse should agree to be respectful to one another during this discussion. If only for this one meeting, you should present a united front.

7. Know that children read the underlying messages. They're going to be watching your body language, listening for sarcastic tones, and interpreting so much more than the words you're saying.

8. Be honest. While full disclosure, especially in the case of adultery, is not always a good idea, it is always in the child's best interest to provide the truth. Telling lies or half-truths at this point

undermines your credibility and your child's trust in you.

9. Do not promise things you can't deliver. If your child asks about issues you haven't yet resolved, don't pretend you know the answer. Simply promise that you'll provide the answer once the issue has been decided.

10. Be ready for tears. The children may react out of surprise or fear, and crying is a common result. Be quick to hold them and provide comfort.

Children's first reactions to the news of divorce commonly take one of the following forms:

■ We can't let this happen.

■ There has to be something you can do.

■ What are we going to do?

But kids can come up with some surprising reactions—here's a few, reported by real parents:

■ I knew this was going to happen.

■ I thought this only happened to other families.

■ What are my friends going to say?

■ Do Grandma and Grandpa know?

■ How could you do this to me?

The experts agree that the one thing kids need at this time is your support. Start by assuring them that they are not losing their parents. Tell them that although you and your spouse are not going to be married anymore, both of you are still their parents. You still love them, and that will never change. Make it clear that parents don't divorce their kids. This is an important issue for kids. They take things personally, wondering what they will lose in this

> **"**
> Remember this: no matter what the situation, no matter what your child's response: Kids are not adults. They'll have their own set of emotional reactions, and from that perspective, they may not agree that a divorce is the right thing to do.
> —Dr. Paula Bortnichak, family therapist.
> **"**

situation. Spell it out for them—they won't lose the love of their parents—and take that pressure off their young shoulders.

Remember also that, no matter their age, the children will still need the chance to speak their minds. Give them the time and opportunity to talk about their feelings, their fears, and their concerns. Kids can't always defer their questions until the most convenient time; they ask them as they come up. So allow them the freedom to come to you at any time for discussions. Remember to listen to them. Realize that your kids are upset and frightened. They're trying to sort out this complicated issue just like you are.

You will undoubtedly see that your child is really struggling with putting his feelings into words. It will become quite clear that your child wants to talk it out, but just doesn't know how. At this time, you need to know what to say to get your child through this. It may help for you to talk to a therapist about how to improve communications with your child. A therapist who is well-versed in how children think may be able to give you some useful insight. At the very least, he or she might be able to give you some specific wording for opening up a dialogue.

If your child is not functioning well in the aftermath of your initial conversation on the subject, and later conversations don't seem to be helping, you might need to seek outside help for them. Look for these signs in your kids to determine whether further help is needed:

- **Personality changes.** For example, your once outgoing child becomes withdrawn, moody, and irritable.

Watch Out!
Thirty percent of American children are in therapy by the time they reach the age of seven. The majority of these children come from divorced families.

- **Loss of interest.** Your child no longer enjoys the things he once loved doing, like a favorite sport or hobby.

- **Withdrawal.** Your child spends more time alone.

- **Mood swings.** Your child cries easily or more often.

- **Disrupted eating habits.** Your child is not eating, or he's bingeing.

- **Changes in sleep patterns.** Your child is either sleeping too much or too little.

These are serious signs that you should get some outside help for your children. No matter how much you try to let them talk things through with you, your children may feel that they can't because they don't want to upset you. A qualified third party may be just the outlet they need to get it all out. Explain that going to a counselor doesn't mean they're crazy. Kids worry about such stigmas. Say instead that this is just an expert who might be able to help them sort out their feelings.

A therapist is not the only outside source of support available to your children. There are many people in a child's life—older, trusted relatives; teachers; religious leaders; instructors; even their own friends.

Your children won't be the only ones in their class to experience divorce. They've heard friends talk about the subject, so they most likely have someone their own age who they can talk to about the divorce. Perhaps your child spends a lot of time at a friend's house, and that friend's parents are divorced. Your child learns by observation of his friend's life that the problem is not insurmountable. His friend may even open his eyes to the benefits:

Unofficially . . .
Thirty-eight percent of all children born in the mid-1980s will experience divorce within their homes.

Bright Idea
As with all kids, some can be little demons. To make sure your kid's same-age advisor is feeding him good and helpful information—not tips on "how to make your parents pay for doing this to you"—make yourself available for heart-to-hearts with your kids on a regular basis.

no more fighting between the parents, having two rooms—one at Mom's and one at Dad's, and so on.

Quite clearly, if your children have close friends they can turn to for support or distraction, it actually helps them to cope better with the divorce. A good friend will talk about his or her own experience and will share the feelings and fears he or she had. In listening, your child learns that his own feelings and fears are normal, and that he too will eventually get used to it like his friends did.

Talking to your parents

It may be hard to tell your parents that you're getting out of your marriage. They, and the rest of your family, are likely to react strongly to the news. Their reaction may be shock or disbelief—or, in the case of abuse or adultery, they may be thrilled that you finally took the step to dump your undesirable spouse. It may help to deal with some of the family reactions you face if you realize where they're coming from.

Most of our parents grew up in an era when divorce was uncommon—maybe even unheard of. The older generations married "for better or worse," and they meant it. They were conditioned to put up with the problems of marriage, and they had a much stronger adherence to traditionally defined gender roles. Fewer women worked outside the home, and the men "ruled the household." Sure, these are old-fashioned notions to some, but these attitudes might influence your parents' reaction to your news of divorce.

If your parents find it hard to accept your divorce, it may have to do with their current status. Maybe they're older. Maybe they're sick or disabled. Up until now, they may have depended on you;

perhaps they were even counting on you—safely married and in a stable home—to care for them in their old age. Having been accustomed to seeing you as being part of a "stable marriage," they may have trouble understanding that your problems cannot be worked out.

And, after all, they *are* your parents. No doubt they're worried about you as well. Will you ever marry again? Will you ever find someone to love you and care for you?

Your parents may also be experiencing a sense of failure. Not *your* failure, though that's what you might expect, but *theirs*. They may very well be asking themselves if this is their fault—if they failed to teach you how to make a marriage work or to persevere. Then again, if your own parents are divorced, they may find it a little easier to accept your decision. They know what it's like to be in a marriage that isn't working. They know how ending it can sometimes be the only answer.

Don't be surprised by any response you get. People don't always know how to express their feelings, especially when faced with something as difficult as a divorce. Remember, if you've been married for any length of time your family has no doubt learned to care for your soon-to-be ex. A friend of mine told me that when her husband left her, her father went into a deep depression, mourning the loss as if her husband had left *him*. My friend's father loved her husband like a son, and losing that son was very hard on him.

Whatever their reaction to the news, remember that your parents know how to push your buttons, perhaps without even meaning to. Having a rational and conclusive discussion about the divorce with

I come from a long line of women who took their cheating spouses back over and over. While I did the right thing in getting a divorce, my mother and grandmother continued to say I should have taken him back.
—Shea, recently divorced

Bright Idea
If your parents insist on involving themselves inappropriately in your divorce, you'd be best advised to find a different confidante. Try a support group. The perspective of objective third parties whose judgments are not colored by knowing you personally all your life could be helpful.

your parents is probably going to take some work. You'll need to convince them that you have thought this through, that the marriage just was not working, even though you made every effort, and that the only solution was to end it. Here are a few tips to make it a little easier to talk with your parents about the divorce:

- Keep the messy or humiliating details to yourself, however much you might be tempted to divulge the intimate details of the dissolution of your marriage.

- Rule out all intrusive discussion. It's good for you to talk with your parents, but you should maintain some boundaries. Make it clear that some questions are off-limits. Some concerned parents can be pushy, wanting—out of concern for you—to dig in and find out everything. Just say "I don't feel like talking about this right now."

- Keep the negative talk about your spouse to a minimum, especially if you have children who will remain in contact with your spouse. Your parents don't need to hear you slam your ex, because that will only make them worry about the children when they see him.

- Remember that your parents love you and want the best for you.

Telling siblings

Breaking the news to your siblings is going to be difficult as well. While they may not have the same hang-ups as your parents, they will have strong reactions of their own. Again, they may feel relief that you're dumping an abusive spouse, but they also might feel uneasy.

Your change of identity affects them. They want to comfort you and support you, but your new status shakes them up a little. How will this affect Mom and Dad, they may worry. What about family parties? What about the kids? The entire makeup of your family changes, especially if you're the first member of the family to divorce. They may not know how to react to you. It will just take time for them to get used to the idea, and then you'll be back to your normal sibling squabbles. Some things never change.

In most cases, your siblings will become your strongest support system. They've known you all your life, and they're likely to be protective of you during difficult times. Lean on your sisters and brothers, just as you'd want them to lean on you during their roughest moments.

Some of your family's reactions may surprise you. You might be taken aback at the level of your family's anger. A friend of mine reports that a member of her family offered to have her ex beaten up. Other recently divorced people report similar reactions from siblings—loved ones promising to get the ex fired from a job or threatening to call the IRS. The desire for retribution is often strong among those who feel protective of and loyal to you.

You're also likely to be in for some surprising revelations. Now that your marriage is ending, everyone is free to tell you what they really thought of your ex. You may hear stories about things your ex did or said that no one ever told you about. These stories can be unsettling. But don't get upset at your family. Know that they're only trying to support you in your decision, or trying to make you feel better about leaving—or having been left.

Watch Out!
Don't encourage your siblings in their more extreme expressions of loyalty. That only creates new problems, and any act of retribution can only backfire and hurt you later, during the divorce itself.

Finally, don't be surprised at unexpected generosity. Siblings may offer to give financial advice or help with the house and kids, or even offer to help out with divorce-related expenses.

Spreading the news

You're going to have to break the news to everyone you know eventually—your co-workers, your friends, your neighbors. Sure, they may hear about it through gossip, but it would be in your best interest to handle the flow of information yourself.

Since everyone must be told sooner or later, it's a good idea to make your own contact list, and make sure it's complete. You don't want to get an anniversary card addressed to you and your ex from some well-meaning but uninformed relative. That day will be painful enough.

As you tell people, you're likely to encounter a fair amount of shock, surprise, and sympathy. Sometimes this will be uncomfortable, but take this as an opportunity to expand your support system. The people you tell may show you great love and concern, calling you often, inviting you out, offering to help in any way. Know that these reactions are genuine and take comfort in that. You have wonderful people in your life.

The elements of a successful divorce

Now that you've taken care of the preliminary business of setting priorities, developing goals, and telling your loved ones about your upcoming divorce, it's time to take one last look at the big picture. Your ultimate goal is to turn this difficult experience into a constructive life-change—to have, in other words, a "successful divorce." A successful divorce includes many elements, all of which contribute to helping

Bright Idea
If you don't want everyone to find out through family gossip, print out and mail an official announcement. The wording can be as simple as 'It is with great sadness that I must share with you the news that we are planning to end our marriage.' This saves you from having to go into great detail, and the job gets done quickly.

you reach a fair agreement with a minimum of confrontation. A successful divorce:

- Is timely and efficient—the divorce doesn't drag out for years
- Is based on open communications between parties, so that both sides are heard and understood
- Indulges no behavior that leads to an escalation of tensions
- Involves the ability, by both parties, to leave hurt feelings and anger out of the decision-making process
- Seeks a fair settlement, not retribution
- Prioritizes the right values, such as putting the children first
- Involves a certain amount of give-and-take

Taken together, all these elements contribute to a fair and equitable agreement that both sides can accept. But not all divorces work out this way. Unsuccessful divorces happen when people fall into certain common pitfalls that make an equitable and amicable settlement impossible and cause needless pain and expense. The hallmarks of an unsuccessful divorce are as follows:

- The divorce process is long and drawn-out.
- Tension and fighting are allowed to continually escalate.
- Communication is lacking between the divorcing parties.
- Retribution, not resolution, is the motivating factor.
- The children are used as pawns in the negotiations.

These elements result in an unsuccessful divorce—one that fails to achieve a fair settlement for all parties involved. Clearly, a successful divorce is far preferable to the other kind.

Looking ahead

At this point, you may feel that you're looking down a long, long road. You're about to begin your journey into a process that you may not yet fully understand. You may have preconceived notions about the divorce process, and these can sometimes be quite scary. You have lots of questions—some realistic, some not. And you no doubt have lots of concerns about not just the divorce process itself but also about how you will cope in your new, post-marriage life. We'll be discussing the actual divorce process in great detail in Part 2, and in later chapters we'll take up the issues of coping, but for the moment we'll take a brief look at what's down the road for you.

If, like many people, this is the first time you've had to cope with a divorce, you may fear that you're facing years of negotiations, a messy court battle, and unrelenting personal attacks. Or, based on what you've seen on television and in movies, you might have an unrealistic expectation that the entire affair can be cleared up in a week's time. Whatever your preconceptions, it's important to get a realistic perspective on the process of divorce so that these expectations do not scare you unnecessarily.

So, what's it *really* going to be like? The answer to this question is different for everyone. A lot depends upon the circumstances of your marriage, the number of sticky issues you'll have to deal with—such as child custody and spousal support, and the particular circumstances of your breakup. A case involving children and property is of course going to take longer and will be more difficult than a simple split between two people who have been married for a year and have no assets to divide. Your divorce, then, is going to be as unique as your marriage was.

In addition, your spouse's behavior will make a difference in how your divorce will proceed. Here you may be able to make an educated guess about how things will go. After all, you know how your soon-to-be-ex reacts and how he or she communicates. Is your spouse stubborn and vindictive, or fair and level-headed? Given the nature of divorce, the personalities of the people involved generally determine the course of the process. You probably can accurately predict what it will be like to work with your spouse on such an important issue as this, especially at a time when emotions are high. In this sense, you know more than your lawyer does. After all, you know what to expect from your spouse—it's the rest of the process that has you feeling unsure. But with this special knowledge of yours, you can at least predict with some certainty some likely outcomes.

If the two of you can agree upon the terms of your divorce, you're not likely to have to face a dramatic court trial. Instead, what you're likely to be up against are multiple negotiation meetings until you can reach a fair settlement. Your lawyers simply file the resulting settlement agreement with the court. No gavel-banging, no witnesses. We discuss the details of negotiating a settlement in Chapter 7.

The court trial is usually reserved for the extremely messy cases where the parties simply cannot reach agreement on central issues or for

Unofficially . . .
It really is best to clear your mind of expectations and fears. Instead of indulging in anticipation, choose to deal with issues and situations as they arrive.

Timesaver
In simple final hearings, the defendant does not necessarily have to show up. If you are the defendant, tell your lawyer that you choose not to attend the final hearing. Since no decisions are being made by the judge, this hearing is ultimately a formality. Many people choose to "no-show" rather than lose a day of work.

situations that involve serious charges such as abuse or adultery. Chapter 7 provides some insight into the court system and gives you some help in handling such a situation, should it become necessary. But for most divorces, there may be a required "final hearing" in court—this is something that varies from state to state. In these cases, however, such an appearance is likely to just be a formal questioning session, intended to make certain that you know what you're getting into. When this type of formal hearing is required, it is followed by the judge's signing of your papers—the whole procedure can take as little as 15 minutes. The judge will have a copy of your divorce complaint, so he or she will know about the circumstances of your divorce. You will be asked to stand before the judge and answer some basic questions to identify yourself and to declare your agreement to the divorce agreement.

One question that's probably at the top of your list is "What's this going to cost?" Unfortunately, this is one question that we can't answer with any exact figures. The cost of a divorce depends upon the scope and duration of the case, as well as the state in which the divorce is filed. But we can tell you this: It's not going to be cheap. If you think about your expenses as an investment in your future, however, they may be easier to take.

By far the biggest chunk of your expenses is going to be your lawyer's fees. Many attorneys demand several hundred dollars an hour, so as the clock ticks during your meetings and negotiations, the tab increases accordingly. But if you have excellent representation, a valiant fighter in your corner who produces the results you want, it's worth every penny. We'll take this issue up in greater detail in Chapter 4.

Time to get started

If both you and your spouse maintain communication, respect, and the right priorities throughout your divorce process, you'll find that you can create the foundation for successful, secure futures and for the protection and nurturing of your children. *These* are the goals of the successful divorce, and they should always be at the forefront of your mind as you chart your course. If you keep these basic concepts in mind as you set your priorities, you'll see that you really *can* have a successful divorce. In the next chapter, we'll deal with the first practical steps you'll need to take to prepare for the actual divorce—steps toward making sure that you, your children, and your financial well-being are protected during this interim period before you have the protection of a divorce settlement.

Just the facts

- Getting your priorities straight is the first step to a successful divorce.

- It's never too early to start forming a plan and setting your goals.

- Your children and other loved ones need to know what's going on—take care in telling them about your split.

- Keep the elements of a "successful divorce" in mind and you can make this experience a constructive one.

Watch Out!
You've heard the old expression "You get what you pay for." Don't compromise the outcome of your case by hiring a professional only on the basis of an extremely cheap fee. Trying to cut costs now could cost you even *more* money in the long run when you have to hire another attorney to get you better results down the line.

GET THE SCOOP ON...
Safety first ▪ Keeping records ▪
Protecting your financial assets ▪
Stopping short of court

Chapter 3

Before You See an Attorney

B efore you see your attorney, there are some steps you should take to protect your interests. The divorce process has not yet begun, so you are in essence out there on your own, without any of the safeguards that the legal system provides. While in this state of limbo, you'll need to be on your guard and to take action to shield yourself from getting taken advantage of or hurt in any way by your soon-to-be-ex. Your primary concerns at this point in time should be protecting yourself physically, protecting your children, protecting yourself financially, and gathering the information you'll need to protect your future. Realizing each of these goals is going to take some legwork on your part, and for now you're doing it alone. Once you've hired a lawyer, he or she can help in all of this, but right now the responsibility falls to you.

Safety first

Before you even begin to worry about anything else, you've got to give first priority to any security issues that may exist in your home. Domestic violence is a frightening reality in today's society, and if it is something that is part of your marriage, you must do all you can to protect yourself and your children. Although acts of domestic violence are often handled as a matter separate from divorce proceedings, it remains true that domestic violence is a frequent cause of, or major contributor to, divorce. So, before you think about anything else, your first concern should be to guarantee the safety of yourself and your children. If there is reason to worry about physical abuse, securing your physical safety should be priority number one. There are a number of ways to protect yourself and your children while preserving the strength of your eventual divorce case. In this chapter we'll outline a few of them, and we'll take them up again in Part 6.

If your spouse is violent, you usually have two options. You can report the violence to the court or you can report it to the police. In either case, you are turning to people who are well-trained in responding to a domestic violence complaint, and who can provide you with the guidance and protection you need.

The most typical case of domestic violence that arises as part of, or in conjunction with, a divorce is when you and your spouse still live together and he or she hits you. Should this occur, immediately contact the local police. An officer will be sent right away to your home or to wherever you are when the abuse is occurring. The first order of business is to secure your immediate physical safety, but the

officer will also be prepared to aid you in obtaining
more permanent relief. One type of assistance that
the officer may provide is helping you to file for a
temporary restraining order. A restraining order is a
court-issued ban that legally prohibits contact
between two individuals—your spouse would be
required to stay away from you, thus protecting you
from further acts of violence. In situations of active
physical abuse, the police may arrest your spouse, or
merely make arrangements to remove him or her
from the house.

Once the immediate threat of physical violence
has been dealt with by the police, the court will be
able to address the issue on a more permanent basis
and may issue a *final restraining order.* Such an order
prohibits your spouse from returning to your home.
If your spouse violates the restraining order, in all
likelihood, he or she will go to jail. In many states,
the response to violations of a restraining order is to
arrest first and ask questions later. In other words,
the court and the police will in most instances protect you to the fullest extent possible.

If your divorce or separation arises directly out
of an act of domestic violence and the subsequent
issuance of a restraining order, the court will often
grant you some immediate financial protection in
addition to securing your physical safety. This protection may include an order for child or spousal
support, pending a more detailed analysis of the situation. For example, the courts are aware that if you
and your children are financially dependent upon
an abusive spouse you may be afraid to seek legal
help because you require his or her income. In this
type of case, in addition to ordering physical
restraints on the abusive spouse, the court will order

Unofficially . . .
The most obvious
example of
domestic vio-
lence is the
physical kind:
Your spouse hits
you. Less obvious
are cases of ver-
bal abuse or
intimidation. All
these types of
domestic vio-
lence are de-
serving of court
protection.

child support or alimony to make sure that you and your children have adequate means to pay your bills.

Sometimes a violent spouse will not respect the authority of the court's restraining order. If this is the case, you may need to take further action to secure your safety. Consider changing the locks on your doors, for example. In some extreme cases, it might be wise to leave the home—in many towns and cities there are shelters that provide refuge from people seeking to escape domestic violence. We will take up the discussion of such extreme situations in greater detail in Chapter 13.

The importance of keeping records

Preliminary concerns that need to be addressed early in your decision to seek a divorce are not only concerned with physical safety, however. In the upcoming divorce process you will be looking at the prospect of deciding on custody, property division, and the allocation of responsibility for debt. As a general rule with regard to financial issues and issues involving your children, the more you can prove, the better off you will be whether you formalize your settlement agreement through your lawyers or in court. One way to guarantee that you can prove your claims is to keep detailed and accurate records. The better your record-keeping, the stronger your claims will be.

Records pertaining to the children

If you anticipate that your spouse will fight for physical custody of your children you should arm yourself with as much hard evidence as possible that will attest to your suitability as the custodial parent. The court will use this evidence in making its decision as

Bright Idea
You can seek a restraining order not only for yourself, but also on behalf of your children or other members of your family that are in fear or danger.

to who gets the children, so meticulous record-keeping and collection of data can only help your case. Here are some steps to take:

1. Begin keeping a daily record regarding all the things that need to be done in caring for your children. You will use this record should you need to demonstrate that you assume most, if not all, of these essential chores. You might find it helpful to set up this record in the form of a daily schedule that shows what needs to be done for which child at what time during the day, and which parent completed the task. It will also be useful when you come to developing a custody and visitation schedule.

2. Keep a record of disciplinary events. If you believe that your spouse uses excessive or improper discipline techniques, you should keep detailed notes of any such events that occur.

3. Keep a record of the children's schoolwork, how their grades are when they're with you, and—if you and your spouse are separated—how their grades are when they're with your spouse.

4. If you are separated, keep records regarding visitation or support payments. This will be invaluable to your case, should you need to prove that your spouse does not make timely payments or visit the children on a regular basis.

Records pertaining to alimony or support

It is often a good idea to start keeping a weekly or monthly record of income and expenses. This will provide documentation for your claims for alimony or support, should your proposed settlement

> 66
> When my wife started clamoring for custody of the kids, I was able to whip out my list of all the times she canceled on taking them, all the times she left them alone at home, all of the rotten things she said and did. That list helped convince the judge that she wasn't deserving of more custody. Case closed.
> —Dennis, recently divorced
> 99

include a request for either. You may wish to keep records of significant changes or events, such as the transfer or expenditure of significant amounts of money, or the receipt of a bonus, by your spouse. *Third-party records*, such as bank statements, are the best kind of evidence from the court's point of view. They are highly accurate and come from an unbiased source.

Accurate notes and records are crucial for your own personal use, too. Without them you may easily overlook important practical matters. By keeping careful records you will be able to provide your lawyer and, later, the judge with the hard facts they will need to formulate their actions and opinions. In addition to allowing you to document your own claims, your records will provide you with the means to *disprove* any false claims made by your spouse.

If you haven't already done so, now is the time to go out and get that notebook we talked about in the introduction—the one that you can use to keep track of everything you need to know regarding your divorce. Set up special sections in which to keep track of all the information we've talked about here. You'll find it an invaluable aid later on in the divorce process.

Protecting financial assets

In anticipation of filing for a divorce, you need to ensure that your spouse does not drain your checking account or build up huge debts on your joint credit cards. Such tactics are common behavior among embittered partners, leaving the other person with no money or assets with which to proceed with the divorce, or with liabilities for which they are ultimately responsible. They can also make it very difficult for the other person to establish credit after the separation, especially if all the accounts held during the marriage were issued jointly. If you take a few simple steps right at the start, you can avoid unpleasant financial surprises later on. We will be discussing many of these issues again in Chapters 7 and 8 when we deal with the division of property in your divorce settlement agreement, but now, *before* you have court-ordered protection of your financial interests, there are some things you must consider.

Charge cards

If you and your spouse have separated, it is probably a very good idea that you cancel all the charge cards that were issued in both your names. This is for future protection, but keep in mind that regardless of how your credit card is titled—whether solely to you, or your spouse, or both of you together—if the debt was incurred while you were married, the obligation for payment will usually be divided between the two of you.

As a general rule, however, once you've separated the credit card company is bound to collect the debt only from the person to which the card is titled. For example, as part of your divorce settlement your spouse may become responsible for some share of the payment of credit card debt incurred on a card issued solely in your name. This is an obligation that is imposed by your separation agreement and enforceable through the court, but keep in mind that the laws governing credit are independent of the laws regarding divorce settlements. In spite of the agreement with your spouse, the credit card company may look solely to you for payment, even if your spouse was an authorized user and was the one who ran up the debt. And a company that issued you and your spouse a joint credit card can

Watch Out!
Believe it or not, some people have no idea what assets they have. One spouse always handled the checkbooks, the credit card accounts, any investments. It was *their* job. Well, if these accounts were also in your name, they're your job as well. It's imperative that you become fully informed of your assets, so that you know what you're dealing with on the financial end of your divorce.

Unofficially . . .
Even during a
divorce, you can-
not financially
abandon your
spouse.

generally seek full payment from either one of you. In either case, it's a good idea to cancel the card in order to ensure that your spouse does not incur debt for which the credit card company will expect you to pay.

Canceling a credit card is an easy task. All you have to do is call the credit card company and explain your circumstances. They've dealt with this situation many times before, so they will be able to tell you exactly what you need to do. In most cases, they will put a "freeze" on your account right away, particularly if you subscribe to the consumer protection service that most card companies offer at a nominal monthly charge. To complete the cancellation and the issuance of a new card in your name alone, you will usually be asked to send the company a letter of notification. In most cases, this process is a swift one, and you should receive your new credit card within a matter of a week or so.

You should not, however, cancel a credit card without telling your spouse. This is especially true if your spouse has been dependent upon the card to pay certain expenses. In these instances, you should speak with the credit card company about re-titling the card and arranging for your spouse to be responsible for future debt.

A friend of mine had good reason to be leery of her spouse regarding financial matters. He was credit card happy, racking up huge bills on their joint accounts every month. Very often she would have to bail the both of them out by putting her own paychecks into paying off their credit. This had been a major cause of contention during her marriage, so she knew quite well that she needed to protect herself now that the divorce was impending.

Right at the start, she drew up agreements between herself and her spouse that read: *I, _____, release from any and all debts incurred by me as of July 1, 1997. I agree that I am solely responsible for these debts, and I release my ex-spouse from any responsibility for them.* They both signed the agreement and brought it to their lawyers for any notarization that was needed. This document gave her some peace of mind, as she knew she could rely upon the document in court, if necessary, should her husband ever run up debt on her credit card that she might be expected to pay. As noted earlier, however, you should be aware that despite such an agreement between you and your spouse, the creditor may still be able to hold you responsible for payment of any debt incurred on a card issued in your name. So make sure that your separation agreement contains provisions that specify your and your husband's respective obligations regarding currently outstanding debt *as well as* any debt that might be incurred by either of you after the separation.

Bank accounts

Unfortunately, once a divorce action is filed, or in conjunction with the filing, it is entirely possible for your spouse to unfairly invade your bank accounts and leave you without your share of the money. If your spouse is the one who has filed for divorce, you may not even have had the opportunity to anticipate this action. In such cases, you may need to petition the court for the return of the money.

If you know in advance that you are heading for divorce, you may want to take steps to divide at least some of your financial assets beforehand. This will forestall any later attempts by your spouse to unfairly invade the accounts. It is usually a good idea to

Bright Idea
If you don't own a credit card that is titled solely to you, it is a good idea to get one *before* you divorce or separate. If your spouse is in a position to cancel all of your joint credit cards, you may be left without any financial options. In the most extreme cases in which your spouse inappropriately takes joint savings, a credit card will at least allow you to pay bills until the court can grant you proper relief.

transfer one-half of any jointly held funds to a bank account that is solely titled to you. Generally speaking, an equal division of liquid assets will not give rise to great resistance from either your spouse or, later, the court.

If you're like many other couples, you and your spouse will probably agree to leave all jointly owned funds alone until the final resolution of your divorce, or you will agree to use the funds to pay monthly bills or other expenses incurred as part of your divorce. For example, if as part of your divorce you require an appraisal of your house, you may choose to pay the appraisal fee out of jointly owned funds. Or you may agree to use these funds to pay monthly mortgage payments or other bills that are considered to be joint marital debt. Keep in mind that no matter who holds the asset, whether it is jointly owned or held solely by you or your spouse, that asset will ultimately have to be divided as part of your divorce. This subject will be discussed in greater detail in Chapters 7 and 8.

Other assets

All of your property is ultimately going to be divided as part of your divorce. But if you and your spouse choose to separate prior to the final resolution of the divorce, you will most likely divide some of your furniture and personal property at the time of your separation. Other personal property like this also typically gets divided along the way and is rarely a subject that gives rise to great dispute. Most of the time the division of such property is based on purely practical considerations of who most needs which item. But, whereas bank accounts are easily traced and valued, personal items are not. Therefore, if you and your spouse own assets of significant value (whether financial or emotional), you may wish to make a record of ownership and value of the asset in anticipation of divorce or separation.

Other types of property, such as pensions, IRAs, real property, or business interests, cannot easily be divided at the beginning of your divorce. You can still, however, take steps to protect your interest in them. For example, you've probably heard the old adage that possession is nine-tenths of the law. Although this is not really legally true, it does have some validity. If you want to keep your house, for example, you should not be the one to move out, because once you give something away, it is often very difficult to get it back. This last example, however, has an important exception—if you are in an abusive marriage and leave the house to seek safety in a shelter or with friends or family, the court is certainly not going to hold that against you.

Often, one member of the divorcing couple may want to take some of the jointly held assets prior to the resolution of their divorce, with the promise that fair reimbursement will come at the end of the divorce. While eventual repayment may be made, it's best to keep in mind that once the money is gone, there is little guarantee that you will get it back. Even though the court may order that your spouse return the asset, if he or she no longer has the means to do so you have no way to enforce compensation. All in all, the best way to avoid these sorts of problems is simply to freeze your assets—in other words, keep them intact until your divorce settlement is final.

Gathering information

Unless you already have a good working knowledge of all your accounts and resources—say you're the

Moneysaver
If you believe that your spouse has depleted assets and that as a result your interests have been or will be compromised, you can petition the court for the appropriate relief by way of a motion or other similar application. Make the court aware of any such problems so as to avoid future invasions and to stake your claim on a share of the account.

one who always handled the family finances during the marriage—it is a good idea to start gathering the household financial information early. Start now to take note of the monthly bank statements, bills, and expenses.

Even if you are positive that your spouse will be completely fair with regard to finances, you should still do your own researching, because any information you turn up will greatly assist you and your attorney when it comes time to fashion an appropriate divorce settlement. It will also probably save you time and money later on in your divorce. The more information that you acquire at this stage of your divorce, the better you will be able to help yourself. The sheer number of records involved in running your household may come as a surprise to you. In addition to bank statements, you should obtain the following:

- Tax returns
- Business records
- Investment account statements
- Tax bills
- Receipts
- Canceled checks from checking accounts
- Savings account passbooks
- Credit card statements
- Expense account statements
- Safe-deposit box activity records
- Children's bank account statements and passbooks
- Diaries

Bright Idea
Access any of your joint financial records kept on your home computer. If you or your spouse regularly record your joint or separate bank and credit card accounts on such a program as Quicken, your task of collecting your financial information will be made much easier. Save the data you find on a new disk, print out the statements, and keep that data in a safe place.

- Medical records
- Phone bills

In short, you should re-create or copy any information that directly or indirectly concerns the family finances. This is of extreme importance if your spouse is much more sophisticated than you are on the subject of financial matters, or you fear that he or she will not honestly disclose all of the assets and liabilities that need to be divided. Although this may all sound very sneaky, you *should* know all about your family finances, even if you are positive that your spouse is not deceiving you. It is important for you to understand your resources as best you can when separating or filing for divorce. If you make yourself fully aware of the assets and liabilities that will need to be addressed as part of your final settlement, you increase your chances of avoiding a lengthy and expensive divorce process. We'll discuss more about discovering details about your financial situation in later chapters.

You still have choices—stopping short of court

You've gotten a lot done already, having fully explored your priorities and securing the safety of yourself, your children, and your finances. You might think that you're ready now to go forward— but there's one last area of decision-making ahead of you as you complete your preparations for your divorce. You may think all divorces are long, drawn-out fights that ultimately wind up in front of a judge. Some are, it's true, but most are not. Depending on your circumstances, you might not need to go through anything so confrontational as a lawyer-led court fight. If you and your spouse can work together cooperatively, you may be able to resolve your differences and issues through a variety of other alternative methods—mediation, arbitration, "do-it-yourself," and uncontested divorce. Now's the time to decide if any of these methods is best for you.

Mediation

Mediation is a method of resolving your differences without involving the court and adversarial attorneys. Instead, a neutral qualified third-party moderator fosters communication between you and your spouse.

A mediator is not a marital counselor. Instead, he or she will assist you in resolving the issues that arise as a result of your separation or divorce. For example, he or she will deal with the fact that you do not have sufficient income to support yourself, or that your children need support, or that your credit card bills need to be paid. The mediator will try to fashion an agreement between you and your spouse that addresses the present and future problems. The mediator's goal is to forge a compromise between you and your spouse, avoiding the adversarial nature of an attorney-led divorce.

In mediation you discuss, rather than fight over, the issues. It involves both you and your spouse meeting with a mediator and openly discussing all the issues that arise as a result of your separation or divorce. The mediator will not *tell* you how to resolve the issues but rather lead you in finding your own resolution, which may later lead to a *separation* or *settlement agreement*.

For mediation to work, both you and your spouse must be fairly equally informed about your finances—there is no "discovery" process (see

Watch Out!
Although the lawyers and the court are doing their job, that does not mean that you are always best served by legal action. Sometimes, this cannot be avoided due to the extreme emotions involved. However, other times you will end up with a much more meaningful resolution if you discuss your disputes, rather than fight over them.

Chapter 6) as is provided by the courts. Rather, mediation assumes that you already know most everything you need to know in order to resolve an issue. Unless you have a good knowledge of your finances, or trust that your spouse will honestly disclose all relevant financial data, it is highly possible that mediation will not result in a just and proper agreement. You and your spouse will both have to deal in good faith and be willing to compromise if you hope for mediation to work well for you.

On the plus side, if you are certain that you and your spouse can negotiate an agreement with the aid of a neutral mediator, this option will often save you money and alleviate much of the emotional distress that is generally associated with the divorce process. But since you are divorcing, you may no longer trust your spouse, or you may be unable to discuss your differences productively. If that's the case, mediation may not initially be a viable option for you. Sometimes, however, you can turn to mediation later in the process for help in resolving specific issues, say custody, even during an otherwise hotly contested divorce.

Choosing a mediator is a lot like choosing a lawyer, and you can turn to Chapter 4 for a detailed treatment of how to accomplish that. Generally speaking, however, what you'll need to look for are credentials, membership in a professional organization, strong referrals from others who have had use of the mediator's services, and general good sense.

When you and your spouse first meet with your mediator you will explain the conditions surrounding your divorce and discuss the major issues involved in forming your divorce agreement. You'll also use this time to identify the subjects on which you and your spouse do not agree.

Bright Idea
Although the mediator doesn't *have* to be an attorney, it is useful to employ one who is also a divorce lawyer, as it is often necessary to understand the law and how it influences the issues and your resolutions. You also may choose a qualified family therapist as your mediator, if child and family issues form the bulk of your disagreements.

Once you've established the areas you need to work on, your mediator will help you keep your communications on a cooperative basis as you discuss your issues, one by one, for as many sessions as it takes to reach an agreement acceptable to both of you. Once all support and custody issues are arranged and all other areas of contention have been agreed upon between the two of you, the mediator may draft an agreement that can be used as the basis for your property settlement or divorce agreement. Each of you will then take a copy to your respective attorneys, who will continue the process from there. One advantage of mediated agreements is that couples are more likely to accept and abide by the terms of an agreement that they helped to draw up themselves. Thus there may not be as much post-settlement fighting and dragging back to court as might occur in the traditional model of divorce.

Arbitration

Like mediation, arbitration can be faster and cheaper than the regular divorce route as well. In this process, your attorneys bring your cases to an outside arbitrator, who then makes a firm judgment based on the case before him. Unlike mediation, in arbitration you (and your spouse) agree to be bound by the arbitrator's decision. This is a good option in a situation where neither side is likely to try to appeal the decision.

For all you do-it-yourselfers: *pro se* divorce

In cases where the issues are simple and both sides have mutually agreed upon the terms of the divorce, you may want to represent yourself rather than hire a lawyer. This type of divorce is called *pro se* (a Latin term meaning "for yourself"), and it's generally an

Timesaver
Before your first meeting, draw up a list of the points on which you and your spouse agree or disagree. Even if you later end up amending it, presenting the mediator with this list could save you a session or two, shaving valuable time off your bill.

acceptable idea if the following conditions are present:

- You have been married for a short period of time.

- You don't have many assets to divide and you agree on how to divide them.

- Your divorce will be uncontested.

- You and your spouse each have jobs of your own and are self-supporting.

- You have the time and ability to handle all of the many tasks and details involved in negotiating your case.

- You have enough of a grasp on your state's divorce laws to prove grounds for your divorce and understand the legal jargon and processes involved in your case.

With legal costs reaching the stratosphere, you and your spouse may consider doing most of the footwork yourselves. There are, after all, divorce software kits that provide you with all the legal forms necessary. But while this may sound like an easy way to divorce, taking matters into your own hands could create more trouble than it's worth. Most likely, if you overlook a major issue in your agreement, you will need to go to court to settle it later. Therefore it is generally a good idea to hire a lawyer to at least review your proceedings and agreement, even if you and your spouse in essence negotiate the terms of your divorce between yourselves.

You can safely do at least *some* of the legwork for yourself—doing so will save you some of the fees you would otherwise pay a lawyer. But at some point you'll want a lawyer to review your forms and tell you what you've overlooked. He or she can point

Moneysaver
Preparing such necessary forms as asset lists using do-it-yourself options such as computer software will save you the expense of compiling your lists during meetings with your lawyer. Of course, your basic list may have to be amended, but your head start is a savings.

out some of the most commonly forgotten issues that do-it-yourselfers normally leave out of their computer-assisted agreements:

- Tax return preparations
- Pensions
- Insurance provisions
- Military benefits
- Property value
- Debt repayment
- Retirement plans

There are also child-related issues that you may not be thinking about now, but that you will have to face at some time in the future, such as providing for college tuition and weddings. By consulting a lawyer, then, you will get advice that may help you to avoid future legal wranglings.

No contest?

If you've reached the point where you agree on the settlement of all issues, you can obtain what is generally referred to as an *uncontested divorce*, in which all issues are resolved between you and your spouse and you have no need for the assistance of the court.

From a legal standpoint, there is no difference whether you receive an uncontested divorce as a result of a settlement agreement, or require a trial to resolve all of your contested issues—in the end, a divorce is a divorce is a divorce. No matter how you go about *getting* the divorce, the court will issue an order to which you and your spouse will be bound until a further court order changes it. The only difference is that if you present a settlement or divorce agreement, the court will typically incorporate your agreement into your order of divorce, thus, in essence, making your agreement a court order. If you do not present an agreement, but rather require a trial in order to determine "who gets what," the court will fashion an order without your input. As is true throughout all of the procedures involved in a divorce, the less you need the court's help, the more quickly you will resolve your case and the more quickly your divorce will be granted.

In the next chapter you will learn what you need to know to effectively choose a lawyer—and even in the case of a pro se divorce you will at least want to secure some legal advice even if you do stop short of taking your divorce into court. Most people find themselves "out of their depth" when faced with the issues and responsibilities of handling a divorce, and need the advice of a legal professional to make certain that their interests, and the interests of their children, are properly taken care of. But all lawyers aren't created equal, and finding the right one can be a daunting task unless you know what to look for. Chapter 4 takes you step by step through the process of researching and interviewing prospective lawyers and gives you a few tips on how best to establish a good lawyer-client relationship for the tasks ahead. Once that's been taken care of, it will be time to move on to Part 2, which will take you step by step through each phase of the divorce process itself.

Just the facts

- Securing the safety of yourself and your children should be your first priority.
- Careful record-keeping will provide you with support for your claims in court.

Watch Out!
Do not be confused between a fault or no-fault divorce and a contested or uncontested divorce. Fault and no-fault refer to the cause of action or reasons behind the divorce, whereas contested and uncontested refer to the issues that must still be resolved.

- Until you receive formal court protection, take steps to secure your financial situation.
- Mediation and arbitration, as well as pro se and uncontested divorces, let you avoid the confrontation of going to court.

GET THE SCOOP ON...
The attorney's role ▪
How to find an attorney ▪ Fees and retainers ▪
The lawyer-client relationship

Choosing an Attorney

Now that you've got your priorities set and identified just what you need to address in your divorce action, it's time to consider how best to accomplish your goals. Some people may feel that they are capable of handling everything from this point on by themselves, but divorces that are so trouble-free and simple are not all that common. Most people find that it is necessary to consult with a legal professional, if only to make certain that they have complete knowledge of the legal requirements for divorcing. But because most of us do not have frequent occasions to turn to a lawyer, finding—and hiring—one can be a little intimidating. In this chapter you'll learn how.

You've heard all of the lawyer jokes, but in the course of your divorce process your lawyer is going to become very important to you. The person you choose to represent you takes your entire case into his or her capable hands, and the outcome depends very much on your lawyer's expertise and knowledge of the statutes that apply to you.

63

Choosing the right attorney, then, can make or break your case.

What does the lawyer do?

Your attorney will play many roles in the divorce process. In many ways your lawyer acts as the "captain" of your team—the person who knows the rules, the plays, and the weaknesses of the other side. He or she outlines a game plan and explains what you need to do to be a team player. To complete the sports analogy, your lawyer is the person who runs with the ball.

In addition to general knowledge of how the law works, your attorney will bring to the table a wealth of particular legal expertise in the field of divorce, which he or she will use to serve your best interests and fight for your rights. If you've chosen well, your lawyer has a great deal of experience in handling cases of your kind, and has learned by now not only what works but also what doesn't work in the settlement and trial processes.

Also among his or her many tasks, your attorney will assume the role of diligent fact-finder. It is a lawyer's job to collect all of the information needed to appropriately address the issues involved in your case. He or she will research the legal precedents that apply, consult law journals and other publications, and perhaps even spend hours on the Internet for your benefit.

Your attorney serves as your answer person as well, addressing whatever questions you may have as your case progresses. He or she understands that you are unfamiliar with all of the terms and statutes involved, and should answer any query you have at any time. Attorneys expect to be called often when new situations, problems, or confusions arise, and a

> 66
> A lawyer's advice is his stock in trade.
> —Abraham Lincoln
> 99

good one will always respect your need to be well-informed.

Your attorney acts as your negotiator. On the strength of your input, he or she will deal with "the other side," initiating the push and pull that is a very big part of the divorce process. Your lawyer will deal with the offers made by the other side, and will send out offers from your's. He or she should be adept at the process, playing well enough against the other side's lawyer to win on your major points, but should also know when to concede if that is appropriate. He or she should keep you posted on all developments in your case as they arise, however—recognizing your need to know.

Finally, your attorney will provide you with moral support. When you're upset or frustrated with the case, he or she will be willing to listen when you feel the need to talk about what's going on. You may not get a shoulder to cry on, but your lawyer will at least acknowledge your feelings and give you the assurances you need to make you feel better, stronger, and ready to go forward.

To sum it all up, here's what to look for when you're ready to select your legal representation:

- **Expertise in the field.** You want at least several years of experience, and a specialty in divorce cases is an important plus.

- **Knowledge.** Your lawyer should know the latest laws on the books in your state. Laws change all the time, and you want to know that your attorney is up to speed on the legal specifications that will affect you. Your lawyer should also be able and willing to explain these laws to you.

- **Confidentiality.** Your lawyer must keep all the details of your case between the two of you. A

Unofficially . . .
Once you have a lawyer, the other side cannot talk to you about legal matters. They must talk to your attorney.

lawyer is bound by what is known as the attorney-client confidentiality relationship.

- **Candor.** Your lawyer should fully disclose all of the problems that will arise in your case, as well as an accounting of costs.

- **Accessibility.** Your lawyer should keep in regular contact with you, promptly return your calls, and be willing to send you any information you need whenever you request it.

- **Meticulousness.** Your lawyer should follow up on all of the information that is relevant to your case, leaving nothing undone.

- **Quick thinking.** You never know what will come up in court or in a settlement meeting, so you want your lawyer to be quick on his feet, ready with the perfect comeback or objection.

- **Ethical behavior.** All attorneys are bound by their State Bar's Code of Ethics, which outlines the types of behaviors and actions which are acceptable or unacceptable within the legal profession.

- **Good rapport.** The two of you should get along.

Since you will be working as a team, your lawyer will expect certain things from you in order to be fully effective:

- **Honesty.** You *have* to be open and honest with your lawyer. One of the most difficult problems lawyers face is when clients fail to divulge a damaging fact (a brief affair, past jail time, etc.). Your attorney can help with damage control early on, but finding out later from your ex's attorney may be too late.

Watch Out!
An unethical lawyer may be subject to review by your state's Office of General Counsel, or a similar oversight group. This review board is like a policing counsel, created to keep up the standards of behavior by those practicing law. Make sure your lawyer has not been disciplined by the state bar or the Office of General Counsel.

- **Timeliness.** Your lawyer expects you to be on time to meetings and conferences. Never fail to show up or cancel at the last minute.

- **Cooperation.** If your lawyer asks you for a list of your assets, you must provide the necessary information. Your lawyer needs to work *with* you to best serve your interests.

- **Realistic expectations.** Your attorney expects you to have a decent grasp on reality, to know what you are and aren't likely to accomplish in your case.

- **Firmness of decision.** No lawyer wants to work with a client who is going to waffle through the process. Your lawyer expects you to be *sure* that you know what you want. If you're seeking a postponement, say so—your lawyer will know how to handle that. But persistent foot-dragging on your part will cause problems.

- **Respect.** Your lawyer is your partner in the process—in court, you won't be helping if you interrupt or express disagreement in front of the judge.

Of course, since this is a business relationship, you and your lawyer are going to deal with each other in a respectful, professional way. You each should acknowledge the other's role in the process. The perfect lawyer-client relationship is a partnership, one based on a willingness to listen, communicate, and work hard together to accomplish your goals.

Where can I get one of those?

Finding a good attorney is far more important than, say, finding a good florist. So you'll need to put in some time and do some serious checking around in order to pinpoint the best representation for you. Here's where to start:

Timesaver
If you have access to your State Bar's Internet address, this can be a quick and easy way to access their list of highly recommended attorneys, as well as valuable information on the most current divorce laws in your area. This option may not be available in all states.

- Call your State and/or County Bar Association. They can recommend suitable candidates for your case, and in most states they can even tell you about the candidates' standing in the legal profession. Where did they go to law school? How long have they been in business? A recommendation from the bar is a good indication of the lawyer's credentials.

- Check with the American Academy of Matrimonial Lawyers for a list of recommended attorneys. They have strict membership requirments, one of which is a mandatory 10 years of practicing law.

- Visit your local public library to look in your state lawyer's directory. This will list the candidate's biography, degrees, specialties, and any notable cases on which they've worked. Look also for the *Martindale Hubbell* directory and *Lawyers in America,* two resource books that rate and locate lawyers across the country.

- Ask around. Ask everyone you know for a referral. Perhaps a recently divorced friend found a gem of a lawyer and will whole-heartedly recommend him or her to you.

- Talk to other lawyers. Perhaps you have a lawyer associated with your business or a lawyer friend who can suggest an associate in divorce law.

- Stop in at the local courthouse and sit in on a few divorce cases. You'll be able to see a selection of lawyers in action, which is a smart way to assess how one will perform in court for you.

- Call your state Legal Aid or Public Defenders office to see if you qualify for their services.

You may have seen those ads on television—a lawyer sits behind a mahogany desk, law degrees framed and hanging on the wall, promising you a win in court. An 800-number flashes on the screen, and a list of legal specialties rolls by faster than you can read it. Or maybe you've seen big ads in the newspaper advertising special rates for "quick, easy divorce cases." They may even provide a coupon. Impressive? Maybe to some. But be smart. Don't choose a lawyer just because they advertise.

Just as there are many different types of doctors—general practitioners, specialists, and so on—there are also many different types of attorneys. As you begin your search, you'll note that some list themselves as handling Family Law, Business Law, Personal Injury Cases, and so on. This is an indication of the lawyer's areas of expertise, the area of legal practice for which he or she has trained, and in which he or she has the most experience.

This is not to say that general practice lawyers cannot handle your divorce. Of course they can, if they're good at what they do. They may even handle it better than an under-qualified divorce specialist. If you're really torn between a general practice lawyer that you know and a specialist that you've only *heard* of, it comes down to being a judgment call. You'll have to judge the lawyers you are considering based on their knowledge of divorce law. They may specialize, and then again they may not. You need to go by what they've done, what they know, and what they can do for you.

Watch Out!
Blatant availability and an aggressive approach to soliciting clients may not be the best indication of excellence in lawyers. It may be a sign that they're hurting for business, or that they're just starting out in the practice.

There's a lot of work involved in choosing the perfect lawyer, but as it's probably the most important step you'll take in the divorce process, it's worth every minute of effort. Resign yourself to spending a good amount of time making phone calls, asking questions, and getting referrals. Remember, this is one of the most important investments you can make and may have a great deal of influence upon whether or not you win your case.

Financial matters

Speaking of investments, your choice of attorney is going to be affected by the amount of money your candidates charge for their services. At this time in your life money is likely to be a sore point, but you must keep in mind the importance of your investment in a qualified attorney.

So, what affects the price tag? First, the issues involved in your case. A divorce between two people with kids, millions of dollars in assets, and a shared business will require greater effort and higher expenses than one between a recently married couple with few assets and no children. Are there the larger issues of adultery, bankruptcy, child abuse, or violence in the home? This too may take more time and expense than a simple, mutual parting of ways. Experts may have to be called in to testify, medical tests may have to be performed, and witnesses may have to give depositions. As a rule, the more that's involved in your case, the bigger the price tag.

Your lawyer's reputation will also affect your costs. If you're hiring Johnny Cochran, you'll pay more than if you hired the attorney down the street. A high-profile lawyer may have a certain edge in the courtroom, but you'd be just as well-served by a highly qualified attorney who *hasn't* been on the news. In addition, your lawyer's billing practices will have an impact. Some lawyers charge for everything—photocopying, phone calls, initial consultations—and others swallow those fees or include them in a general fee. Other factors that may affect your costs include:

- **The duration of your case.** If one side is stalling, the case goes on forever, and the meter keeps running.

- **Assistants' help.** Your lawyer is going to have to pay the paralegals, notaries, and other professionals who must help in your case. These people too may work by the hour, and their tab is often on you.

- **Mandated fees.** There are, of course, filing fees, court fees, subpoena fees, and other expenses to consider as your lawyer completes the basic steps within your divorce proceedings.

- **Your attorney's overhead.** Your attorney has operating expenses which usually maintain his offices and the various mechanics of his business. These charges can include his rent, office equipment, office supplies, insurance, and access to law libraries.

An explanation of fees

So what kind of money are we talking about for your lawyer's fees? Fees vary by state, by the issues involved in your divorce, and by the duration of your case. But certain *kinds* of fees are a standard part of any divorce:

- **Initial consultation fee.** Some lawyers don't charge you for an initial consultation; others will charge you their regular hourly rate.

Unofficially . . .
In many instances, office overhead can account for up to 50 percent of the annual gross income a lawyer earns from his fees.

Watch Out!
Beware of fees
you do not
understand. In
all cases, a good
lawyer will take
the time to
explain his fees
fully in relation
to the services
required by your
case. He or she
should be willing
to provide you
with a fully
itemized written
record of your
payment sched-
ule at regular
intervals
throughout the
case.

- **Retainer fee.** Think of this as a debit card amount or an advance payment for services to be rendered. The lawyer collects a lump sum from you and draws from that "account" throughout your case. Retainer fees can range from \$2,000 to \$4,000, depending upon local pricing structures for legal services, the skill of the attorney, and the issues involved in the case.

- **Flat rate.** Your lawyer might just take a look at your information, assess what will be involved, and charge you a flat rate for the entire thing. As with any flat rate, the actual grand total may be higher or lower than that amount.

- **Contingency fees.** The lawyer agrees to take a percentage of whatever money is won by you through your settlement or trial. You're not likely to come across this option, though, since most states do not allow contingency fees for domestic disputes.

- **Hourly fees.** Your lawyer may charge by the hour.

- **Fixed fees.** Here you pay a specific amount for a specific service.

- **Cost advance.** Through this setup, you will pay a periodic advance payment to your lawyer to cover her expenses as she works on your case.

- **Mixed fee.** This one is very unusual. It's a combination of contingency and hourly fees.

Figure 1 presents a sample copy of a fee agreement similar to one that you might encounter when you are negotiating with an attorney. You'll note that it is general enough to accommodate any one of the several different fee options we've just discussed.

The attorney's fees in this matter will be set as follows:
( ) Fixed fee of $_____
( ) Hourly rate at $_____ per hour plus _____ percent of amount recovered
( ) Estimated fee in the range of $_____ to $_____
( ) Contingent fee of $_____ ( ) saved ( )recovered
( ) Fee determinant on all relevant factors
( ) Minimum retainer of $_____
( ) Hours of attorney's time covered by retainer is: _____
( ) Other: _____
This office will bill you:
( ) Monthly on _____ of each month
( ) Upon completion of case
( ) Other arrangement: _____
ALL BILLS ARE PAYABLE UPON RECEIPT. IF YOU DO NOT PAY WITHIN 30 DAYS OF RECEIPT, YOUR ACCOUNT WILL BEGIN TO ACCRUE INTEREST CHARGES.
RETAINERS:
Retainer of $_____ is to be applied:
( ) Toward fee and out-of-pocket expenses
( ) Toward fee
( ) Toward out-of-pocket expenses
( ) Retainer is refundable
( ) Retainer is non-refundable
COSTS AND EXPENSES
Typical out-of-pocket expenses for this matter may include:
( ) Costs such as court costs, filing fees, process server fees, deposition costs, sheriff or clerk of court fees, investigator's fees
( ) Abstracting charges or title insurance premiums, clerk's recording fees
( ) Photocopying, telephone charges, postage, and travel costs
( ) Other: _____
Estimate for costs and expenses, not including attorney's fees:
( ) Expected to range between $_____ and $_____
( ) Not expected to exceed $_____
( ) No expenses expected
NOTE: This is an estimate for your convenience, not a guarantee.
If the above properly sets forth our agreement, please sign below and keep one copy.
Return the original with a check in the amount of $_____
We will draw $_____ toward attorney's fees and apply $_____ toward out-of-pocket expenses as outlined above. If we do not receive the signed original of this agreement (you retain the copy) and your check within _____ days, we shall assume that you have obtained other counsel and shall mark our file CLOSED and do nothing further. Thank you.
Dated: _____
Signed: _____
Attorney at Law
The above is understood and agreed to by me:
Dated: _____
Signed: _____
Client

Figure 1:
Attorney's Fees

Once you've agreed upon a payment option, you should arrange a payment schedule with your lawyer. This may be monthly, confined to stages of the divorce process, or in the case of extremely complex divorces, quarterly.

Get it in writing

Your attorney should spell out his or her fees in writing. You are, after all, entering into a business agreement, so you should treat this as such. That fee agreement can be presented to you on a general purpose form, like the one in Figure 1, or it can deal only with the specific type of fee arrangement you agree upon with your attorney. Also following is a sample of a specialized fee agreement—a retainer agreement—that you might draw up with your attorney.

Money troubles

It's just good sense to get the best lawyer your money can buy, particularly if your ex has greater resources than you do. It's a sad fact that at this time, as financial resources are split and one partner may be left without substantial income, the choosing of lawyers often leaves one partner outmatched in the legal department. The only recourse that partner has is to do tireless research and get the best lawyer affordable. If things are tight, don't be afraid to seek help from family members. They may be willing and able to help with your fees, especially if custody of the children is in question.

You may think that there's not much you can do to keep the legal price tag down. That's not necessarily so. While you may not be able to talk your lawyer into charging you less money per hour of his service, you can certainly decrease your price tag in other ways:

Client: _____
Attorney: _____

    Following our meetings and discussions, you have requested and I agreed that I shall represent you regarding your matrimonial matter. We shall be guided by the following understandings and agreements:

1. Based on our discussion, there are, among others, the following issues to be negotiated or litigated:

  A. Your Cause of Action for divorce.

  B. Custody of the children and Visitation.

  C. Alimony and Support as applicable.

  D. Equitable Distribution of Property

  E. Evaluation and consideration for Income Tax purposes.

  F. There may be need to negotiate or litigate for interim support, liens and/or Protective Orders until the issues can be settled or litigated.

2. It is impossible, at this time, to predict the nature, extent and difficulty of the contemplated services of attorney's time involved. We shall exert every effort to represent your interests and rights, and if possible, to seek an amicable solution of your claim.

3. It is understood and agreed that our services shall be compensated at the rate of $_____ per hour.

4. In consideration of the services to be performed you are to pay us a retainer of $_____ on account of services to be rendered. Billings and accounting for our services will be submitted at regular intervals. Should the hours and costs of our services exceed the retainer amount, statements shall be payable upon receipt.

5. You are to be responsible for all necessary and reasonable legal costs including filing fees, subpoena costs, deposition costs (if needed), process servers, etc. It may be necessary to hire experts such as accountants and appraisers to assist you. Although I may recommend such, the decision rests entirely with you, and if you decide to hire experts you will be responsible to pay for their services directly.

6. In representing you in this matter, I cannot and do not predict results or final developments. Be assured that it is our full intention to provide you with conscientious, faithful, and diligent service, seeking at all times to achieve solutions that are just and reasonable for you.

(The client and attorney need to sign this letter in the spaces provided below showing understanding and agreement. The client shall present the retainer check to the attorney at the time of signing.)

Consented to and approved:

_____

_____

Figure 2: Sample Retainer Agreement

Watch Out!
Don't hire a lawyer you can't afford, and don't take out a huge loan or a lien on your house if you'll have trouble paying it back. Use your resources wisely.

- Do some of the legwork yourself. The more information you can obtain on your own and bring with you to the first meeting, the less work your lawyer will have to do with the clock ticking.

- Bring any related paperwork you have with you to the first meeting.

- Disclose *all* facts of your case right away, so that nothing has to be done at the last minute.

- Keep your meetings short. If you're as brief and concise as possible, what would have been tackled in two hours might be tackled in one.

- If at all possible, save your questions for your meetings with the lawyer. Your lawyer may add charges for any phone calls that you make to him at his office or home.

- Discuss all decisions with your lawyer fully before signing anything. If you think out your steps, and get full legal advice on them, before acting, there will be less time spent on damage control later on.

Interviewing prospective counsel

As you hunt for a lawyer, arm yourself with a complete list of interview questions and ask the same of all the lawyers on your preliminary list. This way, you can compare and contrast what each one has to offer, and you can better choose the person who fits your requirements. Here is a list of useful questions for you to ask:

1. Have you handled cases that are similar to mine, dealing with the same issues involved (child custody, spousal support, abuse, etc.)?

2. How many cases have you handled?

3. How many of those cases have gone to trial?

4. Will you be willing to take my case to court if we cannot reach a good settlement?

5. Do you have time right now to take on my case, or do you have any big trials coming up?

6. Will you handle my case personally, or do you hand off to an assistant?

7. If you hand off to an assistant, what are the assistant's credentials? May I interview him or her?

8. What are your hourly rates? Do you bill by the full hour, or by portions (quarter or half-hour)?

9. Do you charge a retainer? If so, is the retainer refundable for unused portions?

10. What is your billing schedule?

11. Do you charge extra for outside help from accountants, secretaries, private investigators, or other such services? If so, what are those fees?

12. Do you charge extra for court time, or is that included in your regular hourly rate?

13. Do you charge for copies of paperwork, or do I get those for free?

14. Will I be billed for phone charges?

15. What extra fees do you charge?

16. What about court costs?

17. Will I get regular, itemized bills in writing?

18. What are your office hours?

19. Can you be reached at home? By beeper? By answering service?

20. What laws apply to my case?

21. What is expected of me as far as discovery and attendance at meetings, hearings?

Bright Idea
In your meetings, do not rush your attorney, and don't leave out information just to save time. You want to be brief, not incomplete.

Bright Idea
Photocopy
the Lawyer
Questionnaire in
the Appendix
section, and use
it to record your
notes and their
answers as you
do your phone
interviews.
If any
lawyer's first
few responses
displease you,
don't bother
continuing . . .
thank the attor-
ney for giving
you the time,
and hang up.

22. Do you know my ex?

23. Do you know my ex's attorney?

24. How much input will I have in the case?

25. Will you contact me regularly regarding the status of my case?

26. What do you foresee as the outcome of my case? What are my chances of winning?

Once you've narrowed down your field of candidates, it's time to re-interview the front-runners. Ask each one about the issues involved in your case, and analyze how he or she answers them. Is he willing to take the time to explain things fully? Does she talk down to you? Does he seem to feel that as long as *he* knows what he's talking about, that should be good enough for you? How completely does she answer the question? Is he well-spoken? Make it clear that you're planning on participating in the process. Does she seem to resent that? Does she have a "leave it all up to me" attitude? How does she respond to you as you explain the conditions of your divorce? Does she just sit there and stare at you, or does she seem sympathetic to all you've been through?

While you're at it, check out the office. Is it organized, or are their piles of papers all over the place? Are the "In" and "Out" boxes overloaded? The lawyer doesn't have to have an elegantly appointed waiting room or mahogany paneling, but the office should be more than a renovated closet with a fold-out card table and a pay phone on the wall.

Are you constantly interrupted by a ringing phone? Does the lawyer seem harried and overwhelmed? Ask about his or her caseload. If there's a calendar on the wall, take a look at it. Is it covered with court dates, lots of cross-outs, and any other indications that this person is completely loaded down? It's great to have a busy, sought-after lawyer, but not if this means that you won't have access to his or her services when you need them.

Do you have any preference about your lawyer's gender? Some people are more comfortable with a lawyer who is the same sex as them, others prefer the opposite. Just remember, it's the lawyer's experience and skill that counts. So don't eliminate a great candidate just because of gender.

Creating the lawyer-client relationship

Once you've found the lawyer you want, remember that the key to a good partnership with your attorney is good communication. This is based on openness, honesty, mutual confidence, and reliability.

But there's more to it than that. In a sense you'll be communicating with your attorney the minute you walk through the door. It's important to give the right messages, to present yourself as someone with whom he can work and someone who should be treated with professional respect and courtesy. Here are a few suggestions to accomplish just that:

- Dress nicely. Wear a suit or a dress, and project a serious image of yourself. Give a firm handshake.

- Look him in the eye when you speak.

- Speak clearly. Don't use a lot of "um"s and "uh"s.

- Be calm. Even if you're plate-throwing mad at your spouse, this is not the time to be calling names and using expletives.

- Take notes. Show that you're informed and that you'll be involved in your case.

Unofficially . . .
You might think that a big legal firm is better than a smaller one. That is not so. Lawyers in big firms often hand over their cases to paralegals or young associates. If you're considering a lawyer from the biggest firm in town, make sure you ask about his or her workload, and whether or not he or she will be personally attending to your case.

- Ask questions. This too shows that you're going to be participating in the process.

- Don't be afraid to talk about yourself. It helps establish an air of familiarity with your lawyer if you project yourself as a whole person, not just a divorcing person.

This is the beginning of the process, the meeting at which you'll start to outline your case, determine a strategy, and share the reins with your lawyer. You'll set up a meeting schedule, and your lawyer will tell you what you'll need to bring to the next meeting, what your next steps are, and what guidelines you should follow as the two of you begin to build your case.

Recording all meetings

Bright Idea
Get everything
in writing!

Remember what we've said before about the importance of record-keeping? By all means, you should take and keep notes related to your meetings with your lawyer. Get that file folder we talked about earlier and make a new section so you can use it to store all of your important paperwork and notes. Date your entries and keep everything in order so that you can easily find what's needed and refer to it when necessary.

So now that you've hired your lawyer and had your first few meetings, the actual process of the divorce will begin. In Part 2 you will get the lowdown on the various stages of a divorce, from the initial filing through (should it be necessary) the actual trial. This process can seem intimidating—there are so many forms and terms, and so much information to keep in mind—but if you consider it in terms of several basic steps you will see that this is nothing that you can't handle. Read on for a one-step-at-a-time tour through the divorce process.

Just the facts

- Choosing the right attorney can make or break your case.

- Assess potential attorneys fully—and remember to ask about billing practices and meeting schedules.

- Record any information obtained or questions that arise during your meetings with your lawyer.

Get the Lowdown on the Divorce Process

PART II

Chapter 5

Filing for Divorce

You've made your decision to divorce and you've found a lawyer you feel comfortable with (or—just maybe—you've decided to go *pro se*.) Now it's time to move forward. The very first step in the divorce process is *filing a complaint*—this is the first official notification that you and your spouse are terminating your marriage. You may be the partner that files, or it may be your spouse. Generally speaking, with regard to your legal rights and obligations, it doesn't make any difference which one of you actually begins the process—in some cases you can even file jointly. But whoever files the complaint, there are some general rules of procedure that have to be followed.

What's involved?

When you or your spouse files a *complaint*, you are officially petitioning the court for a divorce. This document informs all parties concerned of the reasons for the divorce (generally known as the "cause of action" or the "grounds for divorce") and sets forth some basic background information

Example 1: Sample Complaint for Divorce citing fault of the defendant (used in the state of New Jersey).

JANE DOE
    Plaintiff
vs.
JOHN DOE
    Defendant   Complaint

Plaintiff, Jane Doe, resides at _____, says:

1. She was lawfully married to John Doe, the defendant herein, on _____, in a religious ceremony.

2. She was a bona fide resident of the State of New Jersey when this cause of action arose, and has ever since and for more than one year next preceding the commencement of this action continued to be such a bona fide resident.

3. The defendant, John Doe, resides at _____.

4. The defendant has been guilty of extreme cruelty toward the plaintiff starting in _____ and continuing until this time. Particularly specifying some of the acts of extreme cruelty committed by the defendant, the plaintiff says:

    (a) Defendant demeans and insults plaintiff. He often criticizes plaintiff in front of the children.

    (b) Defendant constantly demands to know the whereabouts of plaintiff. He has become obsessive and paranoid.

    (c) Despite the fact that defendant earns a good living, he refuses to spend any money on the family, but all too often needlessly spends money on himself.

By reason of these acts, it is improper and unreasonable to expect plaintiff to continue to cohabit with defendant.

More than three months have elapsed since the last act complained of as constituting plaintiff's cause of action. The acts of extreme cruelty committed by the defendant within a period of three months before the filing of this complaint, as above set forth, are alleged not as constituting in whole or in part the cause of action set forth herein, but as relating back to qualify and characterize the acts constituting said cause of action.

5. _____ children were born of the marriage, namely _____.

6. There have been _____ previous matrimonial actions between the parties.

7. Personal property was legally and beneficially acquired by the parties, or either of them, during the marriage.

8. The plaintiff is unable to support herself and the minor children of the marriage.

WHEREFORE, Plaintiff demands judgment:

A. Dissolving the marriage between the parties;

B. Equitably distributing property which was legally and beneficially acquired by them or either of them during the marriage;

C. Compelling the defendant to support the plaintiff and the minor children of the marriage;

D. Compelling the defendant to pay the legal costs and fees incurred by the plaintiff with regard to the within action;

E. For such further relief as the Court may deem just and equitable.

CERTIFICATION OF VERIFICATION AND NONCOLLUSION

I, Jane Doe, do hereby certify that:

1. I am the plaintiff in the foregoing Complaint.

2. The allegations of the foregoing Complaint are true to the best of my knowledge, information, and belief.

3. Said Complaint is made in truth and in good faith and without collusion, for the causes set forth therein.

4. To the best of my knowledge and belief this matter is not the subject of any other action pending in any Court, nor is any such proceeding contemplated at this time.

5. To the best of my knowledge there are no other parties who must be joined in this action.

6. I certify that the foregoing statements made by me are true. I am aware that if any of the foregoing statements made by me are willfully false I am subject to punishment.

_____

Dated: _____, 199____.

regarding you, your spouse, and the conditions of your marriage. As a general rule you must file this complaint in the location in which you have lived for some minimum period of time (this time requirement varies from state to state). Your complaint will therefore contain basic jurisdictional information such as your address, as well as general information regarding your children and household finances. It will also typically set forth your "grounds for divorce" (also known as "cause of action"). The language used in these documents can be somewhat difficult—but don't let the "legalese" put you off. Your attorney can explain each and every item you find hard to understand.

Grounds for divorce

Different states have different names for what is commonly called "grounds for divorce," but all states generally recognize the same grounds as valid. For example, many states recognize some version of *irreconcilable differences* or *incompatibility*. In essence, this particular cause of action permits you or your spouse to obtain a divorce for no reason other than that you want one. Although other states may require more severe grounds be cited, using terms such as "extreme cruelty" or "mental cruelty." In most cases, however, regardless of the cause of action specifically cited in your divorce papers, the court typically will accept your reasons as being true and deserving of a divorce. It will not usually question the appropriateness of your decision.

There are, however, certain instances in which the court may take a more active role in approving a cause of action for divorce. For example, if your divorce is based upon charges of an act of adultery committed by your spouse, the court will want more proof of your allegations than would normally be required. This is because your cause of action not only involves matters that are private to you and your spouse, but also involves a third party. Even in this situation, though, the court will not punish either you or your spouse as a consequence of any acts of indiscretion.

You can get a divorce for almost any reason you choose. However, in your papers, you must specify a cause of action that meets the criteria for a divorce in your state. If your state does not recognize "no-fault" divorce, for example, you may have to cite some cause of action more specific than simple incompatibility. For example, you may base your cause of action upon a claim of "extreme cruelty," and support your charge with claims that your spouse is emotionally abusive, belittles you in front of others, and undermines your career. But whatever your stated cause for action, in the eyes of the court, there is no better or worse reason to get a divorce—all the court requires is that your stated reasons are recognized by the laws of your state as suitable grounds for divorce.

Fault versus no-fault divorce

Some causes of action assert fault on the part of one spouse, whereas others impart no fault to either party. These particular causes of action available for you to cite depends, for the most part, on the state in which you reside. However, most states do have no-fault causes of action—and some states *only* have no-fault causes of action. In these states, the court has taken the position that no matter what your reasons for the divorce, those reasons should remain private between you and your spouse. Some states require that you and your spouse live physically and legally separate for a set period of time before allowing you to file a no-fault divorce.

Although you and your spouse can separate after filing a written agreement with the court, you may not actually be able to begin the divorce process until after you satisfy a separation requirement. If

Watch Out!
Do not file divorce papers with the goal of venting your anger and frustration, or in an effort to hurt or embarrass your spouse. These papers are used solely to set in motion the process by which you will begin resolving the issues that surround you and your family. Using them for retribution will only make your case more difficult down the line.

Unofficially . . .
Many states
impose a 12- to
18-month legal
separation period
before permitting
a no-fault
divorce.

you do not wish to wait so long to obtain your divorce, you can pursue a fault divorce.

Even though the court may technically differentiate between a fault and a no-fault divorce, when dividing assets and liabilities and establishing support it generally will not consider fault. However, some states do consider the cause of action when resolving your case. For example, proof of adultery may influence the court's decision with regard to the award of alimony and child custody.

Since the reasons for a no-fault divorce are kept private, there are no charges against your spouse that you have to prove. The court will grant your divorce as a formality, without inquiring into your reason for seeking it. Instead, it will go on to address the major issues of your divorce settlement—such as child support, alimony, and the division of assets and liabilities.

In many instances, even if your cause of action is based upon grounds of fault, you may not have to prove your cause of action—the court is willing to accept your reasons as being true and valid. However, in such cases where you do, in fact, have to prove your case, you will be required to present evidence at a trial.

Causes of action

As noted earlier, different states recognize different causes of action, but every state permits you to allege fault for the following types of actions on the part of your spouse:

- Cruelty
- Adultery
- Willful neglect
- Incurable insanity

- Habitual drunkenness
- Drug addiction
- Bigamy
- Endangerment of your life
- Physical abuse
- Gross neglect
- Deviant sexual conduct
- Desertion
- Felony conviction

No-fault causes of action include the following:

- Separation
- Irreconcilable differences
- Incompatibility
- Irretrievable breakdown of your marriage

In some of these instances, you and your spouse may actually file together, simultaneously petitioning for the divorce based upon no-fault grounds.

Actions and reactions

Your spouse's reaction to the cause of action you choose will depend upon your allegations. If you are looking for a fight, the fastest way to create one is to be very aggressive and demeaning with your allegations. This, however, is not a constructive approach to take.

To reduce confrontation (and probably to reduce costs as well) consider your spouse's probable reaction to the grounds for divorce you cite. While you may not care about making your spouse's life any easier, you certainly don't want to make your own case harder than necessary by incurring your spouse's wrath. In a perfect world, even though you are getting divorced, especially if you have children,

Timesaver
If you believe you cannot definitively prove your allegations, as with pictures, written proof, or witness testimony, you may wish to use an alternate cause of action that will produce the same results. Avoiding a court battle over hard-to-prove allegations reduces the expense, emotional impact, and delays that may result from a trial.

Watch Out!
While you don't
want to cause
undue confronta-
tion, don't let
your fear of
escalating ten-
sions keep you
from filing the
true cause of
action for the
divorce you seek.
Even if you were
intimidated and
controlled in
your marriage,
you only hurt
your case by
understating
truly serious
charges such
as abuse and
adultery.

you would be able to resolve all your divorce issues peacefully and amicably. Since the divorce complaint can help or hinder that goal, be as honest as possible.

Service

Once the cause of action has been decided upon and the divorce complaint is drawn up, the divorce papers must be served upon you or your spouse. "Service" merely means that you or your spouse has been presented with divorce papers in such a way that a timely and meaningful response to the allegations and complaints can be made, usually by a date specified in the divorce papers.

If you are initiating the action, it is important that you are able to prove to the court that your spouse received the papers, and that he or she was given a reasonable opportunity to respond.

The method by which you serve the divorce papers may influence the process of negotiation and resolution in your divorce. If your spouse realizes that he or she may be served but does not want to be, there may be a string of attempts to avoid receiving the papers. If you think your spouse will attempt to avoid being served, you may wish to use a professional "process server." Process servers are very good at what they do, and eventually will manage to serve the papers. Equally important, the process server will be able to testify that he or she did in fact properly serve your spouse. With the server's testimony that the papers were indeed served, your spouse will not be able to deny having received the papers.

In most cases a professional process server is not necessary. The complaint can simply be mailed and voluntarily accepted. If your spouse already has a lawyer, the complaint may be mailed to the lawyer.

In some states, your divorce papers may only need to assert the reason for your divorce—in other words, they may not provide any formal direction to your spouse that he or she must respond in any manner. In these cases, in addition to your divorce papers, you are required to serve a summons or other directive on your spouse. This document instructs your spouse as to how, when, and where he or she can respond.

Appearance

Once you or your spouse receives the divorce papers, the clock starts ticking. The person being served is typically called the *defendant* or *respondent,* the person issuing the service is generally known as the *plaintiff.* The *respondent* has the right to respond to the allegations and address the issues of the case and has several options by which to do so.

Whether you or your spouse is the *respondent,* your have several ways to answer the service of divorce papers. You may simply acknowledge the receipt of the papers without admitting or denying the allegations. Instead of addressing the allegations, you may just ask for the opportunity to be heard, by the court if necessary, with regard to issues such as finances, custody, and support. This type of response is generally known as an *appearance,* meaning that you have appeared in the case, but not necessarily answered the allegations.

Filing an appearance is generally the least adversarial and least expensive method of responding, and is often appropriate in cases that can be resolved without aggressive legal tactics. If you or

Moneysaver
Professional process servers charge for their services. Speak with your lawyer about saving this nominal fee by having the papers mailed to your ex or his or her lawyer. Although sending papers by registered mail may provide you with proof of receipt, however, this is generally not an accepted form of proof of legal service.

JANE DOE

                       Plaintiff

vs.

JOHN DOE   Acknowledgment of Service

                      Defendant

    The undersigned hereby acknowledges service of a copy of the approved summons and complaint in the above captioned matter on this _____ day of _____, 199____.

Unofficially . . .
The term *appear-
ance* does not
automatically
mean that you or
your spouse has
to physically
appear before
the court. An
appearance can
be accomplished
in writing.

your spouse files an appearance, the court will be able to grant the divorce based on the grounds contained in the complaint that was filed.

Instead of ignoring the allegations of the divorce, however, you may wish to address each and every issue. For example, your spouse may assert some basic information, that you have three children, that you own a house, and that you moved out two months ago. You would admit that these allegations are true. However, your spouse may also include allegations that you have been extremely cruel, that you committed adultery, or that you, in some other way, are responsible for the marital difficulties. You will most likely want to deny allegations that suggest you are at fault in the divorce.

Responding to the specific allegations contained in a complaint for divorce is known as *answer*. An answer allows you to deny any wrongdoing and to detail any inaccuracies which may be contained in the original complaint for divorce.

JANE DOE

      Plaintiff

vs.

JOHN DOE   Appearance

      Defendant

    Defendant, John Doe, hereby enters his appearance in the above captioned action and wishes to be heard regarding the issues of custody, visitation, support and equitable distribution.

Dated: _____

CERTIFICATION OF VERIFICATION AND
NONCOLLUSION

    1. I, John Doe, am the Defendant in the foregoing Appearance to which this Certification is annexed.

    2. The allegations of said Appearance are true to the best of my knowledge and belief. The Appearance is made in truth and good faith and without collusion for the causes set forth.

    I certify that the foregoing statements made by me are true. I am aware that I am subject to punishment if any of the foregoing statements made by me are willfully false.

Dated: _____

Counterclaim

A third way to respond, in addition to either admitting or denying the allegations contained in the divorce papers, is to assert your own allegations in what is called a "counterclaim." That is to say, if you

Unofficially . . .
Even if you don't
want the divorce,
you may have no
alternative if
your spouse
insists. In such a
case, you may
wish to deny all
acts of wrong
doing but forego
a counterclaim.
Generally, the
court will not
find it suspicious
that you did not
file a counter-
claim against
your spouse, and
you will not be
judged nega-
tively in court
for this decision.

are served with divorce papers you may wish to deny all acts of fault alleged against you, and at the same time you are able to allege acts of fault committed by your spouse. Your counterclaim is just like a second set of divorce papers and is often filed as if you were beginning the divorce process.

The counterclaim is a very common response to the service of divorce papers, as it allows the respondent to tell his or her own side of the story. The court will typically grant both plaintiff and respondent a divorce based upon their respective causes of action. In essence, if your spouse files a claim and you file a counterclaim (or vice versa) you are divorcing each other.

Because every divorce is unique, you will want to discuss all of your available options with your attorney. He or she can advise you as to the most appropriate response to make, based on your own particular circumstances.

Finally, in some states, you may not have the opportunity to file an answer or a counterclaim if your grounds for divorce are no-fault, because the court has no interest in the reasons behind the divorce. In these instances, you may merely acknowledge service and begin the process of resolving all issues.

Default

Even if the *respondent* (whether you or your spouse) simply ignores the complaint and fails to respond, a divorce can usually still be granted by way of default. As long as you can prove to the court that your spouse was properly served and was given adequate time to answer the allegations in the complaint, and if there is no legally valid excuse for his or her failure to respond, you may petition the court to grant the divorce by default.

The court will not normally grant you a divorce by default unless it is convinced that your spouse's failure to respond was voluntary. It is therefore very important to carefully follow all the rules and laws in filing for your divorce and serving any papers. Without the aid of an attorney, you may be unaware of all the necessary steps involved in effectuating proper service, so it is highly advisable that you consult legal advice. If the court is not satisfied that the service of divorce papers has been properly handled, it may delay the division of assets or the resolution of issues involving child custody or support.

While it may sometimes seem to a layperson that the requirements of the court are extremely time-consuming and difficult to meet, there are good reasons for these requirements. This is because the court is inclined to give the benefit of doubt to a party that does not appear, giving that person every reasonable chance to be heard. This is why even though the court may grant a divorce, it will often still give the defaulting party an opportunity to be heard on the subject of financial- or child-related issues. When he or she does appear, it is unlikely that the court will vacate its order of divorce, but it will accept arguments about the settlement of particular details in the settlement.

In many cases, after the initial filing of the divorce complaint, an additional set of papers must be served on your spouse. These papers serve notice that the court has granted the divorce but is giving him or her another opportunity to be heard—these papers will stipulate that if he or she continues to

Timesaver
To be sure that your spouse will appear, have your lawyer call your spouse's lawyer to confirm the date and time. It is then your spouse's lawyer's job to remind your spouse to appear.

Example 4:
Sample Answer
and Counterclaim
responding to
the Divorce
Complaint pre-
sented in
Example 1.

JANE DOE
    Plaintiff
vs.
JOHN DOE
    Defendant   Answer and Counterclaim

    Defendant, John Doe, by way of Answer to the Complaint, says:

1. That he admits the allegations in paragraph 1.
2. That he admits the allegations in paragraph 2.
3. That he admits the allegations in paragraph 3.
4. That he denies the allegations in paragraph 4.
5. That he admits the allegations in paragraph 5.
6. That he admits the allegations in paragraph 6.
7. That he admits the allegations in paragraph 7.
8. That he denies the allegations in paragraph 8.

WHEREFORE, the defendant demands judgment:

(a) Dismissing the Complaint of the Plaintiff;
(b) Denying all relief requested by the Plaintiff; and
(c) For such other relief as the Court may deem necessary and proper.

COUNTERCLAIM

    Defendant-Counterclaimant, John Doe, by way of Counterclaim against the plaintiff, Jane Doe, says:

1. The defendant-counterclaimant was married to the plaintiff herein in a religious ceremony on _____.

2. The defendant-counterclaimant was a bona fide resident of the State of New Jersey on the date this cause of action arose, and has ever since and for more than one year next preceding the commencement of this action continued to be such a bona fide resident. The defendant-counterclaimant resides at

_____.

3. The plaintiff resides at _____.

4. The plaintiff has been guilty of extreme cruelty toward the defendant-counterclaimant. Particularly specifying some of the acts of extreme cruelty committed by the plaintiff, the defendant-counterclaimant says:

(a) Plaintiff told defendant-counterclaimant that she no longer loved him and in fact, probably never really loved him;

(b) Plaintiff stays out late at night and refuses to account for her whereabouts;

(c) Plaintiff has become violent toward defendant-counterclaimant. Specifically, following an argument regarding plaintiff's whereabouts, she hit defendant-counterclaimant.

By reason of these acts, the defendant-counterclaimant's health and mental state have become affected and it is improper and unreasonable to expect the defendant-counterclaimant to continue to cohabit with the plaintiff.

More than three months have elapsed since the last act complained of as constituting the defendant-counterclaimant's cause of action. The acts of extreme cruelty committed by the plaintiff, as set forth, are alleged not as constituting in whole or in part the cause of action set forth herein, but as relating back to qualify and characterize the acts constituting said cause of action.

5. _____ children, namely _____, were born of the marriage and they currently are in the custody of both parties.

6. The plaintiff has adequate means of support for herself and to pay for her own fees and costs.

7. Personal and Real Property was legally and bene-ficially acquired by the parties, or either of them, during the marriage.

8. There have been ____ previous proceedings in this or any other Court pertaining to the marriage and its dissolution.

WHEREFORE, Defendant counterclaimant
demands judgment:

A. Dissolving the marriage between the parties;

B. Awarding the parties joint custody of the minor children of the marriage;

C. Requiring the plaintiff to pay the legal fees of the defendant-counterclaimant in the within action.

D. Equitably distributing all property subject to same;

E. For such further relief as the Court may deem just and proper.

_____

Dated:_____

---

ignore the matter, those issues will be decided without any of his or her input.

Except in cases in which you and your spouse have no assets or liabilities that need to be divided, it is highly unusual that both parties do not appear in the case. So don't make the mistake of hoping your spouse won't appear in court and that you'll get everything your way due to his or her absence. That situation is actually a rarity and should never be depended upon or created by deception as an underhanded strategy.

Help in the interim

Once a divorce proceeding starts, you and your spouse are expected to begin to resolve all relevant issues concerning children and finances. What do you do when, despite all good faith efforts, you are unable to reach an agreement with your spouse? In such cases, you may wish to file a *motion* or other similar application with the court which seeks specific relief to your immediate concern.

For example, if you are dependent upon your spouse's income to pay your expenses, you may find it necessary to file a *motion for pendente lite relief* ("motion for temporary relief," or relief pending the final resolution). This is filed when one party to the divorce needs to have access to jointly held assets before the final resolution of the divorce. After all, your day-to-day expenses won't wait for your divorce to become final. The motion for pendente lite relief asks the court to order that your spouse continue to provide financial support (or, alternatively, asks that you be allowed to use some of the family's joint assets) in advance of the final judgment.

When seeking temporary relief from the court, you petition the court in writing. The petition is typically submitted as a *certification*, an *affidavit*, or *affirmation*, explaining the problem you are facing and the relief that is sought. For example, you may wish to explain that you are dependent upon your spouse for support, that the mortgage payment is due, and that you are left without adequate means to buy groceries. Or you may wish to explain that you're caring for two small children and need child support payments to cover their expenses. Your petition may also contain references to particular laws that are relevant to your situation—this is known as a *brief* or *memorandum of law,* and a lawyer will provide the research and information you need for this.

After you file your papers, your spouse then has an opportunity to disagree with your petition. For example, if you have petitioned for the court to order that your spouse provide financial support, he or she may respond to your petition by suggesting you could obtain employment, or that you are not properly budgeting yourself. Once both sides have filed statements affirming their positions, the court may allow or request oral argument—it may ask that your attorneys make an oral presentation based upon the written submissions. Generally, the court will only hear from your attorney—you are not personally expected to argue your position. After consideration of all the papers and arguments, the court will structure a resolution and order that you and your spouse abide by this resolution until further order.

In the above example, the court will most typically ensure that your children are adequately supported, that the mortgage continues to be paid, that the car and credit card payments are made, and that all assets that must eventually be divided between you and your spouse are protected and not unfairly diminished by you or your spouse. In framing a decision, the court must try to divide the total available income in a manner that solves the immediate problem, for example, payment of the mortgage. But the court can't anticipate any future

Watch Out!
As with any other motion, you and your spouse will be bound by the court's order. Failure to comply with the order may be considered to be contempt of the court.

Example 5:
Sample Notice of
Motion for
Pendente Lite
Relief demanding
child support
and alimony, as
well as contin-
ued insurance
coverage, prior
to the final reso-
lution of a
divorce.

JANE DOE
        Plaintiff

vs.

JOHN DOE   Notice of Motion
        Defendant

TO: John Doe
SIR:

PLEASE TAKE NOTICE that on _____, at 9:00 in the forenoon or as soon thereafter as counsel may be heard, the undersigned attorney for the plaintiff shall move before the Honorable _____, at the _____ County Courthouse, _____, ____, for an Order:

1. Compelling the defendant to pay $_____ as child support, directly to plaintiff, for the support of the parties' minor children.

2. Compelling defendant to pay $_____ as alimony, directly to plaintiff, for the support and welfare of plaintiff;

3. Compelling defendant to maintain medical insurance coverage for the benefit of the minor children.

PLEASE TAKE NOTICE that in support of this notice, Plaintiff's Certification is annexed hereto.

Also please take note that a form of Order is annexed hereto.

problems or issues—if your situation changes, you may have to petition the court again and seek further relief.

The *pendente lite* application may be filed to address issues that go beyond financial concerns.

JANE DOE

     Plaintiff

vs.

JOHN DOE   Certification

     Defendant

I, Jane Doe, of full age, the plaintiff in the above refer-enced case, make this Certification in support of my Motion for Pendente Lite Relief, and hereby certify:

1. My husband and I have been separated for the past two months. Last month I filed for divorce.

2. Since our separation, my husband has refused to con-tribute toward the expenses of the house, including necessary expenses incurred on behalf of our two minor children.

3. My husband works full time. I am not employed. Without support from my husband, my children and I will not be able to meet our monthly bills.

4. Further, my husband is provided medical coverage by his employer for the benefit of our children. However, he told me that he was going to cancel the coverage unless I split the cost with him.

I, Jane Doe, hereby certify that the above statements made by me are true. I further certify that I am aware that I am subject to punishment if the above statements made by me are willfully false.

Example 6: Certification in Support of the Motion for Pendente Lite Relief appearing in Example 5.

For example, you may need to file one to resolve problems relating to child custody and visitation. After all, even before your divorce becomes final, you will probably have to work out where the kids will live, and the parent who lives apart from the

children will need some sort of visitation schedule.
If you and your spouse cannot agree on these questions on your own, the court may have to make some
initial determinations.

One area of concern addressed in this way is the
question of child custody, which we discuss in much
greater depth in Chapters 8 and 9. If you and your
spouse cannot agree upon custody, the process of
obtaining evaluations will probably begin as a result
of a pendente lite motion. When it comes to children's issues, the court is inclined to proceed con-
servatively. Because of this, it will often order that
you, your spouse, and your children be evaluated by
an independent advocate or counselor. Until such
evaluations can be completed, the court is likely to
order joint physical custody. This is an attempt by
the court to keep both parents on equal footing.
This does not mean that the court's final determination will mirror its initial order. The court will still
conduct much more extensive hearings and procedures which rely upon expert evaluations before
making a final decision. (We'll discuss this in more
detail in Chapters 8 and 9.) For purposes of pendente lite relief, the court will attempt to maintain
the status quo as much as possible.

It is important to understand that the court, at
this point, is merely addressing the immediate concerns that face you and your family during the
divorce process. For example, your spouse may be
showing up at your house on a sporadic, unan-
nounced basis to see the children, and this may be
causing you problems. In such a situation, you may
request that the court establish regular visitation
days or times, so as to enable you and the children
to maintain some type of regular schedule. Without

JANE DOE

     Plaintiff

vs.

JOHN DOE   Order

     Defendant

THIS MATTER being presented to the court on the application of _____, Esq., attorney for the plaintiff, and it appearing upon a reading of the certifications by the parties and having heard oral argument by counsel; and for good reason shown;

It is, on this _____ day of _____, 199___;

ORDERED, as follows:

(1) That on the first day of each month, beginning on _____ the defendant shall pay directly to the plaintiff the sum of $_____ as child support.

(2) That on the first day of each month, beginning on _____ the defendant shall pay directly to the plaintiff the sum of $_____ as alimony.

(3) That the defendant shall maintain medical insurance coverage as provided by his employer for the benefit of the minor children. Defendant shall be solely responsible for the cost of said insurance.

Example 7: Court Order mandating payment of child support and alimony and the maintenance of insurance coverage for the children as petitioned for in the Motion for Pendente Lite Relief appearing in Examples 5 and 6.

much consideration, the court may order alternate weekends or a similar arrangement just to establish some order.

In some states, as soon as the divorce papers are filed the court may grant some automatic temporary "reliefs" without any need for you to petition. For example, upon filing for the divorce, you and your spouse may automatically be restrained from selling, transferring, or borrowing against any of your property. You may also be restrained from taking a child out of state or canceling or transferring life-insurance policies. However, many states do not have these automatic restraints—make certain you know your state's position on these issues, and file any applications you may need to protect your interests and the interests of your children.

What can you expect?

Watch Out!
Nothing hurts your case more than withholding information from your lawyer. Without full knowledge of the situation, your attorney can not effectively represent your interests. So one of the worst things you can do is fail to tell your attorney the full and honest truth.

While you know your spouse better than your attorney does, your attorney, because of his or her experience with people going through divorces, may be able to predict your spouse's reactions, motives and intentions better than you. It is important to be honest with your attorney as he or she will not be able to properly represent you unless he or she understands all of the facts and circumstances of your case. Many times, people make the mistake of withholding information from their attorney due to embarrassment or other emotional reasons. Your attorney is not judging you. To the contrary, if you are honest, your lawyer will be able to better advise you with regard to all issues of concern.

Expect to have some very frank and difficult conversations with your lawyer. And understand that while your attorney is representing your interests, he or she must do so within the framework of the law. Your attorney may have to tell you that as a consequence of law and/or the facts and circumstances of your case, your demands and expectations cannot be met. This does not mean that your attorney is working against you. For example, the more you fight, the more it costs. Your lawyer may counsel you to move away from confrontation and try a more cooperative approach when you just want to lash out. But your attorney realizes that sometimes you simply cannot afford to continue to fight—for either financial or emotional reasons—and by recommending compromise he or she may be trying to take a longer view toward protecting your interests. If you don't understand why your attorney is taking—or refusing to take—a particular course of action, talk frankly with him or her. Your attorney *will* level with you, if you ask.

Because a divorce involves two parties, you won't be able to control everything that happens. Your spouse can greatly influence the tempo and tone of your divorce. For example, while you might be willing to settle your case amicably, if your spouse is intent on fighting every issue down to the division of the toothbrushes, you are in for a very difficult and expensive divorce. Either you or your spouse generally has the right to contest any and all issues that affect you, your children, your finances, and any other relevant concern. As a result, the court normally will not decide a contested issue without at least some type of hearing or presentation of evidence with regard to that matter. The more contested the issues, the more you will need the court's involvement and the more it will cost you for your divorce.

Through all of this, you should not confuse negotiations and legal posturing with settlement or resolution. Making a demand does not mean that you are going to get it. Just because you and your lawyer agree that you are right, it does not mean that your spouse—or the court—will agree. Just because your lawyer, in very good faith, tells you that you are going to prevail, it does not mean that you will. We'll take up the subject of negotiating a settlement in Chapter 7, but for now keep in mind that it is generally a good thing that you remain open to the possibility of compromising with your spouse. If you cannot, you can expect to spend a lot of time filing motions, going through extensive discovery procedures (see the next chapter), attending hearings, and possibly going to trial.

How long will this go on?

Timesaver
At the initial meeting between your legal team and your spouse's, it helps to state that both sides are interested in a timely resolution to your negotiations. Both sides have much to gain by completing the process swiftly, so setting such a standard helps to establish both sides' willingness to cooperate.

The length of time it takes to get a divorce depends on how long it takes for you and your spouse to resolve all contested issues. If you can resolve your differences without the court's direct involvement, you can be divorced in typically a few months. If, on the other hand, you require the court to hear an issue, you may wait for the court's hearing or decision for many months. This obviously will delay the ultimate resolution of your case. Although most people get divorced well within one year from the time the divorce papers are filed, if your spouse wants to fight, or is, for example, concealing information regarding assets, liabilities, or other significant issues that impact the terms of a resolution, your divorce may take years.

Preparing for the worst

Although far from typical, your spouse may address every issue of your divorce in bad faith, with deceit and ill will. You should be aware that he or she does not have the right to act in bad faith, but as a practical matter it may be difficult, if not impossible, to quickly convince the court that your spouse is either lying or acting against the interests of justice. It will take time and money to prove your spouse to be the louse that he or she has become.

We're fighting about everything!

More often than not, you and your spouse will agree more than you disagree. This is especially true with issues regarding children. Although custody fights can be the worst battles in a divorce, they are not very common. You and your spouse, sometimes with the aid of a mental health professional, can usually agree upon what is in the best interest of your children. If the two of you are going to fight, most often money will be the cause.

Avoiding the worst

One way to help avoid the worst is to make sure that you take an active role in your divorce. This sounds simple, but in times of intense emotional distress, many of us are tempted to throw all our difficulties into our lawyers' laps and expect him or her to solve all the problems. But you should be aware of all discussions, negotiations, and other aspects of your divorce, as each happens. You should not merely hear the conclusion of a negotiation, but rather, you should play an active part. This of course does not mean that you need to be on the telephone all day with your lawyer. What it does mean though is that your attorney should keep you abreast of all events that influence your case.

Privacy issues

All conversations between you and your attorney are confidential and cannot be disclosed without your consent. This is generally known as the *attorney-client privilege*. The privilege belongs to you, not your attorney, meaning that you, although it may not be a good idea, can discuss your case with anyone, but your attorney cannot discuss the matter with anyone

Watch Out! Sometimes, even though you and your spouse can resolve an issue or series of issues, your attorneys may insist on fighting. Remember, your lawyer works *for* you. Do not let him or her dictate your arguments.

other than you. But, although your conversations with your lawyer are confidential, your divorce proceeding is not a private matter.

Generally speaking, court proceedings are open to the public. This does not mean that anyone off the street will be able to obtain your court file and divulge confidential information. However, except for some issues that involve children, your case is generally heard in an open courtroom in front of strangers. As a practical matter though, except for the judge and his clerks, no one will know anything about your divorce. If you have concerns regarding private issues, you should discuss these with your attorney in order to ensure that your interests are protected to the fullest possible extent.

With the filing of the divorce complaint and the response (with or without a counterclaim), the divorce process has begun. Now you turn your attention to how to handle the division of responsibilities, assets, and liabilities that will be necessary when you and your spouse split up. This requires that both you and your partner are equally knowledgeable about your household circumstances, and to ensure that this knowledge is equally available to the two of you, a procedure known as "discovery" is available. In Chapter 6 you will learn about this process, what it's there for, and how to most effectively use it.

Just the facts

- A divorce can be started by either you or your spouse.

- Causes of action can assert either fault or no-fault.

- In addition to either admitting or denying the allegations contained in the divorce papers, you may wish to file your own claims or counter-claim.

- If specific relief for a particular issue is needed prior to the final divorce, you can file a motion with the court for immediate resolution.

The Discovery Process

Chapter 6

In order to settle all of the issues of your divorce, both you and your spouse need to have full access to all the information you need. You recall that in Chapter 3 you were advised to gather together all the information you can on your own before you even begin the formal process of divorcing, and you should have been keeping careful records of any and all events that may have an impact upon your final settlement. But some information is more difficult to come by than the day-to-day records of household. If your spouse has information that you lack, you are given the opportunity to obtain it through a process known as *discovery*—so-called because you are discovering pieces of evidence with regard to your case. The idea behind discovery is that for any settlement or court resolution to be fair and equitable, it must be based upon equal access to all available information.

The need for inside information

Gathering information through discovery is an essential part of the divorce process. Even when both spouses want to resolve all issues peacefully and amicably, some discovery may be needed in order to ensure a fair and equitable agreement— even if only to confirm certain understandings and justifications that underlie your settlement proposal.

Unofficially . . .
Even if your state does not require the filing of a preliminary form containing information about your family and finances, you will be able to obtain this data by way of other discovery methods.

For example, before an agreement can be reached, you must have a full and complete understanding of your finances, including such items as the value of a house, car, pension plan or other assets, wages, debts, expenses, costs of insurance, day care, school, and a multitude of other concerns. You and your spouse may both already have a good idea as to the values of these items—but it is often the case that only one spouse has managed the household finances prior to divorce, and therefore has a significantly better understanding of the family's total financial picture. Through discovery, both parties have the opportunity to level the playing field. Its procedures are designed to uncover any information you may need to resolve any issue arising from your decision to divorce.

The starting point: basic disclosure

Watch Out!
You typically must certify that the information that you provide in the form is true. If you willfully provided incorrect information, you will be subject to the penalties of perjury.

When a divorce is filed, many states require you to file a document to disclose basic information on your family. While the actual content of such forms differ from state to state, the following list provides an example of some of the information that you may be required to furnish. The questions may serve as a good starting point for formulating your discovery demands.

In addition to the general disclosure document, you may also be required to provide a full and complete copy of your federal and state income tax

The basic information list

1. Name and address of parties.

2. Name, address, and birth date of all child(ren).

3. Person with whom all child(ren) resides.

4. Name and address of your employer(s).

5. Name and address of health insurance company(ies) and type of coverage.

6. Name and address of life insurance company(ies) and policy information.

7. Last year's income of you and your spouse.

8. Present income of you and your spouse.

9. Analysis of all deductions from your paycheck, including taxes, medical insurance, life insurance, pension plan, savings plan, wage execution, voluntary retirement fund payments, loan payments, and all other deductions.

10. Budget of monthly expenses, including:

- Rent
- Real estate
- Electric and gas
- Renter's insurance
- Parking
- Mortgage
- Real estate taxes
- Homeowners insurance
- Repairs and maintenance
- Water and sewer
- Garbage removal
- Other mortgages
- Snow removal and lawn care
- Maintenance charges
- Other shelter charges
- Telephone
- Service contracts on equipment
- Cable TV
- Plumber/electrician
- Equipment and furnishings
- Automobile payment
- Automobile insurance
- Automobile registration and license
- Automobile maintenance and fuel
- Commuting expenses
- Food at home
- Household supplies
- Prescription drugs
- Non–prescription drugs
- School lunches
- Restaurants
- Clothing
- Dry cleaning and commercial laundry
- Hair care
- Domestic help
- Medical
- Dental

- Medical insurance
- Sports and hobbies
- Camps and vacations
- Children's private school costs
- Parent's educational costs
- Children's lessons
- Baby-sitting and day-care expenses
- Entertainment
- Newspapers and periodicals

- Gifts and contributions
- Payments to non-child dependents
- Prior existing support obligations
- Life insurance
- Savings/investment
- Debt service
- Visitation expenses
- Professional expenses
- Other

11. Values of following assets and liabilities, including:

- Real estate
- Bank accounts and certificates of deposit
- Vehicles
- Tangible personal property
- Stocks and bonds
- Pension, profit-sharing, retirement plan(s)
- Businesses, partnerships, professional practices

- Whole life insurance
- Other assets
- Mortgages on real estate
- Long term debts
- Revolving charges
- Other short term debts
- Contingent liabilities

returns, W-2 statements, 1099 statements, self-employed schedule C statements, recent pay stubs, bonus information, and any other financial information that is relevant to your divorce. Even if the court does not require these items, you might find it useful to have them for your own records and for your attorney's use.

You and your spouse may find that by exchanging these types of forms, either by way of a formal court procedure or informal swap, you can resolve most, if not all, of your financial issues. This is the first type of discovery; it quickly and easily provides a picture of your present circumstances. If that's true, there may be no need for further discovery. But if further information or clarification is needed, other methods of discovery are available.

Interrogatories

Interrogatories are the next most common form of discovery. These are written questions served upon you or your spouse for which written answers are required. The questions must be answered under oath, meaning that if false information is willfully provided through this method, you or your spouse will be subject to the penalties of perjury. Because interrogatories are answered under oath, they are often very effective in providing accurate information.

Moneysaver
Interrogatories are often the least expensive type of discovery and, as a result, often the first attempt at gathering information.

What can be asked?

An interrogatory may ask any question that is relevant to your divorce. Although the language of a formal interrogatory may be legalistic, the questions are quite basic. The following is a list of some of the questions that may be asked of you—or that you may ask your spouse.

1. Where do you live?

2. Do you own or rent? How many rooms are in your home, and how are the rooms used?

3. Who lives in the home with you? Give names and the relationship of each resident to you.

4. Are you currently employed? If so, give the name and address of your present employer(s), the date you started working there, and your duties on the job, and your weekly pay (gross and net). A copy of one or more recent pay

stubs (usually three) will be required to document salary, as will a copy of the W-2 form(s) on file with your current employer. If you have an employment contract, a copy of that may be required as well.

5. If you've been with your present employer(s) for less than three years, or if you held other jobs as well during any of the past three years, you'll need to provide the same information for each such employment as requested in the above stated interrogatory.

6. Does your employer provide you with any insurance? If yes, you'll be asked to list each type and plan, together with the benefits to which you are entitled. You'll also be asked to provide the nature and value of such coverage.

7. Does your employer provide you with free or subsidized meals, transportation, or other such fringe benefits? If yes, provide the nature and value and basis of valuation of each such benefit.

8. Does your employer pay for any expenses you incur? If yes, you may be asked to provide the gross amount paid by each employer, for each year, during the past five calendar years and list each payment you received and the nature of the expense incurred.

9. Do/did you receive any other income during the current year and/or during the past five calendar years? If yes, you'll be asked to list the type of income and the source from which you received it, and you'll be asked whether that income was included on your Federal and State Tax Returns during the past three years.

10. Does anyone owe you any money? If yes, you'll be asked the name and address of each debtor; the amount of the debt; the date the obligation was incurred; the date it will become due; the conditions for payment of the obligation.

11. You'll be asked about any and all checking accounts in which you had power of signature within the past five years. You will need to provide the name and address of (each) bank, the account number(s), the date you opened the account, the date you closed it (if applicable), the name the account is in, and the name(s) of any other people with legal right or interest in such accounts. You will also be expected to supply the name and address of any other person who had power of signature on any such account; and a copy of the check registers and monthly statements for each account.

12. For savings accounts, money market accounts, or certificates of deposit in which you had power of signature within the past five years, you will be asked to supply similar information, as well as a list of deposits to the account(s) and the source of the funds deposited, a list of withdrawals, and a copy of any bank books or statements for the accounts. You will be asked to itemize the values of certain of your assets, including automobiles, jewelry, boats, collections, furs, household goods and furniture, and paintings or other art work.

13. You will be asked to provide details on any life insurance or annuity policy, or any life insurance program, in which you have an interest.

14. You'll be asked for details about any safe-deposit boxes maintained by you or in which you had power of signature in the past three years.

15. You'll be asked if you've submitted any financial statement, for credit purposes or for any other purpose, within the past three years, and if so, you will be asked to provide details of this action.

16. You'll be asked about any withdrawals or trans-ferals of funds from accounts held jointly with your spouse to any account or investment in your name solely or to any account or invest-ment in which you had an interest together with others, not your spouse, during the course of your marriage.

17. You will be asked if there are any funds, real property, investments, or other assets that you claim should not be subject to division between you and your spouse. If yes, you'll need to pro-vide complete details about such assets, and the justification for holding them apart from the general division of property.

18. You will be asked if there is any property titled in your spouse's name to which you claim a share. If yes, you'll need to describe that prop-erty, including an estimate of the total equity you hold in it and the portion of that equity that you believe should go to you. You will also be asked to explain why you believe you have a right to claim a share.

19. You will be asked to provide the names and addresses of everyone who may serve as a witness to the allegations you are making in your plea. You will also have to indicate their

relationship to you and whether or not you expect them to appear in any court trial.

20. You will be asked to disclose information regarding any gifts or inheritances you may have received before or during your marriage.

21. You will be asked to disclose all your current debts, the parties to whom they are owed, and the circumstances in which the debts were incurred.

22. You may be asked about your mental-health history, or to provide release forms allowing access to your treatment records.

23. You may be asked to provide information on your medical history, or authorization for the release of your medical records.

24. You may be asked about your use of prescription medicines over the past three years, including details on the types of medication and the condition for which it was prescribed. You may even be asked to provide copies of these prescriptions.

Getting the most out of an interrogatory

Depending upon your facts and circumstances, you may wish to ask very specific questions. For example, your spouse may be seeking alimony because he or she can no longer work as a result of a permanent medical disability. You may wish to ask questions about the nature of this condition and you may ask that your spouse provide copies of any reports and medical records that prove the disability. On the other hand, if your spouse is claiming that he or she cannot pay support due to a loss of his or her job, you may ask to see your spouse's resume

Watch Out!
Your state may limit the number or types of questions that can be asked, so make sure your lawyer chooses the questions carefully—don't waste your time asking for information you can get easily on your own.

and a list of all potential employers to whom he or she is presently applying for work.

Sometimes, you may not be satisfied with your spouse's written answers to your interrogatory. The disadvantage to interrogatories is that typically, although the answers are signed by your spouse, the answers are likely to be heavily influenced by the advice of his or her attorney. Sometimes this won't matter—if your question is about the specifics of his or her weekly paycheck there is a pay stub that can serve as concrete evidence. Other information is less easily verified. And there is always the danger that your spouse may simply deny the existence of records that you request.

Depositions

Timesaver
Often, this is a very effective technique in quickly clarifying information that was not fully explained or disclosed by way of interrogatories, avoiding the time and expense of exchanging letters, making phone calls, or scheduling meetings for clarification.

One solution to this problem is to take a *deposition*. Depositions are questions that are answered orally, under oath. The advantage is that your spouse must answer, on the spot, for him or herself, without the benefit of lengthy and careful analysis with his or her attorney. These questions and answers are recorded, typically by a stenographer, and become proofs and evidence in your divorce proceeding.

Generally, you can take depositions from any parties that have direct knowledge about a contested issue in your divorce. For example, your spouse may be a salesman and claim that his wages and commissions have been drastically reduced, coincidentally, at the time of your claim for alimony. You may be able to depose his or her employer to learn more about the circumstances. As a general rule, you are entitled to depose any party that possesses information that is not only relevant but also necessary in order to resolve your case.

JANE DOE
          Plaintiff
vs.
JOHN DOE
          Defendant

          NOTICE OF TAKING OF DEPOSITION ON ORAL EXAMINATION
To: John Doe
     PLEASE TAKE NOTICE that in accordance with all applicable Rules of Civil Practice and Procedure, testimony will be taken by deposition upon oral examination by a person authorized by the State of _____ to administer oaths on _____ at _____ at _____, with respect to all matters relevant to the subject matter in this action, at which time and place you will please produce the following:

Dated: _____.

Example 1: Sample Notice of Taking of Deposition document.

Despite the advantages of depositions, this type of discovery is not typical. It may take you and your lawyer only two or three hours to draft written questions, but all day to ask them and get them answered. In addition to attorney costs, all of the questions and answers are recorded by a stenographer, and he or she must be paid for his or her time as well as for producing a written transcript of the deposition.

Watch Out!
Generally, depositions can easily cost three or four times more than interrogatories and as a result are typically only used when absolutely necessary.

Hand it over . . . subpoenas and demands to produce

Sometimes you do not need an answer to a question, but rather, you need a document, or business records, or bank books, or stock certificates, for example. You may be entitled to seek these documents by way of what is generally called a *demand to produce* or by way of a *subpoena*. Obviously, these are methods which request or order your spouse to cooperate in providing the requested information, thus allowing you equal access to the documents. This type of discovery may be especially important in instances in which one party, to the exclusion of the other, possesses records or documents that are relevant to the issues of the divorce. For example, your spouse may have always done your tax returns and upon your separation, took all the tax related documents with him or her. By way of a demand to produce or other similar document, your spouse is compelled to give you copies of the returns. You may wish to demand any document that is relevant to the issues of your divorce.

The following are general examples of demands you may wish to address to your spouse as a part of your divorce.

1. If your spouse rents his or her residence, a copy of the lease.

2. Copy of any employment contract in effect between your spouse and any employer within the past five years.

3. Copies of any insurance policies that you presently own, including health insurance and life insurance.

4. Copies of expense vouchers submitted to your spouse's employer during the past two years.

5. Copies of all tax returns prepared by your spouse or on his or her behalf during the past three years.

6. Copies of all check registers and bank statements for all checking accounts in which your spouse had any interest or authorization to sign checks or make withdrawals during the past five years.

7. Copies of all bank books or bank statements for all savings accounts, certificates of deposit, money market, or similar accounts in which your spouse had any interest or authorization to make withdrawals during the past five years.

8. Copies of any policies or annuity contracts or similar in which your spouse had any interest during the past five years.

9. Copies of any financial statements prepared or submitted to any company or institution, for credit or other purposes, within the past three years.

10. Copy of any report of any expert who engaged in connection with the divorce.

11. Copy of any will or trust by which your spouse received an inheritance or by which he or she received or will receive any income or principal, or in which he or she has any remainder interest.

12. Copies of all prescriptions for any prescription medication taken during the past three years.

13. A copy of the resume he or she used to obtain his or her present position.

Getting an expert's opinion

Even though you and your spouse share assets, you may disagree about the worth of the assets. The most common instance is when you own a house but disagree as to the fair market value. In order to resolve this type of issue, you may have the right to obtain an expert opinion—often called an *appraisal*.

. . . On real estate

The case of determining the value of a house, for instance, might require an appraisal or a real estate broker's letter. You may wish to obtain something as

Unofficially . . .
As a general rule, real estate brokers, because they want to list your house for sale, provide higher estimates of fair market value than real estate appraisers who are truly impartial and paid to do nothing more than provide an accurate and detailed appraisal.

simple as a real estate broker's letter indicating what in his or her opinion your house is worth, or you may wish to hire a licensed real estate appraiser and obtain a full appraisal of the property.

...On the value of a business

If you or your spouse owns a business, it is often very difficult to accurately estimate its fair market value. In these circumstances you may wish to hire an accountant who specializes in evaluating businesses.

...On medical issues

You may be seeking support as a result of a medical disability or illness. In this case, you may have the right to secure a medical expert to prove your claim, and your spouse will have the right to use his or her own medical expert to challenge or disprove your claim. Often, the most reliable expert opinion in these types of cases is the doctor who treats you for the disability. Although you can hire an independent doctor to support your claim, if your own treating doctor does not support your allegations, you may be hard pressed to convince your spouse and the court.

...On employment issues

Another common example of expert discovery is the case in which your spouse may be seeking support as a result of his or her inability to obtain employment. In these instances, an employment expert may be necessary to either prove or disprove the claim. This type of expert, based upon your spouse's education, work experience, ability, the job market, and other relevant factors, would provide an opinion as to whether your spouse can obtain employment and if so, for how much money.

What an expert witness does

All these experts generally provide a report as to his or her findings and conclusions. The expert may then be deposed or may be asked to render a follow-up report to more specifically address certain issues or address new issues.

Unless the court recognizes someone as an expert, he or she cannot present opinion, but rather, only fact. For example, if you cannot work due to a medical disability, you can testify that you are in pain or feel excessive stress. However, you cannot conclude that you cannot work. Instead, the court will only accept the opinion of an expert, who after examination, can offer his or her findings and conclusions. In this instance, in addition to a medical expert, you may require an employment expert whose opinion will be used in conjunction with the medical expert to either prove or disprove your case.

Whenever you and your spouse cannot resolve an issue that cannot solely be decided on the existing facts, procure expert discovery. By using expert opinions, the court helps remove biased and prejudicial testimony.

When your spouse makes an admission

There are other types of discovery techniques available for your use. For example, you may demand certain admissions from your spouse. Let's say you have discovered evidence that your spouse is earning a yearly bonus that he or she did not previously voluntarily disclose. You may present your proof to your spouse and demand that he or she make a formal admission, under oath, acknowledging the receipt of the bonus. If your spouse does not admit

Watch Out!
Be aware that experts are many times nothing more than hired guns. There are typically a network of experts who for a fee and will testify on your behalf in support of your claim. The same is also true of the experts available to your spouse's side of the case, so make sure your attorney is prepared to disprove a seedy expert witness' claims, if not of professional reputation.

the allegation, he or she is typically required to explain why the allegation is not true. Very often, demands for admissions are a very quick, accurate, and inexpensive way to resolve discovery issues.

The idea of discovery is to allow you the opportunity to learn everything you and, if necessary, the court, need to know in order to resolve the contested issues of your divorce. As a result, generally, so long as you seek information that is relevant and necessary to a resolution, you may seek that information through any appropriate discovery procedure.

Some pros and cons of the process

Although discovery is very useful and sometimes indispensable, it is also often very costly. If you and your spouse have easily verifiable incomes, assets, and liabilities, chances are that you will be able to resolve your case without the need for extensive interrogatories, or depositions, or expert opinions. In cases where you or your spouse is not a straight W-2 wage earner, but instead is self-employed or is paid on a commission or bonus basis, extensive discovery often becomes the only way to satisfy yourself with regard to the family finances. In these cases, you should expect to spend significant time and money in obtaining accurate evaluations. As a general rule, if you or your spouse solely controlled the finances during the marriage, chances are that significant financial discovery will take place. If custody is an issue, very significant discovery will take place. In these instances, you will require very extensive expert reports and evaluations.

In cases of self-employment or hidden assets and income, discovery can lead to very delicate tax issues. For example, discovery may lead to the discovery of unreported cash in a family business. Generally, if the court becomes aware of issues such as unreported income, it will notify the Internal Revenue Service.

Discovery motions

Discovery is typically done on a voluntary basis and although the court may set a discovery schedule and monitor progress, much of the process is dependent upon the cooperation of you and your spouse. What do you do if your spouse does not properly or fully respond to your discovery requests? You can file a motion or other similar application, asking the court to compel your spouse to cooperate. As with any other motion, you and your spouse have the opportunity to file papers regarding facts and law and often have the opportunity to present oral argument.

In a discovery motion, you will most often explain what discovery was requested, the relevancy and necessity for the information and the refusal of your spouse to comply. You will most likely also have to prove that your discovery demands were served in a timely fashion and further in accordance with the applicable court rules.

Unfortunately, your spouse may assert that your demands are not reasonable or not relevant. Or, for example, he or she may claim that the requested discovery does not exist or is not available. After considering the arguments, the court will decide whether your spouse should comply with your demand. Generally, if the court believes that your demands are necessary and reasonable, your spouse will be ordered to provide meaningful and accurate answers. Or, the court may fashion a compromise and order that your spouse furnish answers to modified demands.

Moneysaver
Extensive discovery means an expensive divorce. Use only those techniques that are absolutely necessary. If you are satisfied that you and your spouse can cooperate to resolve all your disputes, discovery may be a wasteful and lengthy exercise. So remember, use discovery only to seek information that you do not already know or for which you require proof or admissions from your spouse.

If the court compels your spouse to comply with your requests, it will typically give your spouse a specific time period, for example, 30 days, to obey, or face possible penalties or sanctions from the court. Other times, the court may appoint a neutral party to oversee the details of your discovery process and ensure that all reasonable and relevant demands are met. In doing so, the court is working to fashion any resolution that aids in the full and complete exchange of discovery information.

From a practical point of view, if there are discovery demands to which your spouse just plain refuses to comply, although the court may order him or her to do so, actually getting the information is often very difficult and sometimes impossible. You may need to file a motion to compel a response to your requests and then a second motion to compel your spouse to comply with the court's previous order. For example, the court may have ordered that your spouse provide you with certain discovery within 30 days, but your spouse still refuses.

You would hope that merely because your spouse did not properly comply, without additional time, money, and motions by you, he or she would be properly punished. This is not necessarily the case. You may have to file another motion to convince the court that your spouse failed to meet the terms of the prior court order as this may not be so obvious to the court. For example, your spouse may have provided some information but not all the information requested. You may find yourself arguing over the completeness of your spouse's compliance, which is often very difficult for the court to determine. You may have requested all records from your spouse's business. In response, then, he or she

Timesaver
To avoid the expense and extensive time required by discovery motions, some states oversee the case by appointing a discovery master or other individual to resolve disputes. Other states set a discovery schedule to which you and your spouse must adhere, depending upon the circumstances.

may provide you with some records and claim that no other records exist. Although you may believe that your spouse is hiding information, it is often very difficult for the court to determine who is right.

As with any court proceeding, credibility is very important and many times the determining factor. In a divorce proceeding, many times the court must simply determine who is telling the truth. It will of course use all of the facts and circumstances of your situation for assistance, but in instances of "he said, she said," you may be frustrated at the court's inability to quickly recognize the complete truth.

Although you may file a motion for the resolution of most any issue in a divorce proceeding, most often, you will not want to. Motions are expensive— a single motion can cost you thousands of dollars in legal fees. Why so expensive? Motions can involve certifications or affidavits, briefs and exhibits of proof, and other documents; they may take many hours to write, compile, and serve upon your spouse. As a result, even before you get to court, your attorney may have spent many hours and billed you thousands of dollars.

Many states actually establish a discovery schedule to be followed by you and your spouse. The schedule provides time limits, for example, to serve and answer interrogatories, take depositions, or render expert opinions. For example, a schedule may provide for the following discovery:

1. Service of interrogatories—30 days

2. Respond to interrogatories—30 days after receipt

3. Depositions—90 days

Moneysaver
Each motion you require can add thousands of dollars to your legal bill. You should keep this in mind when deciding to file a motion rather than compromising. Time in court waiting for your turn is still billable by your attorney. Cutting down your need for court appearances can greatly reduce your legal fees.

4. Expert evaluations—120 days

5. Other written demands—60 days

6. Completion of all discovery—180 days

Your state may not issue formal written discovery schedules, but rather, have rules and regulations which dictate the type of discovery and time periods involved with each method. In any event, over the course of hopefully months, rather than years, you will be able to access all necessary information in order to resolve your case. The hope is that sometime during the discovery period you and your spouse will be satisfied that you have obtained all necessary information, and as a result, can resolve all issues without the need to involve the court. During discovery, unless you or your spouse petitions the court as a result of your spouse's bad faith or failure to cooperate, the court will in large part ignore your case and allow you to formulate your own resolution.

While discovery can take some time, you will eventually have acquired adequate information on which to base your case. At this point you may find that you and your spouse, together with your respective attorneys, are ready to cooperatively reach an agreement on the settlement of your financial and parental issues. Or perhaps you will discover that you need, instead, to turn to the court for help in resolving some items that are in dispute. In the next chapter you will learn the steps involved in formulating a proposal for settlement and you will discover techniques that will help you to participate in negotiating its terms with your soon-to-be ex. And, in the event that negotiations are not successful, you'll get the scoop on just what is involved in bringing your divorce to court.

Just the facts

- Both you and your spouse may obtain information from the other regarding all issues of the divorce.

- Many states require you to file an informational document that discloses basic data.

- If your spouse does not fully respond to your discovery requests you can file a motion asking the court to compel your spouse to cooperate.

- For every motion you require, you can expect to add thousands of dollars to your legal bill.

- Many states actually establish a discovery schedule to be followed by you and your spouse.

Chapter 7

Bringing It All to Closure

Now that you've had the chance to collect and review all the information you need to decide just how you want to divide the responsibilities and property of your marriage, it is time to look at the process of resolution. Divorce proceedings are designed to help you resolve all relevant issues—parental and financial. Often you will be able to settle your case with informal resolution techniques and little court involvement—this is always the best and least stressful way to go, if you can possibly manage it. You might need help along the way, however, and for this reason some formal as well as informal court procedures have been developed for your use.

The basic steps toward resolution

Typically, you and your attorney, along with your spouse and his or her attorney, can identify all the important issues that must be resolved. Those issues may involve the care and support of children, support of you or your spouse, the division of assets, and payment of debt. Once you have identified the relevant issues, you and your attorney can begin to formulate a proposal for resolution.

The most common method of resolution is simple telephone negotiation. From the first time your attorney speaks with your spouse's attorney, he or she can begin to work toward resolving the case. Although there may be practical restraints that prevent you from discussing specific proposals—such as a pending appraisal of your house or business—the most amicable and successful resolutions often begin very shortly after the initial filing of divorce papers. Your attorney might confer with your spouse's counsel by telephone very early in the case in an effort to draw up a plan of settlement based on the information and requirements you already provided.

It is useful for your attorney to begin settlement discussions right from the start of your case. To help in this process, you must decide what is important to you. For example, if you own a house and want to continue living there you'll want to devise a financial plan that allows you to pay the carrying charges and other related expenses. The more definitive your plan, the better your chances of achieving your goals. It is much easier to settle an issue for which there is a clear cut realistic answer. For example, it will be difficult to convince your spouse that you should remain in the house if you have no way of paying the mortgage. Likewise, if your plan does not provide adequate provisions for your spouse, chances are you will not settle.

Preparing your proposals

Once you and your spouse have exchanged sufficient information derived through the discovery process, it's time to prepare a specific settlement proposal. This is a good time to conduct an informal meeting between you and your spouse, in the presence of your attorneys. At this meeting you will exchange settlement proposals with the hope of finding some common ground. Up to now, negotiations will have largely been conducted by your attorneys, as they set about the process of laying the groundwork for settlement. Now, however, a four-way meeting involving you, your spouse, and your respective attorneys will allow you the opportunity to speak for yourself.

Very often, you can settle all—or almost all—of the significant issues in your divorce in a single meeting. Of course, you and your spouse must want to compromise for this to happen. Except in cases that involve custody issues or complicated property valuations, this type of meeting can usually address most of the custody, support, and property-division concerns and at least identify any other areas of dispute that might require additional discovery or court assistance. As a result, informal, lawyer-assisted meetings early in the divorce process can help to save you money and time in resolving your entire case. They provide you with the general outlines for drafting the proposal you will ultimately file with the court for approval.

Negotiating your terms

As noted above, these meetings are the place in which you negotiate the terms of your divorce. There are some basic rules for getting what you

Moneysaver
If all parties to the divorce can meet face-to-face, your issues can be settled in less time and with less expense than if you have to pay hourly for a time-consuming game of telephone tag between your respective lawyers. Remember, you're paying your attorney by the hour, and you may even be paying for each individual phone call.

want from this process. Negotiating is not just a back-and-forth discussion—it's goal-oriented and must be entered into with care and strategy. It is helpful to recognize that there are basic rules to the art of negotiating, and to learn to use them to your own advantage. Here are a few things to keep in mind when you're meeting with your spouse and your spouse's attorney:

- Be firm. If you're waffling on any points, your spouse's attorney will sense that, and you may be shaken by the line of discussion.

- Anticipate the other side's questions and points, so that you know what you'll say when they make their arguments.

- Prepare a formal list of your demands and requests beforehand, so that everything is covered efficiently.

- Take notes of any important new issues that arise during the negotiations.

- Bring copies of all necessary documents or evidence.

- Dress professionally. An official image lends credibility to your position.

- Make eye contact with your adversaries. Breaking eye contact is a sign of dishonesty or a lack of conviction.

- Stay calm. Do not resort to yelling or snapping.

- Do not be defensive.

- Listen carefully. You may be tempted to interrupt, but let the other side complete their statements before you respond.

- Resist making decisions right away. It's perfectly acceptable for you to take as much time as you need.

- Stick to the point—don't let yourself get sidetracked.

- Call for a "time out" if the negotiations get heated. You can't get anything done if you're working in an atmosphere of open hostility. A five-minute break might be enough to let everyone cool down and get back on the negotiating track.

When negotiations don't go well

That last item is very important. Negotiations bring out difficult issues, and often some hurt feelings and bitterness, so the process may become strained at times. It is also common for one side of the negotiations to attempt to manipulate the other by playing on the emotions that arise during divorce proceedings. If you can anticipate that tensions may arise, you can defuse the situation and defend yourself from being manipulated. And if your divorce is particularly adversarial, it is helpful to be aware of some of the manipulative "tricks" that may be used. Some of these include:

- Personal attacks on your personality

- Personal attacks on your appearance

- Personal attacks on your role in the divorce

- Threats

Less openly confrontational, but disturbing nonetheless, are such tactics as:

- The "silent treatment"

- Referring to you in the third-person, rather than directly

- Negative (provocative or dismissive) body language

Timesaver
A list of issues prepared beforehand will greatly reduce the time spent in negotiations. Once each topic is discussed and decided, cross it off your list and consider the issue closed. Rehashing topics you've already covered earlier in the day or at an earlier meeting only wastes time and money.

Such tactics can unnerve you—but not if you keep in mind that, if your spouse is using these childish methods, he or she is doing so solely to manipulate you into giving up what he or she is afraid of losing in the divorce. Your best bet is to let these efforts pass by unnoticed. The less you respond, the sooner any such game-playing will stop.

If you can't resolve, the court will

Bright Idea
Because court conferences, arbitration, and other such procedures give you a chance to hear from someone who is impartial to your case, you can compare your present position with that of the judge or arbiter to see if you are on the right track.

If after discovery and basic negotiations you are still unable to resolve your case, the court may begin to take a more active role in helping you reach a resolution. It may obligate you to participate in a series of conferences with a judge or other professional mediator. It is quite possible that a neutral, independent third party, after hearing the facts and circumstances of your matter at a non-binding arbitration, may disagree with you and your attorney. If this should happen, it's probably best to take it as a very good sign that you are not being reasonable. You may therefore wish to reconsider your demands and expectations. The opposite may also be true— the mediator may find your demands to be very reasonable, but hold that your spouse is the one who is being unrealistic. In either case, the mediator's findings can be very useful in helping you to reformulate your settlement proposal so that it is most likely to attain your goals.

As we've seen, court procedures like mediation may cause you and your spouse to reformulate your demands and reconsider your differences. After a detailed conference with the court, you'll know fairly well how a judge would rule on your case in trial, so you may be able to settle your case in accordance with what the judge is likely to rule. If you wish to settle your case, it is very important to listen, not only to your attorney, but to *all* other parties that affect your case. This means that you must understand what not only is important to you, but also what is important to your spouse, and you must try to formulate a resolution that best meets *both* of your needs. If you or your spouse is completely unwilling to compromise, chances are that your case will result in a trial and the court will impose a ruling upon you. If this happens, neither you *nor* your spouse is likely to feel that the decision is satisfactory.

Going to trial

A trial is your last resort in the resolution of your divorce. Very few divorces actually end up with a trial, and much more often than not a trial is the worst possible way in which to resolve your case. Of course, if you and your spouse, with the help of your attorneys, cannot come to an agreement as to all the issues, you may have no alternative but to go to trial.

No matter how you analyze it, no one wins when a divorce goes all the way to trial. It is an extremely emotional and expensive procedure. It is also highly unlikely that the court will give you or your spouse everything each of you is seeking. As a result, more often than not, both of you feel defeated. It is also highly unlikely that the court will come up with a resolution that takes into account all the nuances and considerations of your family. Instead, based upon limited information and time, the court will tell you what it thinks would be a fair and reasonable settlement. Chances are that neither you nor your spouse will agree.

What are you getting into?

To better understand the process of a divorce trial, it is important that you appreciate that there are generally two types of courts: *courts of law* and *courts of equity*. An example of a court of law is traffic court. If you are accused of driving through a stop sign, the only thing that the court has to consider is whether or not it believes that you in fact stopped at the stop sign. The court's decision is black and white: If you stopped you are not guilty, if you failed to stop you are guilty. Of course, courts of law also hear far more complicated cases, but ultimately the court of law is only concerned with whether or not a violation of law has occurred.

Divorce court, however, is not a court of law. It is, rather, a court of equity, which operates on very different principles. While a court of equity does concern itself with general rules and legal statutes, there is much more latitude for interpretation by the judge who is resolving the case. So, when resolving your divorce, although the judge will be influenced by whatever general rules and laws that may apply, in most instances he or she is ultimately guided by a sense of what seems to be fair and equitable to all parties. For example, there is no definitive law that tells the court how to compensate someone who has been married for 12 years, has three children, and owns a house worth $165,000. The judge, based upon experience, opinions, biases, background, and other factors, will make that determination on his or her own, and the court will order you to obey that determination.

As we've already said, a trial can be a very expensive process. It involves the presentation of all relevant evidence, including all the information gathered during the discovery process, testimony taken from all parties involved, and testimony of any expert or lay witnesses who have information pertaining to the case. The simple fact that your case has ended up in a trial attests to the likelihood that it has been aggressively contested, and as a result the time it will take your lawyer to prepare for trial will most likely be measured in days rather than in hours. In addition, the trial itself will most likely last days rather than hours—and this can only cause your legal fees to skyrocket. And if your case requires that you present expert testimony, you will have the expert witness's fees to pay as well.

As a general rule, the court discourages trials in the case of divorce, and it does not like to make significant decisions in complicated divorce actions. It will do so only when forced to, preferring instead that you and your spouse take every opportunity to resolve your issues on your own. If your case actually goes to trial, it is likely to do so only after you and your spouse have made many unsuccessful attempts to resolve your case personally, and will most likely be viewed in that light by the judge. He or she will seldom blame one or the other of you individually for failing to settle your case, but rather will hold you both equally responsible for the breakdown in settlement negotiations.

Keep in mind, too, that a trial is usually "zero-sum game" situation—what one side wins the other loses. If you and your spouse had been previously negotiating in good faith but could nevertheless not resolve certain issues, the trial forces you to throw away all your earlier efforts and imposes upon you a much more adversarial position. This is because of the way trials are structured: Court procedures force you and your spouse to present your arguments in their most extreme terms. This makes compromise very difficult, not to mention that it causes great emotional strain for everybody involved.

Testimony

One example of the strain caused by going to court is the need to present your case in person. You can expect to be called upon to testify, which can be very uncomfortable. You will have to sit through your spouse's testimony, which may be unpleasant to hear. You will also be cross-examined—that is, questioned by your spouse's attorney. This last is often a very confusing and emotional experience, and your spouse's attorney is not necessarily going to be friendly in his or her questioning. Also distressing is that, depending upon the issues in your case, your neighbors, friends, children, co-workers, and employers may be called upon to testify. It is not unusual for relatives to get involved as well. Most people agree that the worst part of the trial is having to re-live during testimony all of the facts and circumstances that brought about your divorce in the first place.

At the trial, you and your spouse will be given an opportunity to present all evidence in support of your claims, as well as an opportunity to refute each others' evidence. This experience is likely to be very different from anything you imagine. Whereas the old *Perry Mason* TV shows usually concluded with a last-minute, clear-cut solution and the triumph of justice, real life court cases are more often exercises in frustration and even boredom. Specifically, depending upon the issues of your case, the trial may be divided into certain manageable sections rather than treating the divorce as a unified whole.

JANE DOE
      Plaintiff

vs.

JOHN DOE   Subpoena
      Defendant

YOU ARE HEREBY COMMANDED TO ATTEND AND GIVE TESTIMONY

On _____ day, _____ date, at 9:00 A.M., with regard to the above titled action. You are further commanded to bring with you for presentation to the court:

    Failure to appear according to the command of this Subpoena will subject you to a penalty, civil damages and punishment for contempt of Court.

Dated: _____

_____

Example 1: Sample copy of a subpoena.

For example, the court may hear testimony regarding your cause of action (see Chapter 5), custody issues (see Chapters 8 and 9), alimony issues (see Chapter 10), and the division of the marital assets (see Chapter 8). Each section treats a single element of your overall divorce settlement independently of the others, sort of as its own little trial within a larger trial. This can be frustrating, because you may feel that individual issues are being treated out of the larger context.

In some situations the court may elect to hear all issues at once, rather than breaking things up into individual "mini-trials" as described above. When the case is handled this way, one side (usually the one that initiated the divorce) presents its entire case from start to finish, with the other side only later getting a chance to respond. If you were the one who filed the initial complaint, for example, you would present all your evidence in support

of each element of your proposed settlement—
including your case for custody, child support,
alimony, and so on. Only after you were finished
would your spouse then have the opportunity to
refute the evidence on which your claims were
based. Then, your spouse would present all of his or
her own evidence and you would have a turn to
challenge those presentations.

In either type of case, after all the evidence is
presented, the judge will make a decision to which
you and your spouse will be bound. You will have an
opportunity to appeal the decision, but as a general
rule you cannot appeal if the judge disagreed with
your assessments of the facts. In divorce decisions,
appeals are generally only allowed if the judge mis-
applied the law. As a result, most appeals fail.

Credibility is key

Often, a trial involves "he said, she said" types of testimony. This can mean that you and your spouse
present completely different versions of the same
event or issue, because each of you has a different
subjective interpretation of the facts. This is common with regard to the cause of action of your
divorce, but it also occurs frequently with regard to
divided assets, determining who gets custody of the
children, or the division of income. As in any court
proceeding, in these instances credibility becomes a
very important, if not the determinative, factor in
the ultimate resolution of the case.

When there is a dispute as to the facts, the judge
must in large part figure out who is telling the truth.
You and your spouse are being judged, not with
regard to fault, but with regard to honesty and credibility. As a result, how you present yourself to the

court is of the utmost importance in a trial. Is your story believable? Is it simple and easy to understand? Are your conclusions and demands fairly obvious or do you need to do a lot of explaining? What do other witnesses think of you and your situation? What do the facts and circumstances suggest? These are the types of questions that the judge must answer and will typically apply the answers to these questions to the applicable law when making his or her final decision regarding your case. Because these are the *judge's* concerns, they are also *your* concerns.

Regardless of the judge's decision, both you and your spouse might resent the fact that the judge can ultimately render the final decision. And neither one of you is likely to be entirely pleased by the results. Each of you has constructed your case believing that your position is the correct one. If your expectations of the final resolution of the case are not met, your disappointment is likely to be very great.

For all these reasons, most people—even in the most heated of contested divorce cases—typically try to settle without having to go to trial. The expense, the emotional strain, the embarrassment, and the loss of time consumed by trial make it very much worth your while to focus on resolving the issues and keep fighting with your spouse to a minimum.

If your case does result in a trial, despite all of the above mentioned problems, you should not feel that all is lost. Even with the best will in the world, you cannot force cooperation from your partner if he or she insists on fighting things out to the bitter end. Instead, you must focus on developing the evidence that will best convince the court that you, more so than your spouse, are in the right. Most often, you will have to rely upon your attorney to do this, because your attorney is more familiar than you are with the specific laws and rules of the court that will govern your presentation at trial. You can help yourself the most at trial by strictly following your attorney's instructions. The trial is an arena in which you probably have no experience and therefore it is very important that you trust your attorney's experience and judgment. And this brings up another reason why, whenever possible, you should seek a resolution of your divorce prior to trial—once in court, even the procedure of a trial is out of your hands. You have far less control over how things will be done.

Mini-trials

Before you require a trial to hear all the issues of your case, you may require smaller-scale, evidentiary type *hearings*. These are special-purpose appearances in court similar to the "mini-trials" mentioned earlier in the discussion of ways that divorce cases may be handled. For example, you may have to bring a motion to compel the immediate payment of proper support from your spouse. This could occur when, although your spouse has agreed in principle that you require support, he or she claims to presently be unable to pay as much as you demand—say, because of involuntary unemployment. To resolve this single issue, you request a hearing. As part of your motion papers, you may present a report from an employment expert stating that, based upon your spouse's training and resume, he or she could obtain employment and therefore pay significant support. However, as part of your spouse's papers, he or she may present a report from a different employment expert stating that there are no available jobs in your spouse's field. Further, your spouse might include a list of all the firms to which he or she has applied for work. What should the court do?

In these types of cases, the court understands that you require support right now, and as a result the resolution of issue cannot wait until your final divorce settlement. Therefore, the court will often hold a "mini-trial," or hearing, that addresses the specific issue. These types of trials are fairly common since, often, without a court hearing, you will not be able to resolve an immediate concern. As these small-scale trials involve only limited issues, they are typically not nearly as emotionally or financially draining as the full-scale divorce trial. Many times, the results of this type of hearing help resolve many other issues of your divorce, as the court's decision with regard to specific issues may suggest its ultimate decision with regard to the remainder of your disputes.

In proceeding through your divorce, your attorney usually will have an eye toward trial even though the chances are that you will not require one. He or she must, however, always plan for the worst-case scenario. For this reason, it is always important to take your attorney's advice with regard to legal matters and procedures.

From a strict legal standpoint, the court system, and ultimately the trial, is designed to resolve your disputes. However, from a practical standpoint, you will most likely not have a trial and, instead, will resolve your disputes with the assistance, rather than at the demand, of the court. This is often perceived as a great contradiction of the court system when viewed by the public.

Putting it on paper: the written settlement agreement

Your ultimate resolution will most likely take the form of a written settlement agreement. It is this settlement agreement that in essence comprises the law of your divorce. So long as the agreement is reached voluntarily, absent of undue influence, coercion, duress, or fraud, it will serve as the final resolution of your case. Generally, except in instances where the agreement is blatantly unfair or in cases in which children are not properly provided for, the court will assume that you and your spouse can and will live by the terms of the agreement.

Timesaver
Get it right the first time. It is bad enough that you have to negotiate the terms of your divorce one time. You do not want to have to revisit the same issues year after year because of a vague or incomplete agreement.

But time can bring changes that you originally failed to anticipate. When this happens, the agreement may have to change. For the most part, however, you are bound by the terms as agreed upon at the time of your original divorce. Therefore, it is very important that your make certain that your written agreement contains all of the understandings that you and your spouse have reached and that it is as specific as possible. It is also important that the agreement address as many potential issues of future conflict as possible, so as to avoid later misunderstandings and disagreements.

As no one can predict the future, understandably, no agreement can be a timeless solution. However, your agreement can anticipate some likely events and as a result, save you from later disputes. For example, in instances that involve young children, you can anticipate that as time passes it will probably cost more and more to support them—due to inflation and other factors. If at all possible you must try to anticipate such problems. For example, you can make sure that you include in your agreement an automatic increase in child support consistent with the increase in a cost of living index. If you're unsure about how to figure a realistic figure increase, then make your settlement plan include a request to revisit the issue of child support every so often—for example, every two or three years—at which time you can recalculate the needs and expenses of the children. To this end, many experts remind you to anticipate that the costs of day care or private school will increase over time.

As another example, let's say that you and your spouse currently own a house and agree that it will sell at some point in the future. Your settlement agreement should anticipate the mechanism for getting it sold, so it should include provisions specifying hiring a real estate broker, setting a listing and sales price, and determining exactly how you are going to distribute the proceeds from the sale. It should also make specific recommendations as to the way in which all this will be accomplished.

All too often, post-divorce conflicts arise that could easily have been avoided if these types of issues were addressed in the original settlement agreement. For example, if you agree that your house is going to be sold three years from now, you may not wish to pick a broker or set a listing price right now—the housing market may change or that broker may not be in business when you're ready to sell. However, rather than merely agreeing that the house will be sold and the proceeds be divided, you can at least agree that the listing price will be set in accordance with a market analysis done by a specific local broker. And you can establish general

Bright Idea
You can avoid the problem of predicting exact dollar values by defining each party's responsibility as a percentage of the total cost, rather than as a fixed dollar amount.

rules governing the ultimate selling price—you can specify that it will be no less than, for example, 95% of the listing price. These types of specific agreements help avoid later conflicts.

The power of your final resolution

You are legally bound by the resolutions contained in your agreement. Generally, your resolution, whether it comes by way of a voluntary good faith negotiation or by way of a trial, becomes an order of the court. This means that any failure to comply with the terms of your resolution is not only a breach of contract, but also a violation of the court's order or demand. In other words, if you or your spouse violate the terms of the agreement, you're not only breaking a promise that you made to each other but you're also breaking a promise made to the court. As a result, if either one of you violates the agreement, it is the same thing as violating a court order, for which you can be held in contempt of the court and for which you may be legally punished. For example, a spouse who is in violation of child support agreements may end up in jail. The violation of other terms usually result in less severe penalties.

The fact that your agreement becomes a court order generally prevents you from raising later arguments about the basic merits or fairness of the terms. If the order is as a result of a trial, the court has already decided that the resolution is fair and proper. If the settlement agreement is as a result of a good faith negotiation, then it is assumed that you have voluntarily entered into the agreement and, for the most part, the court will assume that the terms of the agreement are fair. Even though the court may not have passed judgment on the merits

Unofficially . . .
There needs to be very little legal magic language in your agreement. For the most part, your agreement should be easy to read and answer all present and obviously anticipated questions.

Example 2:
Sample Judgment
of Divorce,
legally terminat-
ing the marriage
of Jane and
John Doe.

JANE DOE
                Plaintiff
vs.
JOHN DOE   Judgment of Divorce
                Defendant

This matter having been presented to the Court on the
_____ day of _____, 199___, by _____, Esq.,
attorney for the Plaintiff, and the Defendant being properly
served and having filed an Answer with the Court, and the
Court having heard and considered the complaint and
argument presented, and it appearing that the plaintiff and
defendant were married on _____, and the plaintiff having pleaded and proved a cause of action for divorce,
in such case made and provided, and the parties having been
bona fide residents of this State for more than one year next
preceding the commencement of this action, and jurisdiction
having been acquired over the defendant pursuant to the
rules governing the Courts;

It is on this _____ day of _____, 199_____,

ORDERED AND ADJUDGED that, pursuant to the
statute in such case made and provided, the plaintiff and
the defendant be divorced from the bonds of matrimony
for the cause aforesaid, and be freed from the obligations
thereof.

---

of your voluntary agreement, it may order the
agreement to be fully binding.

Coping with changing circumstances

Times and circumstances do change, however, and
of course you will not be able to anticipate all future
events. As a result, there may come a time when you
feel that you cannot comply with the terms of your
agreement or that the terms are no longer fair
and equitable. In these instances, your best first step
may be for you to discuss the issue with your ex-
spouse, either directly or through your attorneys.

For example, maybe you have been paying child support or alimony but recently lost your job and as a result, feel that your payments should be reduced. Through discussions with your ex-spouse, you might be able to resolve this issue by way of a compromise. For example, maybe your spouse would agree to a temporary decrease in payments while you are out of work, and expect an increase once you again find employment. Cooperation of this kind is sometimes the best solution.

However, there may come times when despite all good faith efforts, you and your spouse cannot come to a consensus as to how to modify the terms of your divorce agreement. In these cases, you may wish to make a motion or similar application to the court and ask that the agreement be modified.

Unofficially . . .
Although the court expects you to be bound by all the terms of your divorce agreement, it generally understands that as times change, the agreement may require some revisions and as a result will generally help resolve future disagreements based upon a change of circumstances.

Generally, once your final settlement has been ordered by the court, a significant burden is placed on you to prove the terms of your divorce should be modified. And filing a motion for modification is not enough to change your settlement. It is important to remember that until the court modifies the agreement, the terms remain in effect and you remain bound by them. So if you and your ex-spouse can come to a privately negotiated modified agreement, it is generally a good idea to present the modification to the court for approval so as to establish a new court order. This is generally an inexpensive and simple procedure, usually done by way of something called a *consent order*, or an order that is agreed upon by all parties. Much like when you came to your divorce agreement, the court does not pass judgment on the terms of your modification, but rather, based upon your representation of fairness, assumes that the modification is fair and assumes that you agree to be bound to the terms.

However, in cases in which you and your ex-spouse are unable to agree upon a consent order, as a general rule, you will have to prove to the court that an unanticipated, permanent, and significant change of circumstances has occurred since your divorce agreement was entered into. For example, if you lose your job and seek relief immediately thereafter, the court may assume that you will in fact soon obtain another job for similar money. As a result, it may refuse to decrease your support obligation. But if you lose your job and despite all good faith efforts are unable to find another job for an extended period of time, or if you are forced to take new employment for significantly less income, the court may well agree to reduce your support obligation.

In the end, final resolution of your case will take as long as it takes for you and your spouse to come to a settlement agreement. It can be a matter of weeks, or it may take substantially longer. As we've noted, the court will typically establish a schedule with regard to discovery (see Chapter 6) and schedule divorce trials on its calendar.

In this part of the book we have been concerned with providing information on the divorce process itself—but that is really only part of the story. Everyone's divorce is different, because everyone approaches their divorce from a unique set of circumstances. Some marriages are childless, and when a divorce looms on the horizon their primary concern is simply to equitably divide up assets and liabilities. Other divorcing couples have children, and the issues that they must address are extremely important and very different from deciding who gets to keep the family car. In Part 2 we turn to a

Watch Out!
If you merely present a claim of medical disability without providing any medical evidence, you will probably lose your case. However, if you are able to present a medical report or other expert evidence of your disability, you may be able to convince the court to reduce or eliminate your alimony obligation.

careful consideration of the issues that underlie divorce and that must be resolved, from custody to the division of property. We turn then to a detailed discussion of the single most important issue that any divorcing parents can possibly address— minimizing the effect of divorce on the children. Finally, we take up the concept of alimony in its several forms.

Just the facts

- Preparing your proposal involves learning the fine art of negotiation.

- If you and your spouse fail to negotiate an agreement, the court will do it for you.

- Trials are an expensive and emotional way to resolve your divorce, but sometimes they're the only way to get things done.

- Your final settlement agreement has the legal weight of a court order.

- If your circumstances change dramatically after the divorce becomes final, you may petition for changes in the settlement through the court.

Get the Lowdown on the Big Issues

PART III

GET THE SCOOP ON...
Physical and legal custody ▪ Evaluating
financial assets ▪ Division of property and debt

Family Values

Chapter 8

Now that you've got a good idea about the *how* of the process, it's time to explore the big issues you'll be settling in your divorce. You've had years together with your spouse, and together you have built a home, and possibly a family. Your settlement is the way you will divide up all the responsibilities and property that you used to share. But before we even begin to think about dividing up the property acquired during your marriage, the single most important set of decisions you face are those concerning your responsibility to your children.

You and your spouse can speak for yourselves, hire attorneys and other experts, and otherwise act to protect your own interests. Your children don't have that luxury. Even teenagers—normally quite capable of speaking up for themselves—may find it hard to make their needs known during the emotional trauma of divorce. Because of this, the court will maintain a watchful eye on the interests of the children, and has established basic rules and regulations when it comes to issues that involve them—issues like *custody, visitation,* and *support.* In this chapter we'll take up the basic legal concerns regarding the division of responsibility for children between divorcing parents, but custody involves more than simply determining who lives where. Turn to Chapter 9 for a more in-depth treatment of issues involved in custody, visitation, and child support.

Custody

When you and your spouse separate and/or divorce, the two of you will have to develop a parenting plan to cope with your new situation. First and foremost, you will have to decide where your children are going to live. Will they live solely with you, solely with your spouse, or will you try to arrange things so that they share time between the two of you? The daily or permanent residence of children constitutes *physical* or *residential custody.*

Physical custody

Unofficially . . .
Although recent figures report that 85 percent of custodial parents are the mothers of the children, both the mother and father have an equal right to physical custody.

Sole physical custody means that the children will maintain their primary residence in one spouse's house. You and your spouse can come to a very quick and easy decision as to custody by simply adapting your present parenting strategy to your new situation. For example, if, during the marriage, the mother assumed most of the daily parental responsibilities, it often makes sense that upon the divorce she assumes physical custody.

Typically, the spouse with sole physical custody will be subject to what is generally known as liberal and reasonable *visitation* by their ex-spouse. That is, if the children primarily live with their mother, their father has a right to visit and to share in the parenting process. Visitation is a very important part of resolving the issue of custody and is an essential part of any parenting. Although the children may live primarily with one parent, it is important that they spend sufficient time with the other as well.

Shared physical custody means that the children have two residences—one in each of the parents' homes. In cases where both parents have been very active in raising the children and have both assumed many of the daily parental responsibilities, this is often a good option and one that can take many forms. You and your spouse may agree that the children will truly have two primary residences and spend equal amounts of time with each of you. For example, the children may spend one week with you and the next with your spouse and so on and so forth. Or, you may wish to divide the days of the weeks, or months of the year. What is key is that you base your arrangement on what works best for the children.

If you and your spouse are going to truly share physical custody, you may have to live in the same town. For example, if your children are of school age, both of you must make it possible for them to attend school and after-school activities, as well as regular contact with their friends. For this to be possible, you will most likely find yourself living in relatively close proximity to your ex-spouse. You may also find yourself closely involved with each other for the purpose of arranging the children's schedules. This need not be a bad or awkward circumstance. In fact, many people get along much better after their divorce, especially regarding issues involving their children. It is important to remember that the whole concept of shared physical custody assumes that you and your spouse, after your

Watch Out!
The most common child custody mistake is withholding visitation from a non-custodial spouse. Never attempt to punish your ex by preventing him or her from seeing the children. The court has given you custody, not supreme power over your ex's parenting rights.

divorce, will be able to effectively communicate and cooperate with each other.

Legal custody

In addition to physical or residential custody, you and your spouse may wish to decide who will make the major decisions affecting the welfare of the children—you may even decide that you will share this role. The parent that assumes physical custody will typically also make day-to-day decisions regarding the children, but the non-custodial parent may want some say in such major decisions as education, medical care, and religious training. This is known as *legal custody*. Legal custody may be independent of physical custody as it determines who will make major decisions for the children and not where the children are going to live.

Unless there is good reason to decide otherwise, both you and your spouse will most likely share legal custody. This does not mean that you take turns making major decisions, but rather that both of your viewpoints are taken into account. While it doesn't mean that you will always agree with your ex-spouse, it does mean that the two of you are compelled to *reach* agreement when deciding how to handle issues regarding your children.

If you and your spouse cannot work together, the parent with physical custody will make all decisions for the children. This may happen even if your divorce agreement states that both parents should be afforded equal input because such an agreement is extremely difficult for the court to police.

As with physical custody, if you and your spouse can't agree on legal custody, the court will seek the opinions of experts before making a determination. In deciding this issue, the court is not necessarily concerned with the daily routine and responsibilities of you, your spouse, and the children, or with safety and welfare issues, but rather your ability to make responsible, educated decisions. The court will also consider the ability of you and your spouse to work together in the children's interest. If you simply cannot work together in the best interests of your children, the court will be hard pressed to order joint responsibilities.

Developing a plan for custody

Ultimately you and your spouse both remain responsible for the support of the children no matter what you call your custody arrangement. However, depending upon the state in which you live, it may be very important how you characterize your parenting plan since the terminology that you use may significantly affect your receipt or payment of child support. For this reason, it is often very important that you speak with an attorney when finalizing a parenting plan.

As you'll remember from our discussion about drafting your proposal (Chapter 7), it's always a good idea to try to anticipate any possible future events that could dramatically affect your parenting plan— you want to make provision for them in your custody settlement now rather than having to deal with making changes later. For example, if your children will be attending school in two years and you and your spouse share custody, you may wish to request that your spouse move to a town within your school district within the next two years. Of course, you will not be able to anticipate everything, nor will you be able to effectively resolve all future issues, but generally, the more that you can resolve now, the more easily your parenting plan will be implemented.

Bright Idea
Keep in mind that your ex-spouse will *always* be the children's parent and for the benefit of the children, should always be considered and respected in this manner.

Unofficially . . .
Some states, as a matter of law, give the custodial parent more specific responsibility in decision-making; others allow parents a broader, more general sense of responsibility. Some states may specifically separate the concepts of physical and legal custody; others intertwine parental responsibilities. Further, the terminology of custody differs across the states.

In the children's best interests

In determining physical custody, the court will generally consider what it believes to be in the best
interests of the children. This is *not* a judgment on
who would be a better parent. Instead, the court will
generally consider issues such as the children's
age(s), child/parent interaction, any history of violence or other detrimental conduct by the parents,
the safety of the children, and the parents' ability to
communicate with each other.

Financial ability is typically *not* considered when
deciding the issue of physical custody, because no
matter which parent assumes physical custody, both
continue to be obligated to support the children.
For example, if your spouse earns substantially
more income than you and would be able to provide
a nicer home, this financial factor, in and of itself,
will not give your spouse any more right to physical
custody than you. This is because, if you are granted
physical custody, your spouse would be ordered to
pay you child support to help ease your financial
strain. Because of the expectation that child support
will be paid by the non-custodial spouse, finances
are typically not considered.

In addition to looking at the parent's respective
roles in raising the children, the court most often
will also seek expert opinions. These may be
solicited from a psychologist or other mental health
professional, who may be asked to evaluate you,
your spouse, and your children before submitting a
recommendation as to what parenting arrangement
will best meet the children's needs.

In many custody cases a psychologist will interview all relevant parties, including you, your spouse,
your children, possibly other family members, or

anyone who is an important part of the children's lives, and may involve some psychological testing as well as interviews. The psychologist will not necessarily determine who is the "better" parent, but rather, how the children will best be served. A copy of his or her written recommendation will be made available to you, your spouse, and the court. This recommendation will touch upon many factors, including the history of your marriage, the reasons for your divorce, and the children's wishes and emotional attachments. It may also include practical considerations. For example, after your divorce, you may wish to move out of town, but the children may want to stay where they are so they can continue in the same school.

In addition to requesting a psychological evaluation, depending upon the ages of the children and their need or desire to be heard, the court may appoint a guardian other than you and your spouse to represent their point of view. The guardian— usually an attorney or other professional familiar with the custody process—is asked to evaluate the circumstances and present the children's viewpoint. The guardian's recommendations are very important, especially when older children are involved, because as a practical matter, the older the child, the more consideration the court will give to his or her preference. With younger children, the guardian is often able to obtain information that would not otherwise be presented to the court.

No matter how much you try to shield the children from involvement in your divorce, they *are* directly involved in the outcome and the process. This is even more true if you are involved in a custody dispute, because parents often confuse their

Unofficially . . .
The court may consider your willingness to attend parenting classes when deciding custody. In New Jersey, for example, the State Senate is considering legislation that requires divorcing parents to attend a parenting course designed to help them guide their children through the divorce process. Failure to comply with such a request will be held against you in court, so don't scoff if this request is made of you.

Bright Idea
In addition to any court-appointed psychologist, you and your spouse may each want to hire your own independent expert for an assessment. Because the interests of the children are at stake, the court will evaluate as much information as possible before making any decision, and your initiative at taking this step *does* impress the court.

own desires with the welfare of the children. For this reason, the court may give the children an alternative sounding board, to allow them to express their interests apart from those of the parents. It does this through a "best-interests evaluation," which may be broader in scope than that covered by the psychologist's recommendations.

A best-interests evaluation may take into account issues such as appropriate housing and other physical necessities to the proper raising of the children. It may be performed by the court, or it may be assigned to an approved agency. It is often very useful when factual rather than psychological issues are involved. Such issues may include anything from cleanliness to excessive lifestyles involving alcohol or drug abuse. For example, your spouse may be living in an unsafe neighborhood, or in an apartment that is not large enough or properly equipped to raise children.

In some cases the judge may wish to speak directly with the children. When necessary, this is done privately in the judge's office or chambers, so as to minimize any discomfort that speaking to strangers may cause the children. This private interview helps ensure that the children are actually voicing their interests, concerns, and preferences, and not just saying what the parents or the attorneys might want them to say.

Like all the other issues of your divorce that involve expert opinion, you and your spouse have the same access to the expert's reports and records as does the court. If you are working in good faith toward the best interests of your children, you should be able to resolve the custody issue in accordance with the opinions of the experts. If you and your spouse can't agree, you are entitled to a hearing. The court will base *its* decision on the same evaluations and recommendations that you have refused to accept.

Unfortunately, some custody disputes occur not so much because one party really *wants* physical custody, but rather as a means of leverage to negotiate a more favorable financial settlement or to avoid being liable for child support. Or they may be seeking the right to claim the child or children as tax deductions. Most often, tactics like these become apparent to the court once the experts have filed their evaluations, but the evaluation process can be slow and costly. Therefore, you should discuss with your attorney all the reasons you and your spouse might have for wanting custody. If your spouse's motivations are financial, perhaps you can find a way to address those financial issues elsewhere in your settlement.

Economic interests

Another difficult area that you and your spouse will need to resolve is the division of your assets and liabilities. After all, disagreement over money issues is one of the most common reasons for the end of a marriage in the first place. As divorce looms, you'll have to think of all sorts of financial hot topics as you consider how to divide your home, property, assets, investments, expenses, and debts.

You may find this hard to be dispassionate about. After all, financial decisions you once made together with an eye toward future goals are now just dollar figures on a certificate with a symbolic line drawn through the middle of the page. And now that you are splitting up, you're facing

> **"**
> The court will usually go to great lengths to protect all privacy interests of children and, as a result, will not conduct children interviews or hearings involving sensitive children's issues, in public, or in an area that is potentially open to the public.
> —Brett Levine, attorney at law
> **"**

questions you never used to worry about—perhaps
the most troubling one being: How will you make
ends meet after the divorce?

There's property . . . and there's property

When two people get married, they bring into the
marriage a certain number of personal belongings.
During the marriage, the couple accumulates more
and more belongings as they build their household.
You may have accumulated assets solely in the name
of your spouse, or perhaps you maintained jointly
titled assets. No matter—all property, no matter
how it is titled, must be accounted for in a divorce.
Depending on where you live, the sum total of all
your household belongings will be classified by one
or more of the following labels: "personal property,"
"marital property," and "exempt property."

Watch Out!
In some states,
personal property
is classified as
exempt property,
that is, it's not
subject to divi-
sion. So if your
spouse is going
after a personal
item of yours,
find out your
state's defini-
tions regarding
the various
classes of
divisible and
non-divisible
property.

- *Personal property* refers to the belongings you
  bring with you into the marriage, any gifts you
  personally receive during the marriage, and
  anything you personally inherit during your
  marriage. So your grandmother's wedding ring,
  if given to you, is your personal property.
  Depending upon the state in which you live,
  some personal property may be subject to division at divorce.

- *Marital property* is everything the two of you have
  acquired during your marriage, regardless of
  whose name it's in. It is generally subject to division at the time of a divorce.

- *Exempt property* is any property that is not subject
  to division at divorce.

States differ as to how they assign property to the
categories of "personal," "marital," or "exempt."
In addition, several states recognize a further

concept—*community property*. At present, California, Idaho, Louisiana, New Mexico, Texas, Washington, and Wisconsin are community property states, and they approach the division of assets according to a specific set of rules:

- Any property owned by the husband and wife prior to their marriage is their personal property, exempt from division.

- Anything gained during the marriage is shared property and must be divided equally between the two spouses—a 50/50 split, for the most part, right down the line.

Some states practice a policy of "equitable distribution" with regard to marital assets. These states do not draw distinctions between property acquired before and after marriage. Instead, they divide all shared property equitably, no matter when it was obtained. Many people believe that this is the best system, since it does take into account the personal responsibility for ownership.

Although states differ on the specific laws governing the division of assets and liabilities, generally, if the asset or liability was acquired while you were married, it must, in some manner, be divided at divorce. It generally does not matter who's name is on the title to the property. For example, if while you were married, your spouse bought a car that titled solely in his or her name, you are still entitled to receive some value for a share of the car. The same holds true for debt—if your spouse ran up a $5,000 credit card bill during your marriage, upon your divorce you still share responsibility with your spouse for some portion of the obligation.

Even if you don't live in a community property state, you're generally entitled to receive approximately

Timesaver
Check where your state stands as far as division, and ask your lawyer at the outset about any specific rules that apply to the division of your property. Knowing these rules can immediately squelch any of your spouse's efforts to wrongly procure your belongings.

50 percent of all assets and liabilities acquired during your marriage, unless there is a particularly compelling reason to support a different division. Of course this rule assumes that you are not bound by a valid prenuptial agreement.

Ours? Yours? Or mine?

What *exactly* happens to property that belonged to you or your spouse prior to your marriage? Does it get divided as part of your divorce? As noted above, different states have different answers. Some states divide all property, no matter when it was acquired. But many states exclude any property that is brought into a marriage from division, so long as the property was not *co-mingled* during the marriage.

For example, you may own a house prior to your marriage. Upon marriage, your spouse moved in, but the house remained solely titled to you. In many states, upon divorce, the house will remain solely owned by you. However, any increase in its value that occurred during the marriage may be subject to your spouse's claim for a share. In addition, your spouse may be entitled to reimbursement for any improvements made to the house during your marriage.

But if you transferred an ownership interest in that same house to your spouse's name you have "co-mingled" the asset and, as a general rule, co-mingled assets are subject to division. This is true regardless of when the asset was originally acquired. The same principle applies for bank accounts—if you bring money into a marriage and place it in a joint bank account it is generally considered to be co-mingled, whereas if you kept the money separate and apart throughout the marriage it is not. But it's extremely tricky to differentiate between what is and what is not exempt when talking about liquid assets like bank accounts. Unless you have a specific agreement on record, like a prenuptial agreement, that specifies that this money is exempt, you may find it very difficult to keep the money from being divided.

In many states, direct gifts and assets obtained by inheritance are also exempt from the division of property rule, but here too, if you co-mingle an inheritance or gift it is no longer exempt. For example, if, while you are married, you inherit $10,000 and place the money in a joint bank account, you have co-mingled the money. Like a premarital account, even if you keep the money solely titled, you may unknowingly co-mingle it. For example, if you place the money in an account solely titled to you but use the money to pay the household bills it will be difficult, if not impossible, to maintain a claim that this money is exempt from division.

Bringing in the experts

A veritable tornado of fears can fill your mind when you think about the financial end of your marriage. Is it best to handle all financial issues through your attorney? Part of your attorney's job is to get you the most fair and equitable settlement possible, but neither lawyers nor judges are financial experts. You may therefore want to consult a financial specialist to help your case.

The court is going to make every effort to be fair—if you exercise basic caution you needn't fear that you'll be left penniless after the divorce. In order to reach that fair financial settlement, you must provide the court with a complete financial picture of your marriage. If you omit something of great value, your spouse is "off the hook," and it will take greatly expensive and time-consuming

Unofficially . . .
Your financial expert will analyze your household finances, assets, and debts and then prepare charts and graphs to help you map out your financial future. In addition, he or she may serve as a witness in court, and in cases when the court has to resolve the division of assets, the financial expert's advice is weighed very heavily.

measures to go back to court to amend for addition of that item.

So, how do you go about dividing up your assets? Many couples start off by listing their assets, with intention of picking and choosing off the list. Let's look at the list drawn up by a couple we'll call Pam and David:

Pam and David's Division of Assets List

- House
- Toyota Celica
- Ford Explorer
- Vacation home in Florida
- Office equipment
- Home furnishings
- Art collection
- Gold coin collection
- Wedding crystal set
- AV system

In Pam and David's original agreement, she took the house, the Celica, the office equipment, the art collection, and the wedding crystal. David got everything else. In the beginning, this arrangement was fine for them, but then David did some figuring. When he added up the dollar value of the assets Pam got, he saw that her "half" of their assets was worth about $30,000 more than his. He stewed over that for a week and half, and then he voiced his objection in a letter to Pam's lawyer. They then had to re-figure the split of their assets, running up more legal fees in the process.

Clearly, then, the financial value of assets should be taken into consideration first when deciding who gets what. While your financial advisor will also start with a list of assets, he or she will be looking at the *values,* not the *types* of assets on that list. And while you might think that the financial advisor's list will look a lot like the one Pam and David put together, you will be mistaken. Their list was woefully incomplete. Before you start thinking that you could certainly do better than they did, however, here's a little test for you to take: Close this book now and make a list of the assets you think will need to be divided during your divorce. Take your time about it and be as complete as you can, then come back and check your list against the one below to see what you've left out.

Most Often Forgotten Assets

- Life insurance
- Health insurance
- Retirement plans
- Mutual funds
- Stocks and bonds
- Rental property
- Frequent flier miles
- National Guard and reserve pay
- Military benefits
- Benefits from primary wage-earner's job

Now, when most of us think of the word "asset," we generally think only of our belongings: the house, the car, the furniture. Or we think of things like the savings account, that mutual fund, the money in the checking account. For Pam and David, these were the easy things to come up with for their list. But there are other valuable, intangible assets, like your spouse's future earning power, that you also need to consider. And the primary

Watch Out!
Never guess at the value of an asset. Get specific information on the exact values of all of your assets.

wage earner—whether that's you or your spouse—
often receives benefits in addition to a paycheck that
you may need to consider when dividing up the
household assets. Such benefits may include a pension plan, health and life insurance, disability insurance, stock options, vacation pay, and sick pay.
These are items that most couples forget to include
when they draw up a list of divisible assets.

Unofficially . . .
When you divide
assets, consider
only the present
value of the
asset—not a
speculative
future value.
For example,
although today
the house may
be worth
$100,000, years
from now it may
be worth consid-
erably more. But
for purposes of
dividing assets,
you should deal
with present
value.

When considering each spouse's rightful share
the court always takes into consideration the non-
wage-earner's contributions to the breadwinner's
career, but this too is an item that couples frequently
overlook. This can become a major sticking point in
divorce negotiations: The principle wage-earner
may resent having to give half of his or her income.
The non-wage-earner may fear that his or her
contributions—keeping the house, raising the
kids—will go unrecognized and unvalued. But from
the court's perspective, running a household is
treated as a real and valuable contribution to the
marriage that is deserving of recognition in the
financial settlement of your divorce. You should
therefore consider it in your own efforts to draw up
a settlement.

Determining the value of assets

Once you've identified which of your assets is subject to division, the next step is to determine their
value. For bank accounts, mutual funds, stocks, and
bonds, the answer is clear: The dollar amount is
clearly printed on a statement. Your other assets,
however, will have to be assessed. This can best be
done through the services of a qualified appraiser,
whose assessment of the value of your property can
be used in the final settlement agreement.

Let's look at some of the major assets more closely:

Your house. For many couples, the largest single asset they own is their house. The simplest way to divide this asset is to sell the property and divide the proceeds. However, the divorcing couple often doesn't wish to sell—one or the other wants to retain ownership. One way to handle this is to trade the value of the house for another asset. For example, if your house is worth $100,000 and you and your spouse also own bank accounts worth $100,000, one can keep the house and the other can keep the bank accounts. There is another alternative—one of you might consider buying out your spouse's share. To do this, you may need to refinance the property.

There are some situations where one partner is permitted to remain in the house even though they can't trade for or buy out the other's share. This usually occurs when the divorcing couple has small children and the custodial parent wants them to stay in the home that they've always known. In such cases, it is not uncommon that the sale and division of the house is postponed—until, say, the children graduate from school. At that time the house can be sold and the proceeds of the sale will be divided.

If one spouse remains in the house, provisions will have to be made for the payment of the mortgage, property taxes, insurance, repairs, and other household expenses. And be aware that title to the property does not always coincide with potential liability for the mortgage. If, for example, your spouse agrees to buy out your share of the house, you will transfer your ownership interest in the property. But the transfer of ownership will not relieve you of your

Moneysaver
It is important to discuss your plans to divide assets not only with your attorney, but also with an accountant, as tax laws may influence your decisions regarding financial issues in your divorce.

mortgage obligation. If your name remains on the mortgage you remain legally responsible for its payment, regardless of any agreement you may have reached with your ex-spouse. If your ex-spouse fails to pay the mortgage, the mortgage company will look to you for full payment—and if you fail to make payment, you could get sued. To avoid this, you may want your spouse to refinance the property in order to pay off the joint mortgage and assume a mortgage solely in his or her own name. With refinancing, you assign your ownership interest in the property to your spouse by way of a *quit claim deed.* With this, you legally quit all claims of ownership on the property.

But what if your spouse can't afford to refinance and so can't remove your name from the mortgage? Then you may want your spouse to sign what is known as a *hold harmless and indemnification agreement.* This agreement, which can form a part of your settlement or separation agreement, obligates your spouse to make all payments and states that he or she will reimburse you for any damages that you incur as a result of his or her nonpayment. In other words, if your spouse misses a mortgage payment and you get sued or are forced to make the payment, your spouse would be obligated by the indemnification agreement to compensate you for your damages.

While this sounds like a good solution to the problem, beware: It is often unenforceable. After all, it stands to reason that if your spouse truly cannot afford to make the mortgage payments, chances are that he or she will also be unable to reimburse you for your damages. Therefore, you'll want to include some additional safeguards in your agreement. You

Watch Out!
You should consult your financial expert when making any decisions regarding selling or transferring assets.

might, for example, require the automatic sale of the house if your spouse misses a mortgage payment. Or you might stipulate that you can take over ownership of the house if your spouse is unable to make the payments.

Liquid assets. As noted earlier, liquid assets, such as bank accounts, are easily divided by simply splitting the balances in half. Assets such as stocks and bonds can either be divided by transferring title or by selling the securities and dividing the proceeds.

Household property. These assets are usually divided according to practical need as opposed to their specific dollar value. For example, if the children are staying with you and your spouse is moving out, you'll obviously want to keep the children's bedroom sets and other belongings. On the whole, there are really no rules for dividing this type of property. You can, of course, have everything appraised and then divide it all up according to value, but considering the relatively low value of used furniture and personal property, the expense of an appraisal is not cost effective.

Automobiles are a good example of property divided according to use. You will generally keep the car that you drive and your spouse will do likewise. However, the values of the cars may differ. If you each keep the car that you drive, but there is a great disparity in their values, you can request that the difference be made up in the form of cash or other property.

Pensions. Pensions are generally valued by the court as part of jointly owned property, so they are usually judged as "splittable." In splitting a pension plan, you usually have two options: a buyout or a deferred division. In a buyout, the spouse who holds the

Moneysaver
Keep in mind that used furniture and other related objects are worth only a small fraction of what you paid for them. You are almost always going to be better off if you divide the property rather than sell it.

pension may buy out the present value of the other spouse's share. In the deferred division option, on the other hand, each spouse gets a share of the payment when the plan is paid out according to its normal terms. The type of pension plan you have may or may not allow the buyout option, so it's important to check.

If you and your spouse cannot agree on how to handle dividing a pension, the court will often impose a *qualified domestic relations order* (commonly referred to as a QDRO) and rule that you both receive benefits at the time of retirement. This court order directs your pension plan administrator to divide the pension plan payments between you and your ex-spouse at the time you qualify to receive your benefits.

Social security. You may think that you will automatically get half of your spouse's earned social security benefits. But this is only true if you are over 62 years old; were married to your spouse for at least 10 years before the divorce was finalized; you never remarried; and you do not have a retirement plan of your own that is worth more than half of your ex's social security benefits. If your spouse dies after the divorce, you are entitled to receive full "widow's benefits" only if you are over the age of 60 (if you are disabled, the minimum age is 50) and you meet the criteria listed above.

Business interest. It is often difficult to value an ownership interest in a business because, in addition to the tangible assets, goodwill, customer lists, and loyalty, not to mention the company's anticipated revenues, must also be considered. You'll need an expert—known as a forensic accountant—to determine the present value of the business.

Bright Idea
By way of a court order, you can generally divide the IRA or 401(K) and place the proceeds in separate accounts for you and your spouse. This easily avoids the problem of one spouse continuing to accrue benefits to which he or she should not be entitled.

One final note: In many small, family owned businesses, it often happens that only one spouse has controlled all the records. This makes it difficult for the other spouse to establish an accurate sense of the value of the company, and it might be necessary to resort to one or more of the discovery techniques discussed in Chapter 6. If you need to appear in court to settle this issue, this is also a time when you may need to call on the services of an expert witness.

Other assets. You may own other assets that are not easily valued, for example, a stamp or coin collection, jewelry, artwork, or other assets of significant value. In these instances, too, you will need to obtain an appraisal in order to fairly divide property.

Some assets are more easily assessed than others. If, for instance, you have frequent flier mileage or season tickets to a sold-out stadium, you might divide them up by use and need. If you like football, you may wish to take the tickets; if your spouse likes to travel, he or she takes the mileage.

Dividing liabilities

If you have outstanding credit card debt, loans, or other obligations that were incurred while married, these, too, will need to be divided equitably. But, as our discussion of the household mortgage noted, your divorce agreement won't necessarily relieve you of the responsibility for a debt. For example, you may have a credit card that's solely in your name, but the debt on the card may have been incurred to pay for household goods during the marriage. Divorce law may say that your spouse is responsible for a share of this debt. However, the credit card company generally cannot try to collect

Unofficially . . .
Have the shared family business appraised by a certified business appraiser specializing in forensic accounting. It is always a good idea to have an independent appraiser do this job, since you cannot guarantee that the company's own accountant will provide the fair and accurate value of the business.

Watch Out!
If the court is asked to evaluate the business and it believes that the records and returns indicate a potential tax fraud or impropriety, it may refer the matter to the Internal Revenue Service for further investigation.

the debt from your spouse, because his or her name isn't on the account. How, in such a case, can you ensure that your spouse pays his or her fair share? If you and your spouse have sufficient assets, you may simply decide to pay off all marital debt at the time of the divorce. Alternatively, your spouse may agree to "buy out" his or her portion of the debt.

If you have a joint credit card, you will be liable for payment even if you and your spouse agree that he or she will be solely responsible for the entire debt as long as your name appears on the account. You can try the *hold harmless and indemnification agreement* we mentioned in our discussion of mortgages, but as we've seen, this is not always an enforceable solution.

If your spouse files bankruptcy in an effort to discharge his or her debts, be aware that you may be listed as a creditor. This can relieve him or her of the obligation to pay any agreed upon financial obligations arising from the division of property— but it will *not* relieve your spouse of an obligation to pay child support or alimony. To protect your share of the property division, you may want to consider including language that specifically prohibits your spouse from discharging any debt owed to you as part of your divorce. For example, you and your spouse may have agreed that, instead of paying you alimony, your spouse would assume responsibility for all of your significant outstanding debt—you will want this agreement to be specifically referred to in the settlement agreement. By incorporating this specific language, if your spouse failed to pay the debt and later filed for bankruptcy, you may be able to convince the court that your spouse's obligation was really a form of alimony and, as such, a non-dischargeable debt.

A good understanding of the issues surrounding custody of the children is important, but it is by no means the whole story. Your children will be facing a great many changes, many of them frightening, all of them difficult. And sometimes divorcing parents cannot cooperate well enough to work out a custody plan together. Fortunately, there are ways to handle this situation, including formal provisions within the legal system that exist solely for the purpose of making sure that the children's own concerns are addressed. In Chapter 9 you will learn about how to handle custody disputes and about the procedures and resources for protecting your children's interests that are available through the court.

Just the facts

- Resolving your custody issues is the single most important task facing you as you prepare for divorce.

- Joint physical custody requires physical proximity of the divorcing parents and a high willingness to cooperate for the sake of the children.

- The children's interests in custody negotiations are strongly protected by the court.

- Different states have different laws regarding the distribution of your assets.

- The debts and financial obligations of your marriage are shared even after you divorce.

Bright Idea
If you believe that your spouse is a good candidate to file a future bankruptcy petition and you fear that he or she will seek to discharge money due to you, consult with an attorney who specializes in bankruptcy law before finalizing your divorce agreement.

The Children's Hour

We touched upon the legal considerations of deciding custody and support in the previous chapter, and we discussed the ways you might go about developing a custody and visitation plan. But there are circumstances when cooperation between divorcing parents just can't be managed. Because this is the single most important responsibility you and your spouse will share, long after your divorce is final, it merits a more in-depth discussion.

When it comes to their children, most couples are able to agree more than they disagree. You may have differences regarding some of the day-to-day decisions that must be made, but generally you have a common perception of how the children will thrive and how they should be raised. This shared concern for the children makes for an easy custody case and allows a parenting plan to more or less naturally fall into place. But sometimes things just don't turn out so well, and the worst happens—you find yourself—and your children—involved in a custody fight. Battling over the children is *never* a good thing, so it's wise to do all you can to anticipate, and avoid, the problems that make one likely.

When battles begin

Moneysaver
The only way to save money on a custody dispute is not to have one. Avoid the need for costly evaluations by working with your spouse to form a workable custody arrangement.

Generally speaking, you can expect a bitter custody battle to arise in one of two instances: if your spouse wants custody because he or she sincerely believes that the children will be better off with him or her, or if your spouse knows that by battling for custody he or she will most likely force you to accept a less favorable financial settlement. No matter the motivation of your spouse, he or she typically has the right to seek custody.

As noted in Chapter 8, you can expect to be evaluated and re-evaluated in the course of a custody suit. You can also expect very large attorney and expert-witness fees. A custody case is extremely costly because not only do you have to pay your attorney for many hours of preparation and court time, but you will also have to pay psychologists as well as possible guardians and other mental health professionals. It is not unusual for the retainer fees of these experts, cumulatively, to cost thousands of dollars.

More importantly, you can expect that during this process your children will be under tremendous pressure from both you and your spouse, no matter how much you might try to shield them from the situation. Children will want to please both parents and as a result may find themselves in the middle of the case. This happens when you or your spouse intentionally or unintentionally tries to influence your children about custody or other issues. These disputes should remain between you and your spouse—the children should *never* be involved in them.

But no matter what you do, it is a mistake to believe that you can completely insulate your children from the effects of a custody dispute. This does not mean that your children will forever be adversely affected by your arguments, but it does mean that you and your spouse should do everything in your power to settle the issue between yourselves quickly and with a minimum amount of strain. You may also wish to obtain counseling for your children to help them adjust and cope with the issues of your divorce.

One charge that is commonly leveled by parents in the midst of a custody fight is that the other spouse is "turning the children against me!" No matter who ends up with custody, the court will usually order or direct that neither you nor your ex-spouse alienate the affections of the other. Although this is most often impossible to enforce, it *is* extremely important. For example, if your ex-spouse constantly bad-mouths you in front of the children when they are alone with him or her, the court will agree that this is extremely detrimental behavior. However, except in extreme circumstances, there is little practical action that the court can take to alleviate the problem.

Mediation

To avoid custody trials and to keep the children's involvement to a minimum, many courts attempt to resolve the custody issue by way of mediation or some form of counseling. Whereas the court is an adversarial process, these non-adversarial techniques allow you, your spouse, and the mediator or counselor to focus on the issues positively and constructively. Nonetheless, many of the same evaluations required by the court (see Chapter 8) are

Watch Out!
Before you do or say anything that may alienate your children from your ex-spouse, remember that it is the children who will be hurt most by your actions.

Bright Idea
Check the media-
tion section in
Chapter 3 for
reminders of the
mediation
process.

useful when mediating a custody dispute. So, instead
of fighting over your children, you and your spouse
may wish to hire a neutral evaluator and agree to be
guided by his or her findings. This will not only save
you enormous amounts of time and money, but it
will also help to ensure that the children's best interests are met.

Like most other issues in your divorce, the more
you need the court to address, the longer it will take
to resolve. This is especially true in the case of custody, as not only are you dependent upon the
court's schedule, but also upon the schedules of psychologists and other evaluators. Because children
are directly involved, the court will probably try to
resolve issues of custody before financial issues.
However, the process will certainly take many
months and it is not unusual for a hotly contested
custody dispute to take more than a year to fully
resolve. When it comes to issues involving children,
the court will proceed slowly, taking the most con-
servative course of action.

You may have heard about couples who fight in
court over legal custody of their pets. Especially in
cases of childless couples who count their family pet
as their "baby," this issue often does have to come in
front of a judge. While the process is not likely to
include psychological testing of the "parents," the
judge does have to render a decision. According to
recent studies, the wife gets custody of the pet in the
majority of such cases.

Visitation

As part of your parenting plan, if you and your
spouse share physical custody, you have a right to
spend significant and meaningful time with the children. If one spouse has sole physical custody of the

children, you will have to develop a visitation plan in order to ensure that the non-custodial parent has adequate opportunities to involve him- or herself in the lives of the children.

Understandably, a non-custodial parent has a right to see his or her children. Generally, a non-custodial parent has the right to liberal and reasonable visitation. There is no set definition of how much time should be allocated; many factors—the children's ages, school schedules, activity schedules and interests, as well as the parent's work schedules and living arrangements—must be considered in establishing a reasonable plan.

Visitation is not only an opportunity for the non-custodial parent to spend time with his or her children, but is also time for the parent with primary physical custody to relax and to get away from the pressures of taking care of the children, however briefly. A non-custodial parent often desires overnight and weekend visitation with the children to allow them an extended period of time to spend together. This is generally a good idea for both you and your spouse, and it is almost always good for the children. If you have sole physical custody, overnight visitation at your ex-spouse's house will give you a night of rest and relaxation. Weekend visitation will give you a chance to get away or pursue a social life. Overnight and weekend visitation also allows the children to spend significant time with your ex-spouse and forces your ex-spouse to deal with all the child-related problems that you encounter on a daily basis.

Your visitation schedule will have to accommodate your work schedules. For example, if you have primary physical custody and your spouse works on

Bright Idea
If you and your spouse work Monday through Friday, consider taking the children on alternate weekends.

Saturdays, maybe rather than alternating weekends, he or she can pick up the children every Saturday night and keep them until Sunday evening. There is really no right or wrong visitation schedule, as long as it allows the children to spend quality time with the non-custodial parent.

Often, visitation schedules naturally fall into place. For example, teenagers may have after-school activities on Tuesday and Thursday, but have Wednesday evenings free from activities. As a result, Wednesday nights may be a good time for the children to have dinner with the non-custodial parent. Or, for example, maybe the non-custodial parent works nights but is available to visit with a pre-school-age child during the day. Fitting visitation into that spouse's time off from work can substantially reduce child-care costs for the custodial parent if he or she works during the day.

Moneysaver
The best and cheapest form of day care is with a parent.

A very practical visitation schedule for pre-school-age children when the parents work different hours is one that takes advantage of your different periods of availability for watching the children. For example, you may have physical custody and work 9:00 a.m. until 5:00 p.m., and your spouse may not begin work until 6:00 p.m. This is a natural and perfect opportunity for your spouse to have visitation during the daytime, which not only provides significant time to spend with the children, but would also reduce or eliminate the cost of day care.

Although there is really no right or wrong visitation schedule, you should always keep in mind the best interests of your children. For example, if your children are of school age, although you may wish to schedule extensive week night visitation, it might be better to tailor your visitation so that it does not

interfere with your children's schoolwork or partic-
ipation in sports or other after-school activities. The
children have enough to deal with just handling the
fact of your divorce. You don't want to add another
disappointment to their lives by telling them that,
because of visitation, acting in the school play is not
a possibility. This will only cause resentments.

In addition to daily or weekly visitation, typically
you will want to address the issues of holidays and
vacations. Although you and your ex-spouse may
always want to spend Christmas with your children,
the children obviously can only be in one place at
one time. To remedy this, you may decide to alternate the holidays. For example, if you have the children this year on Thanksgiving, your ex-spouse may
have them next year. Or, you may decide to divide
the days. For example, you have the children on
Thanksgiving until 2:00 p.m. and your ex-spouse has
them the rest of the day. There are generally no set
rules so long as both you and your ex-spouse are
provided ample opportunity to spend holidays with
the children. Most often, you will want to resolve
issues of visitation on major holidays and, more
practically, you may need to address visitation during school holidays.

If your children are of school age, you may need
to address visitation or day care during school
breaks, such as winter and spring recess. If you and
your ex-spouse both work, these holidays are often a
scheduling problem, but if the non-custodial parent
can arrange for time off during these periods, it
may serve as a very good time for extended visitation. If the non-custodial parent is unable to schedule time off around the children's vacations, the
parent with primary physical custody will most often

be responsible for them. Additionally, if both you and your ex-spouse plan to take a summer vacation, you should schedule summer visitation to complement your respective plans. You may agree on a fixed time, for example, the first two weeks of August, or consult one another each year about your respective vacation plans.

Moving and visitation

You may have a more difficult time scheduling visitation if one of you has primary physical custody of the children and the other moves too far away to effectively schedule weekday or weekend time. In this case, you and your spouse may wish to arrange visitation around holidays and vacation times. This may mean that you'll need to compromise a little more than you'd like—you may have to allow your ex-spouse some additional time during these breaks from school or work. But that compromise is important—just because your ex-spouse has moved, it does not diminish his or her right to visitation, nor does it reduce the children's need to maintain a good relationship with the non-custodial parent. The two of you will simply have to address the distance factor as best you can.

When one parent lives far away, transportation of the children for visitation may become an issue. When there is a significant expense, such as train or plane fare, or additional time and effort involved, such as a four-hour drive, you and your spouse will have to decide who should bear the burden of these added costs and this extra effort. In deciding who should bear the costs, you might take into consideration the reasons *behind* the move. For example, if you and your children live in the cold northeast and after your divorce your ex-spouse decides to move to the warm southwest simply because he or she prefers the weather, you would probably not be inclined, nor generally expected, to share in the costs of transporting the children. But if the move is involuntary—say your spouse has been transferred to an office in another state and must go or lose his or her job, it may be reasonable to treat the transportation costs as a shared expense.

If you have physical custody of your children, your ex-spouse may file a motion requesting that your divorce agreement be modified to prevent you from moving with the children. This would be done to make certain that he or she has guaranteed access for visitation. In the case of a job transfer, you would have to certify that your employer *requires* you to move and you will lose your job and be unable to support yourself if you do not comply. Your ex-spouse may object, claiming that he or she will no longer be able to spend significant time with the children, but generally, if you are forced to move for economic reasons, the court will permit you to do so. Of course, as part of your move, the court will most likely order a visitation schedule that permits your ex-spouse as much time as possible with the children.

Disputes

In the normal course of events, a divorcing couple should be able to schedule visitation without any involvement from the court because the family's specific circumstances—particularly the parent's work schedules—frequently dictate what will be a practical and equitable schedule. Visitation disputes tend to occur most frequently in situations where one spouse considers the other to be unfit or incapable of proper and safe visitation with the children, when the visitation parent demands more

Unofficially . . . Because visitation is generally considered a right, although the non-custodial parent may move, the parent with primary physical custody is often prohibited from moving without the consent of the ex-spouse or court order.

visitation than the custodial parent believes to be reasonable, or when the visitation parent consistently violates the visitation schedule.

If you believe your spouse should not be entitled to visitation because he or she is unfit and therefore detrimental to the safety and welfare of the children, the court will have to decide the issue in a manner much like that employed in a custody dispute. You will need to first convince the court that you have good cause for concern. For example, if throughout your marriage your spouse watched the children every night for two hours until you got home from work, you will probably not be able to convince the court that he or she should not have liberal and reasonable visitation—after all, you have trusted the care of the children to your spouse in the past. However, if your spouse is an alcoholic and drinks while caring for the children, the court will be more likely to consider your objection and may request more extensive testimony and evidence. It may also seek the advice of expert opinions and evaluate the facts and circumstances in much the same way it would if it were asked to decide custody.

As with all other divorce issues involving children, the court is really only interested in what is best for the kids. Unless there are very significant reasons to suggest that visitation should be limited, the court tends to be generous in allowing the noncustodial parent time with the children. It will typically allow visitation during weekends or alternate weekends, on holidays, and even time during the school week if that is not disruptive to the children's schedules. The court tries to establish an alternating schedule whenever possible. It may alternate weekends, holidays, and summer months.

Unofficially . . .
If you or your spouse remarries or moves in with his or her boyfriend or girlfriend, this does not mean that visitation should be altered, unless of course, the new partner can be shown to be unfit to be around the children. Involvement with a new partner is not grounds in and of itself for changing the terms of visitation.

What it cannot do is tailor a visitation plan to suit the specific details of your schedule. This being the general rule, try to agree upon a plan that best suits your specific needs and schedules without the aid of the court.

But what happens when your ex-spouse either refuses or fails to appear for scheduled visitation? Since visitation is considered a right not an obligation, you cannot force someone to visit his or her children. Visitation disputes can occur when your ex-spouse is chronically late or fails to show up at all. When this happens, you may find yourself constantly arguing over the issue, and you will find it difficult if not impossible to plan anything around the scheduled visitation times because of your ex-spouse's unreliability.

To alleviate this problem and to protect the children's best interests, the court may decide to restrict or rescind the right of visitation when the non-custodial parent habitually fails to adhere to a visitation schedule or in some way abuses it. This does not mean that the court will take an action if, on occasion, your ex-spouse arrives or returns the children 30 minutes late. However, if he or she constantly comes late, or cancels, or involves the children in activities that are against their best interests, you may apply to the court requesting that it narrow the scope of visitation.

A visitation dispute may also arise as a result of financial issues. For example, you may have sole custody of the children and your ex-spouse may visit on a regular basis but may not pay timely child support. Keep in mind that visitation is viewed as an issue that is independent of financial concerns. Do not retaliate for late or missing support payments by

Watch Out!
The court gener-
ally excludes
finances from its
list of considera-
tions in deter-
mining custody
and visitation.
Don't try to
intertwine the
two issues.

withholding visitation—that only puts you in violation of the court's order. Instead, petition the court
for assistance in collecting the child support.

Unless there is a very good reason to order
otherwise, visitation is normally allowed to be unsu-
pervised. In other words, during his or her allotted
time for visitation, your ex-spouse and the children
are free to go and do whatever they wish. This is
almost never a problem. However, in extreme situations, you may feel that your ex-spouse should be
restricted in the location or manner of visitation.
For example, you may have an infant and your ex-
spouse may not really be capable of caring for the
baby by him- or herself. You may want another
adult, such as your ex-spouse's parent, to be present.
Or your ex-spouse may be battling a drug or alcohol
problem, in which case you may wish to limit the
location of the visitation and insist upon some
supervision. If your circumstances dictate such
restrictions, present your concerns to the court.

Child support

While visitation is considered a right, child support
is always treated as an obligation. Both parents,
regardless of the circumstances, have a responsibility to provide financial support for their children
until the children are emancipated. A child is typically considered to be emancipated anywhere from
the time he or she turns 18 until the time he or she
finishes college or enters the military.

Regardless of income, both parents are obligated to pay child support. The custodial parent, in
essence, pays support by paying for the household
expenses. For example, if you have primary physical
custody, some portion of the food that you buy and
the rent that you pay represents support for your

children. The court has ways by which to determine how much of your household bills it believes are in fact attributable to your children's support, but as a practical matter, it does not bother with that level of detail. It simply assumes that if you are maintaining a home for the children, then you are supporting them on a daily basis.

The non-custodial parent fulfills his or her end of the financial obligation by making regular child support payments to the custodial parent. As a general rule, the custodial parent is free to spend the child support in any manner he or she feels necessary for the benefit of the children. It is assumed that the money will be used appropriately. In order to ensure that the children are adequately supported, and further to reduce disputes regarding child support, every state has developed child support guidelines that recommend the minimum amount of support that should be paid by a non-custodial parent. The guidelines indicate what the court believes the children's needs to be, and weighs the costs of these needs against the ability of you and your spouse to pay those necessary expenses. The guidelines are a mathematical chart that tells you and the court how much money should be paid to support your children.

All states work under the general principle that support is calculated as some portion of your income and the number of children that you have. For example, many states use a very simple formula: For one child, you are required to pay 20 percent of your net income as support. For two children, you are required to pay 25 percent, for three children 30 percent, for four children 35 percent, for five children 40 percent, and for six children 45 percent. It

Unofficially . . .
According the U.S. Census Bureau's 1997 numbers, more than four million American households receive child support payments.

does not matter how much money you earn because the support obligation is based upon a percentage of your income. As you earn more money, you pay more support. As a general concept, the better you do, the more money your children should receive.

Other states modify this calculation by decreasing the percentage of child support that is due as your income increases. This is a more complicated calculation, designed to account for what are generally fixed child care expenses. Depending upon your state, the child support calculation may be based on your gross income or on your net available income.

As a rule, you can expect to pay or receive between 15 and 22 percent of your net income for the support of one child, 22 to 28 percent for the support of two children, 28 to 34 percent for the support of three children, 34 to 46 percent for the support of four children, and so on. If you are the support-paying parent, this may seem high, but it is in fact a reasonable level of support. And as many judges have stated, if you cannot afford to support your children, you should not have had them. The fact that the state-imposed guidelines may leave you very little income to support yourself is *not* the concern of the court. Unless presented with very good reason to do otherwise, the court will ensure that child support is paid in accordance with the guidelines.

Child support is intended to cover expenses of children associated with household overhead, necessities such as clothing and food and, to some extent, entertainment and other extra-curricular activities. It is *not* intended to cover the costs of private school or college, day care, medical care, or

Unofficially . . .
If you voluntarily have money taken directly from your paycheck and put into a pension or savings plan, the court will generally consider this money to be available for child support and include this income as part of child support calculation.

other extraordinary expenses. Also, the child support guidelines may not be applicable to cases in which the custodial parent does not incur all of the expenses typically associated with child care. For example, if the custodial parent lives rent-free, the court may determine that he or she requires less support than is recommended under the guidelines.

Suppose you have two children, earn a net income of $20,000 per year, and your spouse earns $40,000 per year. Child support may be calculated according to the following formula. Between you and your spouse, the two of you have a total income of $60,000 per year available for the support of your children. Assume that the child support guidelines chart calculates that 25 percent of your income should be paid as support. In this example, the guidelines indicate that you and your spouse would pay 25 percent of $60,000, or a combined $15,000 per year as support for your children. Since you earn one-third of the total income and your spouse earns two-thirds, you might be held responsible for one-third of that $15,000, or $5,000 per year. Your spouse would be responsible for covering the other two-thirds of the total support, or $10,000. On the other hand, your state may only consider the income of the non-custodial parent. In this example, if you have primary physical custody, you would calculate 25 percent of your spouse's income, which again comes to $10,000 per year,

As a general rule, the child support guidelines will determine how much support you should pay or receive. Regardless of your personal opinion of the level of support they stipulate for you, the court will adhere to the guideline recommendations. But the

Moneysaver
The child support guidelines may not apply to parents who have extremely large incomes, as the percentages would result in extraordinarily high payments, beyond what might be considered necessary and reasonable to cover the expenses of the children.

Bright Idea
Support is gener-
ally ordered to be
paid on a weekly,
bi-weekly, or
monthly basis.
When calculating
support, remem-
ber that for pur-
poses of the cal-
culation there are
4.3, not 4, weeks
in every month
(52 weeks ÷ 12
months = 4.3).

guidelines are based upon typical circumstances
and cover a typical family, with typical expenses, so
if you can prove that you have exceptional circumstances suggesting that the guidelines should not
apply, present that information to the court. In
instances in which the court does not believe that
the guidelines should apply, it will base its support
calculations on the basis of actual spending habits
and needs.

Other expenses

In addition to child support expenses, you may
encounter other child-related costs that need to be
covered, such as costs associated with medical care,
day care, or tuition. Like child support, these
expenses are generally the responsibility of both
parents and are generally paid as a ratio of each parent's income as it relates to total income. For example, say you earn $20,000 and your spouse earns
$40,000 net per year. Generally, you would be
responsible for one-third of the cost of day care,
non-reimbursed medical expenses, or summer
camp, and your spouse would be responsible for the
remaining two-thirds. Day care expenses are generally considered to be a cost that should be shared by
both parents when they are necessitated by the custodial parent's employment.

As an equitable principle, both parents typically
share to the best of their ability in the costs of raising children. However, there is no formal chart or
guideline that dictates the terms of sharing
expenses other than child support. You and
your spouse will need to develop your own plan,
depending on your specific facts and circumstances,
to ensure that these extraordinary types of expenses
are paid. For example, we noted earlier that the

costs of private school and college are not covered by child support payments. Instead, these are considered as extraordinary expenses and are often divided as a ratio of your earnings. But since public schools are available for secondary education, there is no requirement to pay for private school costs. You and your spouse will have to mutually agree to send your child to private school and establish your own plan for dividing the costs. Regarding college costs, many states do not require that either parent make any contribution toward a child's college education. However, some states do require contribution if the child is inclined and has the opportunity to go to college and the parents have the financial ability to afford a contribution. And college financial aid offices expect both parents to contribute to tuition costs, regardless of who has physical or legal custody.

Bright Idea
No matter how young your children are at the time of your divorce, you may wish to address the issue of possible college education so as to avoid a potential argument many years from now.

Although you may not know whether you or your ex-spouse will in fact be able to contribute toward a future college education, you may wish to at least resolve the issue in principle. Like other expenses involving children, a general rule of thumb is to divide the expense as a ratio of your earnings to total earnings. Further, if you and your spouse are determined to help your child attend college, you may wish to consider establishing a method to save together in order to cover the expenses. Considering the often extremely high costs of college, you may need all the time you can get in order to save.

Modifying child support payments

More than any other term of your divorce agreement, the amount of child support, over time, requires modification. This is especially true in the case of very young children. As children grow older, the amount of support will generally need to increase. Inflation alone will require an increase in child support. As a result, you may wish to consider a regular increase in child support consistent with the rate of inflation or other economic indicators, for example, the consumer price index. Or, you may wish to consider a periodic review of child support in consideration of the actual expenses of the children, your income, and your spouse's income. Whatever the case, you may wish to recalculate the guidelines on a periodic basis in order to keep pace.

Enforcement

If your spouse does not pay his or her child support obligations, you do have several options of recourse. For instance, Child Support Enforcement Agencies (CSEA) are established in every state and are usually a part of the State Department of Social Services. These agencies can help enforce child support, help collect back payments, and help locate an absent parent. Your lawyer can put you in touch with the appropriate agency in your state, and you can use that agency's resources to pursue your case.

In order to ensure the payment of child support, it is often the case that you can have your ex-spouse's wages garnished and the money sent to you from his or her paycheck. Sometimes the court system or local probation or sheriff's department will become directly involved in collecting child support for you, either from your ex-spouse or from his or her employer. This ensures the timely payment and receipt of these funds. In fact, some states automatically garnish wages when requested to do so, in order to ensure the timely and proper payment of child support.

If child support is not paid, most states have laws that automatically enter a judgment against your ex-spouse for his or her failure to pay. They also have a wide variety of child support collection mechanisms at your disposal. For instance, Minnesota recently passed a law which suspends the driver's licenses of any person who has not paid child support for the last three months.

While some states are on the right track regarding the gravity of delinquent child support payments, not all states have fully addressed and acted on this issue. The General Accounting Office reports that state governments only succeed in collecting child support payments in one out of five cases. The states have been given money to pursue a workable solution—more than two billion dollars in federal funds have been allocated to establish a nationwide computer registry to this effect over the past two decades. But although that money was accepted by all 50 states, fewer than half have actually established the systems for which that money was targeted.

This glaring misuse of the funds has not slipped by unnoticed. At present, several government officials have proposed a new plan that would make the collection of child support a responsibility of the Internal Revenue Service. Under the proposal, every parent who is responsible for paying child support would fill out a form in the workplace. The employer would then withhold their child support payments from their paycheck, much as is done for pension plan payments. The IRS would then forward that money to the Social Security Administration, which would issue a check for the appropriate amount to the custodial parent. If you

Unofficially . . .
In several states, including New Jersey, wage garnishing is no longer used only as a punishment in the case of a spouse who fails to pay child support on his or her own. It is now being used as a standard child support collection mechanism, unless both sides agree on another method.

support this bill, write to your state senators and congressional representatives.

Whatever your state's stance on the issue of collecting child support, one standard remains: Every time your ex-spouse does not pay, the unmet obligation is recorded as a collectible debt. There is no excuse for not paying child support—regardless of your financial circumstances, you always have a responsibility to support your children. The court will take aggressive measures, including incarceration, to ensure that children are properly supported. If support is collected through the court or sheriff's department, for example, that entity may automatically issue an arrest warrant if it does not receive a timely payment.

Unlike other applications to the court, your ex-spouse does not really have any good faith defense for not paying support. Even if he or she has become unemployed, the court does not consider this fact to relieve him or her of the basic obligation to support the children. The court may modify the amount of future child support payments, but it will only on rare occasion modify money that is past due.

As should be clear by now, the court will place your children's needs well ahead of your own. The court will not seriously entertain arguments claiming that, after the payment of guidelines-calculated support, you do not have enough money to meet expenses. Therefore, if you find that you truly cannot pay support (for example, if you lose your job), you can petition the court for a reduction in child support based on your new financial hardship. Nevertheless, keep in mind that you still have to pay your present level of support until a new court order is established.

If, on the other hand, you are the parent to whom support is paid and you discover after the divorce that the amount ordered is too low, you may file a motion seeking to increase your support payments. But, like all other modification motions, the burden will be on you to prove that there have been changes in your circumstances significant enough to warrant changing the amount of support. Unless you can prove that the current level of support is no longer sufficient, your ex-spouse's ability to pay additional support may not be a consideration. For example, even though your ex-spouse may have gotten a raise at work, if the level of support you are currently receiving is sufficient, the court may not be inclined to increase the amount of the payments. This works both ways, however. If *you* receive a raise at work, this fact will not be enough to permit your ex-spouse to stop paying support.

In the end, it is important to understand that neither parent has the right to desert his or her responsibilities with regard to the children, and the courts and social service agencies have become more and more strict in enforcing children's rights. The legal system recognizes that children have needs and rights independent of the preferences of their parents—needs for financial support, for a secure home, and for ongoing contact with both parents throughout their lives. The simple fact that the parents are divorcing does not change these basic rights of children.

Just the facts

■ The non-custodial parent has a right to adequate opportunities to spend time with the children.

Timesaver
If you cannot locate the paying spouse, you can make an attempt to locate that person through the services of a Parent Locator Service (PLS), providing them with your spouse's birthdate and social security number. You can find a PLS through your local CSEA agency.

- Both parents, regardless of the circumstances, have a financial responsibility to support their children.

- Most states have laws that automatically enter a judgment against your ex-spouse for his or her failure to pay child support.

GET THE SCOOP ON...
The different types of alimony ▪ Taxes
and alimony ▪ When payments end

Chapter 10

What'll We Live On?

According to the U.S. Census Bureau's 1997 report, only 250,000 American households receive alimony payments. Alimony, or spousal support, is designed to help you or your spouse support him- or herself after your divorce. It is typically based upon your financial needs and ability to meet those needs. For example, in instances where your spouse is employed and during the marriage you stayed home with your children, upon divorce it may be impossible for you to pay all of your bills and living expenses without some contribution from your spouse. Or, maybe you have not worked for a very lengthy period of time and lack the requisite skills and training to enter the job market. These are two typical examples of when alimony is necessary and ordered by the court.

Alimony is *not* intended to guarantee that you or your spouse can maintain the lifestyle to which you've each become (or would like to become) accustomed. Rather, its aim is to allow each of you to best support yourselves. It is granted only after taking into consideration your available finances and your ability to earn a living. In fact both you and your spouse will probably have to *reduce* your standard of living after your divorce, because whatever income you and your spouse once relied upon to support a single household will now have to stretch far enough to support two.

Alimony: who gets it?

Alimony is generally awarded when you and your spouse have a significant difference in income—or in the ability to *earn* income. An obvious example is the case when one spouse has not worked in many years and the other has an established career. A less obvious example may be when one spouse worked a full-time job throughout the years of your marriage and earned perhaps $20,000 per year, whereas the other spouse's job pays substantially more—let's say $60,000 annually. While the couple was married, they together enjoyed a household income of $80,000 per year—and no doubt most of that income went toward household and family expenses. But once they got divorced, the income available to each of them dropped precipitously—most dramatically for the spouse that earned the least. On just his or her own income that spouse would not have sufficient means to support himself or herself. There would be a need for support from the more lucratively employed spouse, beyond the funds that would be available for child-support.

For example, assume that you have children and will be receiving $15,000 per year from your spouse as child support. Using the figures in the paragraph above, you'll note that on paying the $15,000 in child support, your spouse will still have $45,000, while your total income for the support of yourself and your children will total only $35,000 (your

$20,000 salary plus the $15,000 in child support). In this example, even with the receipt of child support, you have less money to support yourself and your children than your spouse has to support him- or herself.

How much money are we talking about?

Unlike the situation in figuring appropriate levels of child support, there is no chart or set of official guidelines that establish a specific amount of alimony based upon the amount of money you and your spouse earn. Some states have developed formulas to assist you and the court in determining a proper and fair amount of alimony. Alimony calculations are based upon equitable considerations, such as your marital history, the length of your marriage, and the ability of each spouse to earn a living, as compared with your necessary living expenses. Most importantly, alimony is typically based upon your need for additional income and your spouse's ability to provide that income. In order to be held liable for alimony payments, your spouse must have sufficient extra income to supplement your needs. Likewise, the court will not require you to make alimony payments that exceed your means.

How do they decide how much?

Alimony may be affected by the division of your assets and liabilities. For example, if you and your spouse have significant assets and you receive a significant share of those assets, you may require less alimony. Here's an illustrative case in point: if, as part of the division of your assets, you receive $200,000 from the bank accounts, and your spouse takes $50,000, you'll obviously have significantly more principal upon which to draw than your

Unofficially . . .
Alimony is generally not ordered as a form of punishment. It is a means of reaching an equitable and fair financial settlement between you and your spouse.

spouse does. In addition, you will be able to earn interest or investment income on the money. Taken together, these two considerations can be viewed as diminishing your need for alimony. Or, you and your spouse may have very significant debt. If your spouse assumes most of these obligations, the court may determine that you require less alimony.

As in all other issues of your divorce, you and your spouse, with the aid of attorneys and various resolution techniques, may be able to agree upon a just and equitable amount and duration of alimony. Your attorney can be very helpful in this regard because he or she has likely had experience in this area and should be able to advise you as to the court's likely ruling if the matter went to trial. If your attorney and your spouse's attorney agree fairly closely upon the court's most likely ruling, you and your spouse should be able to find a common ground. However, like all other issues of your divorce, if you cannot agree as to the amount and duration of support, the court will, after hearing evidence from you and your spouse, resolve the issue for you.

Watch Out!
The court will generally be less sympathetic to emotional appeals and intangible issues and will generally view the matter in strictly financial terms. In most cases you will be much better served if you do not need the court to resolve this issue.

Alimony types

Alimony can be agreed upon or ordered for many equitable reasons, based upon financial need and the ability to meet your necessary expenses. It is often useful to consider the idea and necessity of alimony as three separate concepts: permanent, rehabilitative, or reimbursement alimony.

Very few states actually name the type of alimony you will receive. Your divorce agreement will most likely simply state that you shall receive alimony, or spousal support, and will probably not elaborate any further on the concept or reasoning behind the award. Nevertheless, there are three basic types of spousal support, and an understanding of the concepts that underlay them may be useful in determining whether you or your spouse is a candidate for alimony in the first place.

Permanent-type alimony

Permanent-type alimony is financial support that is ordered to be paid on a permanent basis, without any definitive ending point. Some states, if left to the court's discretion, refuse to allow permanent alimony. Most courts will grant this type of alimony only if you and your spouse have been married for a long time and your spouse earns significantly more than you do. But even if you are granted permanent alimony, it will not actually last forever, regardless of what the name suggests. Permanent alimony typically ends upon your remarriage, or at any time that you set up housekeeping with an unrelated partner, because the court sees that the income available to support your household has increased, thus decreasing your need for financial support from your ex-spouse.

The general idea behind alimony is that, at some point in your marriage, you and your spouse must have established certain expectations and abilities with regard to supporting your household. However, even if you and your spouse agreed on the first day of your marriage that you would stay home and he or she would support the family, you are not automatically entitled to permanent alimony should you become divorced two years later. Although you expected to stay home—you and your spouse specifically agreed to this—a two-year marriage is considered to be a short-term marriage, and the court is unlikely to order permanent alimony in the case of

Unofficially . . .
There is no set definition for a long-term marriage. A 30-year marriage qualifies as long-term but a 5-year marriage does not. Depending on circumstances, a marriage lasting 12 years may or may not. Ask your lawyer how the court will view your marriage because it makes a difference in your chances of receiving or avoiding paying alimony.

Unofficially . . .
The court no longer assumes the concept of the traditional marriage, wherein the husband works and the wife does not. Supporting the court's views is a recent report from the U.S. Census Bureau that shows that the percentage of married women working outside the home has doubled in recent decades, reaching 60 percent in 1997. Of working women with children, 70 percent maintain outside jobs.

short-term marriages. It will assume that you can obtain employment and support yourself because, after all, you had only been away from the workplace for a short period of time.

The situation is very different, however, if you were married for 12 years and during that period were unemployed or only held a part-time job in order to stay home with the children. In this situation you may have a good case for requesting that your spouse pay alimony. If your children are quite young, you may wish to remain out of the job market for a considerable amount of time even after your divorce, say until they are ready to attend school. The court may consider that this necessitates permanent support. And even if your only reason for staying home during your marriage was because your spouse earned sufficient income to support the two of you, the court understands that an absence from the job market for as long as, say, 12 years may make it very difficult for you to re-enter the job market and support yourself. In this instance, your age, education, training, and other such factors regarding your ability to earn a living would have to be considered by the court.

Equitable considerations in instances such as these may dictate permanent alimony—but spousal support is *not* intended to allow you to remain permanently unemployed, especially if you have an employable skill. And remember, permanent alimony only refers to the duration of payments, not to the amount. In other words, maybe you couldn't work right at the time of the divorce, but later on if you manage to get a job your level of alimony may change even though it may not stop entirely. And maybe you can and will work, but even *with* a job you can't earn sufficient income to fully meet your expenses—then you may be granted alimony, but only as a supplement to your income.

Disability may also be a factor in the award of permanent alimony. For instance, although you and your spouse may not have had a long-term marriage, you may have a disability that renders you incapable of supporting yourself. This circumstance may result in a court order of permanent alimony, recognizing that you need some form of income. And age may be another important consideration when the court goes about determining the necessity for permanent alimony. For example, let's say you got married when you were 20 years old, you had two children early in your marriage, and you did not work for the duration of your marriage.

If you got divorced after 15 years of marriage, you would only be 35 years old, and your children most likely would no longer require you to stay home. In this scenario, considering your age, the court may assume that you will at some point in the future be able to support yourself. But if, after that same 15 years of marriage, you were 55 years old and had not worked for the past 15 years, the court would be more inclined to believe that you would have a great deal more difficulty obtaining meaningful employment. In this case the court would more likely order permanent type alimony.

Other considerations, such as your educational attainments and training, will also play an important role in the awarding of permanent alimony. Because the duration of alimony is influenced by need, the more education or training you have the more the court is likely to assume that you will be able to support yourself at some point in the future. The more limited your skills, experience, and/or education, the stronger your case will be for permanent alimony.

Rehabilitative support

Where permanent alimony is inappropriate, for whatever reasons, there are other forms of spousal support that may apply. One such form is known as rehabilitative alimony. This type of support is generally intended to allow either you or your spouse a period of time in which to establish a skill, to get a job, or to obtain necessary education or training.

Rehabilitative support is often ordered in divorces when the marriage was not long term and for which permanent alimony is not required. For example, maybe you once worked as a secretary and earned $20,000 per year, but you have not worked since your children were born eight years ago because you felt it was important that you be home with them when they were young. Upon your divorce, you may not immediately be able to re-enter the job market because your skills are a little rusty— for example, you may not have the necessary skills in using the latest office computer software. Rehabilitative alimony may be deemed to be necessary in this instance—it provides you with support for the time you need in order to get the requisite training and skills to re-enter the job market.

Or, perhaps your skills are good enough that you *could* get a job right away, but your youngest child will not be ready to enter full-time kindergarten for another two years and you and your spouse agree that you should remain home to care for the children until then. This too may be a case for rehabilitative alimony—not to allow for training, but to best meet your family's needs.

Perhaps you have the requisite training to immediately enter the job market, but require some transition time to adjust to your divorce, new financial situation, or other considerations. For example, you may be 35 years old and not have worked for eight years. While your skills may be good enough for you to obtain employment fairly quickly after your divorce, at an income level high enough to support yourself, you may still need some time to adjust to the dramatic changes in your new, post-divorce life. Rehabilitative alimony may be ordered in this case, to provide you with support while you take a little time to get your feet on the ground. You will still be expected to ultimately support yourself, but the alimony would serve to allow you to make a gradual transition into the job market.

Perhaps you are presently working but do not earn enough income to solely support yourself. It may be anticipated or assumed that in three years you will be able to earn more income—either as a result of natural advancement in your industry or for some other reason. Rehabilitative alimony could be used to aid or supplement your income for this three-year period.

Naturally, you will be expected to obtain some type of employment—the days of assuming that one spouse simply need not actively seek employment are over. If you are *able* to work and earn some income, the court will most likely assume that you *will* work, and it will calculate your alimony requirements based upon the amount of money it believes you can earn. The court may decide to do this regardless of whether or not you actually obtain employment.

There is no standard time limit set for the payment of rehabilitative alimony. Rather, the duration depends upon the facts and needs of your individual case. For example, if you require three years to obtain necessary training to enter the job market, you may be awarded three years of alimony. If you require five years to stay home with your children, then you may be granted five years of alimony. The important point to remember is this: Rehabilitative alimony is intended to be a short-term answer to insufficient income.

Reimbursement alimony

Reimbursement alimony is intended to reimburse you for income and opportunities that were lost as a result of the agreements or arrangements made between you and your spouse during your marriage. Reimbursement alimony can be set for any duration of time, including permanent, depending upon the income or opportunities you or your spouse may have lost. For example, even if you took a significant amount of time off from your career in order to stay at home and raise your family, you may be able to find employment and even re-establish your career. But it may be the case that, as a result of the time off, your position, salary, pension, and other benefits may be far less than they would have been had you remained active in your career. The court may recognize that, had you stayed on your career path you may have been promoted many times, accrued significant pension benefits, and currently be earning a significant salary. In this instance, you may in essence be entitled to compensation for the loss. The amount of compensation—and its duration— will generally depend upon your ability to recoup that loss without alimony. Although this is not a typical reason for the payment or receipt of alimony, if either you or your spouse gave up a career as a result of your marriage you should consider the use of reimbursement alimony.

The concept of reimbursement alimony may be closely linked to the division of your assets. For example, if as a result of having left your original career path you failed to accumulate significant retirement benefits while your spouse has accrued a substantial pension, you may be awarded a share in his or her benefits as compensation for what you've lost. If this is the case, the share in the pension benefits will replace any dollar amount in reimbursement alimony this situation might otherwise have entitled you to.

Dividing your assets as a form of alimony

You and your spouse may agree that you should receive some amount of alimony, but your spouse may be reluctant to commit to making payments over the long term. This may be especially true in the case that your spouse is planning to re-marry. In such cases, you and your spouse may agree that instead of dividing your assets on a 50-50 basis, you will receive substantially more of the assets, say, 75 percent. The extra 25 percent is intended to provide you with the extra money you need to get on your feet after the divorce that would otherwise be addressed by alimony, but it is paid "up front."

Taxes and alimony

It is extremely important to consider the tax consequences of alimony when structuring such a settlement. We will discuss this in some depth in Chapter 15, but a few preliminary remarks are in order here. For example, your division of assets and liabilities is

Bright Idea
Alimony is generally subject to modification by the court if there is a change of circumstances. Because of this, it's often a good idea to take as much money up front as possible.

Unofficially . . .
There is a movement beginning among recently divorced people challenging the fairness of taxing the recipient of alimony while giving a tax break to those ordered by the court to pay. If you see this as unfair, be sure to contact your state senator to request a modification of current alimony tax laws.

generally done tax-free, but alimony payments must be included as taxable income on your federal tax return, and the payment of alimony is tax deductible. This alimony is different from child support, which is neither taxable to the recipient nor tax deductible for the payor.

All things considered, it is very important to understand the tax implications when thinking about whether or not to request alimony. It is also very important to specifically state in your divorce agreement the type of support you are either paying or receiving. You should always discuss the tax consequences of alimony with your attorney and/or accountant and specifically address how your payment or receipt influences your tax obligations.

What it's there for, what it isn't there for

In some states, the award or lack thereof of alimony may be influenced by the cause of action for divorce. For example, in some states, alimony may be reduced or eliminated, regardless of need, if the spouse to whom it would have been paid is found to have committed adultery. Although in most states support is *not* influenced by the reasons behind the divorce, it does happen sometimes. You should check into the laws of your state to find out if your request for alimony might be affected by the grounds for divorce cited in the complaint.

It is also not generally the case for alimony to be awarded solely in order that the receiving spouse can maintain the lifestyle to which he or she had become accustomed during the marriage. Except in instances of *very* significant income, divorce will most often result in financial hardship for *both* you and your spouse. One thing is likely to be true, however—whether you are receiving or paying alimony, you will not be happy with the amount. Unless you and your spouse saved significantly and earned excess income during your marriage, both of your lifestyles will suffer.

Whereas child support may be modified many times during the course of a child's development, as a general rule, the terms of alimony will not be modified as frequently. Because of the minor status of children, the court will always look out for their best interests and as a result will be willing to re-evaluate child support payments whenever good cause may be shown. However, the court will not typically take such an active role with regard to alimony—so it's very important not only to take into consideration the present circumstances, but also to try to anticipate future needs as much as possible when proposing the amount and duration of alimony payments. If you later wish to change the terms of alimony as set forth in your divorce agreement, you will find that there will be a substantial burden placed upon you to prove why the original terms are no longer fair and proper.

How long will it take to receive payment?

You and your spouse can agree to begin alimony or support payments at any time. If you have separated prior to your divorce, you may need to begin the payments before your divorce actually becomes final. In this instance, you and your spouse can determine the necessary amount and frequency of support payments, either by voluntary agreement or through court order. You may also wish to address the ultimate duration of the payments. For

Moneysaver
The court may have ordered, or you and your spouse may have agreed upon, temporary support payments pending a final resolution of your divorce. It is important to address the tax consequences of this situation with your attorney, accountant, and the court. For example, although you may be separated, you and your spouse may need to file a joint tax return.

example, you may be separated for one year prior to your divorce and agree only that support will be paid for this one-year period.

Enforcement issues

Unlike child support, a judgment will not be automatically entered against your spouse if he or she fails to make timely alimony payments, and there are no automatic procedures in place for the collection of owed money. However, your alimony terms will become a part of your final judgment of divorce and therefore will constitute a court order. As such, if your ex-spouse fails to pay alimony, he or she may be found to be in violation of the court order—effectively, in contempt of the court—and may be punished accordingly.

If your alimony payments are not arriving, or are consistently significantly late, you will most likely have to petition the court for relief by way of a motion or other similar application. At this time you will present the facts of the matter and provide evidence of your ex-spouse's violation. Often, this is very simple: You simply present the court order (your divorce decree) as part of your motion papers and allege that your spouse did not make the requisite payments. However, your spouse *will* be given the opportunity to respond and either disagree or explain why he or she did not comply with the terms of alimony.

In your spouse's response to you or your lawyer, before he or she addresses the court on the topic, you will most likely receive sob stories about banks forgetting to process deposits, increased car insurance payments, or the unreliable U.S. mail. But just as those excuses do not impress the court, they should not impress you or affect your demands in any way. Remember that your spouse has a legal obligation to make those payments. Very few excuses are acceptable, and poor budgeting is decidedly *not* one of them.

If the court believes the violation to be willful, it will most likely direct punishment. In cases of willful violation, you may be entitled to have your ex-spouse's wages garnished and the payment sent directly to you from his or her paycheck—this is one way to avoid future violations. Even if the court does not believe the violation to be willful—for example, your ex-spouse may have recently lost his or her job and at least for the present truly does not have the money—he or she may still be found to be in violation of the court order. In these types of cases, the court frequently rules that you are entitled to any arrears due to you, but may, at your ex-spouse's request, modify the terms of future payments to accommodate the change in employment circumstances. And keep in mind that although the court may punish your ex-spouse for failure to comply with the terms of its order of alimony, collection of the money due you may be difficult, if not impossible, if your spouse truly does not have the funds.

In alimony issues as in any other, remember that unless you tell the court there is a problem, it cannot take action. For example, you may have been ordered to pay alimony and may do so on a timely basis for a while. But later on, if you find you simply cannot meet your obligation—let's say you've been laid off—you *must* inform the court of your change in circumstances. Until the court order is modified, your obligation to pay continues according to the original terms of the divorce, despite the fact that

Bright Idea
If, at the time of your divorce, you and your spouse reach an agreement on the specific term of alimony payments, specify in writing the date that payments commence. You may assume that they started on the date of your final divorce; your spouse may have begun "counting down" from the date of separation. A written stipulation will save you from future conflict.

Timesaver
Don't bother calling your lawyer or running to court if your spouse is habitually a week or two late with your payments. While you may find it unforgivable that your spouse is tardy with the checks, the court will allow a grace period. It's not worth your time or money to pursue legal action unless your spouse is falling significantly behind in his or her payments.

you can no longer make the payments and you cannot assume that the court will modify your obligation retroactively.

Let's look at this situation a little more closely. Let's say that you've missed six months of payments. Your ex-spouse may petition the court for relief—specifically seeking the payment of that six months of alimony. You cannot assume that the court will deny your ex-spouse's application merely because you were unemployed. In other words, if you want the court to consider your period of unemployment as a reason for not making timely payments, you may wish to petition it for relief yourself. Remember, when it comes to alimony, if you want to modify the terms of the original court order, the burden is on you to affirmatively seek the modification.

When the money stops

Alimony payments may end for a variety of reasons, including your ex-spouse's ability to pay. Even though you may continue to require support, a court may be hard pressed to order your ex-spouse to pay if he or she, in good faith, cannot afford to do so. For example, if your ex-spouse retires or becomes disabled, alimony will most likely cease. These possibilities should always be discussed by you and your attorney when considering alimony and your future lifestyle.

In addition alimony, like child support or other forms of ongoing support payments, is subject to the review of the court if a significant change of circumstance occurs that makes it inequitable for you or your spouse to continue to make and/or receive the payments. Much like any other modification of your divorce agreement, if you can prove to the court that due to a significant change of circumstance such that the present payments are no longer fair, the terms of alimony payments may be changed or modified. You or your spouse may make such a request by filing a motion with the court. At that time you will be expected to prove the validity of your request. For example, you will have to prove that your petition to lower or terminate your alimony payments is not due to bad faith on your part, but rather to a change in your circumstances that make it impossible for you to continue providing support at the levels originally ordered.

To make this a little clearer, here's an example. Let's say that you have been paying permanent alimony but you file a request that it be eliminated due to your retirement. If you are age 65 and retiring in the normal course of business, your chances of eliminating alimony are substantially greater than if you decide to retire at age 45. Of course, if you are forced to retire—due to disability, perhaps—then even at the younger age you may be able to eliminate your obligation. But the court will expect that you present medical evidence of your disability. Keep in mind, however, that before eliminating or decreasing the payment the court must fully consider your ability to pay the obligation. So, for example, even though you can demonstrate that you no longer have a job, the court will most likely take into account any assets that you own that could be used to pay the support. For example, if you retire but receive a substantial pension income, the court may view your pension as income available to you to use to continue paying the alimony. If your pension income is sufficient to allow you to continue to pay the support obligation, the court may decide not to grant your requested relief.

Watch Out!
It is almost never a good idea to make or receive alimony payments in cash: You'll have no record of your payment in the event that you or your spouse make a claim of non-payment. A cashed check is many times the best form of proof that you have made your payments on time.

Looking toward a new day

As you look forward to your new and newly single life, you will begin to recognize that the legal institution of divorce can only address some of your concerns. You've worked out a custody plan and sorted out the financial division of household, but there are still a great many important issues left to be addressed. In fact, what you are likely to be discovering is that it is now time to stop looking backward, at the marriage that used to be, and to start looking forward—to the life that you are now about to begin. It won't always be easy, but it *can* be an adventure if you take care to avoid some common pitfalls and learn to develop a good, positive attitude.

In Part 4 you'll learn some of the classic situations that can make the time during and just after a divorce so difficult to get through—but you won't stop there. Yes, it can be tough to figure out just how to start your new life, but others have managed it successfully and so can you. In the next few chapters you will learn about the changes that everyone faces post-divorce, and how best to handle them. You'll learn to recognize the difficult emotions that can get in your way of moving on with your life, and you'll get the lowdown on where to turn for support and advice in coping with them. Finally, you'll learn some proven tricks for coping with stress, so that you can come through the divorce process stronger, smarter, and better than ever.

Just the facts

- Alimony, or spousal support, is designed to help you or your spouse support him- or herself after your divorce.

- Alimony is typically based upon your financial needs and ability to meet those needs.

- Some states have developed formulas to assist you and the court in determining a proper and fair amount of alimony.

- It is extremely important to consider the tax consequences of alimony when structuring such a settlement.

- If your ex-spouse fails to pay alimony, he or she may be found to be in violation of the court order and may be punished accordingly.

Get the Lowdown on Coping

PART IV

GET THE SCOOP ON...
Post-divorce life changes ▪ Handling stress ▪
Dealing with family and friends ▪
Managing your career

Surviving the Ordeal

When you first face the prospect of divorce, the very foundation of your world is shaken. Everything you once believed in, everything you worked for, is gone—just gone. You're likely to feel hurt, angry, frustrated, and sad. Some people react by taking to their beds for months. Some people just can't stop crying. While it's true that everyone's reactions to the upheaval in their lives may be different, it's also true that everyone needs to learn to cope with those reactions. They need to be able to get themselves and their families through this process. So do you. That's what this section of the book is here for—to help you discover ways to not only survive your divorce, but to come out of it stronger than ever.

When you think about the end of your marriage you may be overcome with emotion at times— crying, not sleeping, fearing the future. And you may not believe the people who tell you that time will heal your wounds. At this time in your life, you may feel very isolated in your suffering. If you don't know any other divorced people very well, you

227

66

I felt like I was living in a bad dream. . . . I took it badly. I cried. I lost weight. I didn't sleep. And I didn't believe all the people who told me that time would heal my wounds. 'Yeah, right,' I said. But you know what? It really does. That and a lot of talking and seeking support and thinking it out. —Chris, recently divorced

99

probably feel that no one else could possibly understand how you feel. But that just isn't so. What may be most surprising to you, and perhaps most comforting, is that you're not alone. And it's not just that other people have gone through this before you. Yes, there's some comfort in knowing that you're not the only one to face these problems—but there's another sense in which you are "not alone." All you have to do is look around to realize that there are people just waiting to help you through this time.

Change and constancy

In the beginning of coming to grips with your divorce it can seem as if everything in your life is now going to change. This is probably one of the most distressing things about facing a life-change as big as a divorce. But you'll be surprised to learn that whole portions of your life will *not* change. Think of these unchanging things as the constants of your life—good things that you can cling to for support when the going gets rough. And after awhile you'll begin to realize that although it may *feel* like everything is different—after all, your marriage is over— if you look closely, you'll discover that many things that are essentially *you* have remained. You'll see that your marriage isn't all that you are about. Here's a list of some of those constants:

- Your children still love you and need you.
- You still have your life's work—whether that's your career or your responsibilities in the home.
- You still have your friends and family.
- You still have your talents, skills, and personal strengths.

- You still have your religious beliefs, your faith.

- You still have your connections to the community—your neighbors, charity works, and so on.

Take a moment right now to think about the things in your life that will remain constant. Then make a list, and post it prominently, somewhere where you'll be able to see it when you need a boost. These constants will sustain you during and after your divorce.

I'm not trying to kid you—I'm not saying that your life won't change at all. It already has, and it will certainly continue to do so. But it's best to start out by remembering what you have, not by dwelling upon what you may have lost. This way, thinking about all that's gone or different is not quite so devastating, and you'll be ready to gain some perspectives on the things that *will* change.

Who am I now?

It can be very disconcerting to find yourself single, especially if you were married for a long time. Suddenly you're no longer part of a couple. In marriage you were a "we," but now you have to learn to be an "I." That's an extremely difficult adjustment for some people to make, depending on how fully they merged with their former partner.

There's a line in the movie *Jerry Maguire* where he says "You complete me." In your marriage ceremony, the officiant may have spoken about how "the two become one." Now that your marriage is over you may feel like half a person—after all, during your marriage you may have done most everything together with your partner. You went to the movies together, entertained friends as a couple, and

> 66
> Look at what will endure, the things you've personally worked on.
> —Dr. Paula Bortnichak, family therapist
> 99

so forth. Perhaps that's the hardest thing to adjust to—you're no longer so-and-so's husband or Mrs. so-and-so.

But when you start feeling like "just a half," think of the starfish—you read about them in seventh-grade science class. When a starfish loses an arm, another one eventually grows in its place. Keep that image in mind—if you feel like you've become half a person, remember that what's missing will slowly grow back. You will someday feel whole again.

Some people find adjusting to their new "singleness" more difficult than others do. People who have been married a long time often lose the habit of thinking of themselves as individuals. This is most commonly the case if you married young—if you moved straight out of your parents' house into your married home you may never really have had the chance to create an identity for yourself. Whatever the case, it's time now to redefine yourself as an individual, beyond the roles of "husband" or "wife." Now is the time to remember all the other things you are: a mother, father, sister, brother, or friend. Most important of all, though, is to remember that you are an "I."

If remembering this is difficult to do right now, while you're still struggling with the divorce process or in the immediate aftermath, here's a trick that might help. Take some time now to make another list—in this one write down all of the roles you play in life—from mother, father, sister, brother, to painter, sports fan, good student, volunteer. Every time you make another entry on the list, you are acknowledging the many aspects of your individuality.

Revised routines

Another thing you might find tricky to get used to now that you are no longer part of a couple is the change this makes in your day-to-day activities. Think about the daily routine you followed during your marriage. You woke up together. You got ready for your day. You went to work. At the end of the day, you returned home or you heard your spouse's key in the door. Maybe you did things together in the evenings, like reading or watching TV. You slept together. Over time, this routine became comfortable to you, so much so that it may have been hard to imagine any other. It was the makeup of your life. Now, with your partner gone, your daily routine is entirely different, and for some people it is very hard to get used to the change.

But change doesn't *have* to be negative. Now that you are on your own, you may find that the change in your daily routine is a relief, a liberation. You suddenly have the freedom to alter it in any way that works best for you. Still, even when you're happy to leave the old ways behind, if your daily routine is drastically different now you may need a little help in getting used to it. The best advice is simply this: Look for the positives. Acknowledge to yourself that there are things you don't miss, and establish new routines that suit you best. Include a little pampering for yourself in these new routines: Take a nightly bath, for example. Read before bed. Watch the television shows *you* like for a change. And remember to remind yourself, as many times as it takes to sink in, that you *enjoy* having control over your daily routine.

You might find that weekends are particularly hard—many newly divorced people do. This is probably the time you usually used to spend together,

Watch Out!
If you have kids, though, keep their routine as normal as possible. They've had enough change. A dependable home routine gives them stability.

Bright Idea
Check the community bulletin board column in your local paper—you'll find a wealth of local events listed according to category: lectures, plays, comedy, movies. Circle the events that you may be interested in. It just may open up a world of possibilities that you never knew existed.

having fun or working on the house or running errands. Your tendency might be to look at weekends as an endless chasm, but if you indulge this attitude you'll only be emphasizing your feelings of aloneness. Take a cue from how your weekdays might sometimes seem easier to get through. During the week you have work to keep you busy. Take a hint from that fact: Instead of just hanging around the house, try to fill your weekends with activities—the kinds that *you* like to do. Maybe your former partner wasn't into museums or sporting events. Well, now you have the time and freedom to enjoy these things, so go ahead and indulge yourself. Here are a few ways you might choose to expand your weekend horizons:

- Attend sporting events. They could be pro ball games, or the Little League match-ups at the park—it really doesn't matter which, as long as they are events that you enjoy.

- Take a class. Check with your local adult education center or YMCA/YWCA. The options are endless—from dance classes to cooking classes to professional certifications. It will give you something to do, and along the way you may discover a whole new talent. You will at least meet a few new people.

- Volunteer your time. Help out at a local hospital's children's wing or serve meals at a local shelter. Nothing helps beat bad feelings like the sense that you're helping others.

- Take a walk—in the mall, on the beach, or explore neighborhoods in your town. It will get you out and about, and you'll begin to establish a new, single-you identity for the rest of the world.

- Visit a day spa for a massage, a manicure, a facial. Whatever particular form of pampering appeals to you. After all, you deserve it.

- Start a big project. Paint a room, put up wall-paper, install a ceiling fan.

- Take up a new hobby. It's never too late to learn to play tennis, do ceramics, or play a musical instrument. And it can be lots of fun.

- Load up on the latest best-sellers at the library and get lost in the adventures.

- Go for a drive. Destination unknown. Especially in autumn, take in the scenery that's not too far from your house.

- Plan events for your family. Picnics, parties, reunions, dinners—all these will help to bond your family together in an enjoyable way, and they'll help overcome any feeling of aloneness that you might be indulging in your private hours.

- Make a list of new area restaurants you'd like to try out, and go to one each weekend. Be adventurous—now is the time to replace those old favorites (that maybe have too many memories attached to them) with a few new hangouts.

- Visit old friends you haven't seen in awhile. Maybe there are a few that your ex never really got along with so you lost touch. But there's nothing to stop you now, is there?

Whatever you decide to do, the important thing to realize is that now there's no one to put their plans ahead of yours. This can be a very positive realization, and you'll soon learn to relish this new freedom to indulge your own interests.

Role changes

If your ex had always assumed the majority of the child-rearing, you are probably suddenly discovering that you now have to come up with ways to provide the kids with a whole new level of care than you once did. Similarly, if your spouse always handled the finances when you were married, you're suddenly going to have to learn about balancing the checkbook, paying the bills, and handing insurance. And if your spouse was the social secretary, now it's you who'll have to keep on top of birthdates and holiday preparations. Suddenly having all these new things to learn can throw a lot of people.

When a marriage dissolves it seems as if your workload suddenly doubles—and at first it can be frustrating to have to suddenly learn a myriad of new skills. But think of it as a challenge: A friend of mine spent six hours trying to assemble a toy for her son that, she knew, her ex-husband could have had put together in one. But she was going to get that stupid toy assembled if it killed her! And she succeeded.

It sounds daunting, but there's a positive way to look at this change, too. Many divorcees find a particular satisfaction in being able to handle the jobs that used to belong to their ex. They learn that they can do all sorts of things they never thought they could—handle the money, whip up a decent meal, change a blown fuse, or sing a lullaby—necessity makes a great teacher. If you think of this as a lesson of self-sufficiency you can actually learn to enjoy it.

Social life? What social life?

As you may have already noticed, some of the people in your life are not going to take the news of your divorce very well. It might make them

Moneysaver
When it comes to minor home repairs, you might be tempted to hire professional help to take over your ex's old chores. But you can learn to perform these jobs on your own—for example, by attending free how-to courses offered at such stores as Home Depot.

uncomfortable. Your married friends may hesitate to invite you to dinner if they're used to having you as part of a couple. They may measure their words when they speak to you. When called on it, they may say—and it may be genuine—that they didn't want to make you uncomfortable. If you and your spouse were particularly couple-oriented, your old friends may simply not know how to deal with the newly single you.

And it's not just that you're no longer part of a couple. If your divorce was particularly unfriendly, people may wonder if you're still angry or moody or upset. Will you be bashing your ex in front of everyone? Will you bring everybody down? If they're not sure of how you're handling your divorce, they may just be trying to give you time and space to get your emotions sorted out.

You'd be surprised how people think and how they interpret your situation. It is not unusual for friends to overcompensate for your perceived pain. For instance, if it is common knowledge that your spouse cheated on you, your friends may suddenly find themselves uncomfortable going to the movies with you if infidelity is even a small part of the storyline—even if it doesn't bother you in the slightest. Divorce is still a difficult issue for most people to handle, and they may express their problems with the issue by simply avoiding you. And, of course, there are the people that you might lose to "the other side." Friends you made through your spouse may stop calling. Your in-laws may distance themselves, even if they don't blame you for the divorce.

The most difficult thing to do is to keep from taking all this personally. Try to maintain a common-sense attitude by acknowledging that some people in your old social circle are simply going to

> 66
> Your friends' and family's reactions strongly depend on where they're coming from within their own lives.
> —Dr. Paula Bortnichak, family therapist
> 99

go, no matter what you do. But remember, too, that other people will stay. And the good news is that you'll know that the people who stand by you are true friends.

In fact, it's not unusual for a recently divorced person to grow even closer to friends and family during this time. As your loved ones provide you with their support, send you cards and funny e-mails, and tell you to call them, no matter what time—well, they're showing you just how much they really love and appreciate you. This is very important. You may have taken them for granted when you were all wrapped up in the day-to-day demands of your marriage, but you can value it now. Consider this new-found appreciation of your friends and family as another fringe benefit to your divorce.

Sex is just a three-letter word

Now for the tricky subject—sex. Even if you and your partner's sex life hit a slump toward the end of your marriage, it's a little distressing to realize that suddenly even the *option* of sex is not even there anymore. For many people this is a real blow to their self-esteem. They suddenly start to worry about all sorts of things:

- Will anyone else find me attractive?

- Will anyone else find me satisfactory in bed?

- How will it be when I'm with someone else?

- Why wasn't my partner satisfied with me?

Before going any further, let's get one thing clear right away: It's a smart idea to put the whole issue of starting a new relationship out of your mind during the early days of your divorce. You can acknowledge that you'll never sleep with your spouse again, and you may miss the romantic moments you used to enjoy together, but it's counter-productive to worry about new relationships while you're still working your way out of the old one. There will be plenty of time for that once the divorce is behind you.

Of course, there is more to the issue of sex than just the love-making part. Your partner's physical presence is gone—and that's often the hardest thing to get used to. You may find yourself, quite simply, lonely. You miss the simple awareness of having someone near. But don't confuse these feelings with wanting your spouse back—probably, what you're really lonely for is simply physical intimacy. *That* will come to you again. And change in your love life *will* come, and it can open up new and positive opportunities.

Recognizing and handling stress

As I've mentioned earlier, divorce ranks second—right behind the death of a loved one—as a cause of stress. For many people, the end of their marriage means that their greatest fears have come true. They feel betrayed, abandoned, hurt, rejected, thrown away. They're afraid for their future and afraid of the prospects of starting over. Some people have to deal with difficult revelations about their spouse— that he or she cheated on them perhaps. And even if all these negatives are absent, the simple fact that your life is changing so extensively is bound to cause you to feel some stress.

The important thing is not to let stress run—or ruin—your life. And it can indeed cause some serious problems. You've read the articles and seen the TV shows—you know what stress does to your physical health. It can give you high blood pressure or heart palpitations. It can lower your immune

Bright Idea
So much will change in your life now, but the best way to handle it is to think: Change is good! It helps you develop under-used skills. It opens up new opportunities, a whole new road to follow.

system, making you more susceptible to colds, flu, viruses, even cancer. Your body *does* suffer under extreme or prolonged periods of stress, so it's best to learn to get a handle on it before it destroys your health.

While many people don't recognize stress as a medical disorder, they're wrong. Stress, if left unchecked, can escalate into serious physical and emotional disorders. The most common stress-based psychological malady experienced by the recently divorced is called "adjustment disorder." The symptoms include depression, anxiety, or a mixture of both. While it's a completely normal state, considering the stress involved in ending a marriage, it can last for as long as a couple of months. But if you take proper steps the feelings *will* go away. If your symptoms are severe and have a negative impact on your ability to handle your life's responsibilities you may want to see a therapist—in extreme cases you might explore the possibility of medication.

After a separation or divorce, some people neglect their own health and well-being. They don't eat, they don't sleep, they obsess. They lose weight and grow weak. Alternatively, they may go in the opposite direction—they may begin using food as comfort, and they gain large amounts of weight. This is not something you want to allow to continue for long. After all, although the breakup of your marriage may have hurt you, you don't have to hurt yourself.

Here are a few things you can do to keep your health together and your stress levels in check:

- **Eat something.** Like most people in the earliest and most intense periods of your divorce

66
It's important for you to get what I call a 'reality check.' Just talk to your primary care physician, your gynecologist, or a therapist about the severity of your stress symptoms, and the two of you can work out a plan to handle your symptoms and help you get better.
—Dr. Paula Bortnichak, family therapist
99

process, you may gag when any food comes near your mouth. If this is the case, you'll probably be relying on what I call "flu food": chicken soup, applesauce, juices, Jell-O. However, in order to maintain optimum health, make sure your food choices include protein, vegetables, fruit—plenty of nutrients. Drink plenty of water to keep from getting dehydrated and take your vitamins!

▪ **Exercise.** You've read and heard enough to know that exercise is good for you. It helps keep your energy up, it produces endorphins (the body's feel-good hormone), and at the very least it distracts you from your troubles for a while.

▪ **Meditate.** Yoga or other meditation techniques will help teach you to calm down. Many people report that their first attempts at meditation or relaxation exercises was the first time their shoulders came down from their ears. Buy or rent a yoga or meditation video, and see what it does for you. Other calming activities: taking a warm bath, reading a great novel, watching a favorite movie again.

▪ **Get a massage.** Most doctors and chiropractors are now quite happy to recommend a qualified massage therapist, and your insurance may even cover it if your doctor recommends it as an antidote to stress. If your doctor cannot get massage therapy added to your stress-fighting regimen, look in the phone book for The Great American Backrub, a chain of storefront massage therapy clinics that's spreading across

Bright Idea
If you do choose to exercise—as you should—and if you are interested in yoga and meditation, seek out an inexpensive class.
Beyond the benefits of the activity itself, you are also getting yourself out into the world and making human contact.

the country. Stop in for their 10-minute back rub. It's an inexpensive option with great advantage to your health.

▪ **Get your feelings out.** Start a journal in which you can record all of your thoughts. Simply putting your words on paper can provides release of the pressure that cause you stress.

Take care of yourself and keep your health in check. Do it for yourself. Do it for your children, and do it for your family. Do it so that you're strong enough at all times to take care of the business end of your divorce as well.

Managing your career

Somewhere in the middle of all this upheaval, you still have to continue to take care of your responsibilities—whether that means running your household, taking care of the kids, or holding down a nine-to-five office job. You need to think clearly enough during your working hours (whatever they may be) so that you can stay functional. And newly divorced people who have to work outside the home run into a special set of problems, because they are out in public view during this difficult time. It would be unrealistic to tell you to keep the divorce entirely out of the office, but you can protect your best interests by establishing a few ground rules for yourself:

▪ Don't cry. The office is not the place for emotional outbursts.

▪ Do not work on your divorce process from the office. Give your lawyer your home phone number and speak with him after hours.

- If thoughts about the divorce sneak into your mind, distract yourself. Lose yourself in the job-related task at hand.

- Don't discuss your divorce in the office. Just acknowledge it, accept consolations, and move on. Your colleagues do not need to be kept up-to-date on your legal proceedings.

- Don't converse or argue with your ex while you're at work. Tell your ex to call you at home.

- Show your boss that your work will not be affected by your situation. Even if it means working twice as hard, you must make every effort to keep up your usual standards of excellence.

- Tell your boss directly about the situation. Don't let her hear about it through office gossip. If she knows what's going on, she will understand any changes in your habits or demeanor.

- Don't allow your divorce schedule to interfere with your work schedule. Your boss will *not* be pleased if you keep taking off in the middle of the day to meet with your lawyer.

The people in your office are going to be very curious about your situation. Perhaps you've told them directly, they've overheard at the water cooler, or they've noticed you're not wearing your wedding ring anymore. There may be whispering at first, or a sense that people are "walking on eggshells" around you, or maybe a stream of consoling comments from your colleagues. Some people will respond by expressing support, but others may avoid you. As with your friends, some of them may just be uneasy about their own feelings about divorce, while

Watch Out!
While you may have a good support system in your friends at the office, you may also become a target for your competitors. Don't bring your divorce into the office—you don't want anyone taking advantage of your distress to hurt your career chances.

others may be sincerely concerned but want to avoid upsetting you.

Whatever else is going on, it is very important that you take action to make sure that you're able to function well at the office. If you're a total wreck, you need to consider taking some time off so that you can straighten yourself out without your having to deal with your colleagues. It might be a very good idea to take a few vacation days—you can use them to regroup. Do what you must to make yourself stronger, then go back to the office ready to plow into your work. Show your boss and co-workers that you're a real pro, completely dedicated to your work, and still the reliable asset to the company that you always were.

Getting over it

Unofficially . . .
For most people, it will take a solid six months. Some recent divorces report that it took closer to a year to get back to 100 percent. Your sadness will likely continue, but the suffering part will be over.

You may not believe it now, but you *are* going to get over this. The best cure of all is just *time.* If you keep yourself positive and open to all the new opportunities that will arise in your life, the symptoms of stress and suffering are going to fade, and eventually they will disappear.

To speed your healing, one of the first positive steps you can take is to refuse to think of yourself as a victim. One big danger during difficult times is that it is easy to get used to feeling bad. Suffering becomes a habit, and some people cling to their pain for far too long, just because it's a familiar feeling to them. But indulging in negative emotions will only prolong the agony and keep you from recovering.

Many divorced people I consulted readily offered their secrets to getting over it. Some of their ideas may surprise you, but they are proven to be successful:

- Allow time to pass.

- Talk it out, even if you have to repeat the same things over and over again.

- Don't dwell on it. If you catch yourself, consciously distract yourself.

- Tell yourself "I deserve better."

- Lean on your support system.

- Actively work on your future. Search for a new job or work toward an advanced degree.

- Make changes to help you feel better about yourself—get a makeover, get a new work wardrobe.

- Lean on your faith.

- Stay busy. Plan out every minute in your day so that you don't have empty time to think.

- Read encouraging or inspirational books.

- Don't be sentimental about your past. Yes, it was good at times, but it wasn't that good.

- Don't over-dramatize.

- Don't be fatalistic.

- Tell yourself "Better days are coming."

Sometimes it helps to hold onto the inspirational thoughts of others. Following is a sampling that some of the newly divorced interviewed for this book have used. Cut out the ones that seem helpful to you and stick them on your refrigerator door or tack them up over your desk at the office.

All of the divorced people I spoke to agreed on two points: No matter what you do, you will eventually get tired of feeling bad, and you will one day wake up and realize that you are so much better off.

> **66**
> I completely gave my ex too much credit. I thought that just because he left me, there must have been something I did. I wasn't good enough. But you know what, he's not the supreme judge of character. He left because of a weakness in him.
> —Jessica, recently divorced
> **99**

> *The courageous man is the man who forces himself,*
> *in spite of his fear, to carry on.* —General George
> S. Patton
>
> *Courage is resistance to fear, mastery of fear—not*
> *absence of fear.* —Mark Twain
>
> *Courage is grace under pressure.* —Ernest
> Hemingway
>
> *I'm not afraid of the storm, for I'm learning how to*
> *sail my ship.* —Louisa May Alcott
>
> *If we did the things we are capable of, we would*
> *astound ourselves.* —Thomas Edison
>
> *Recall your courage, and lay aside sad fear.* —Virgil
>
> *If peace be in the heart, the wildest winter storm is*
> *full of solemn beauty.* —C. F. Richardson

Happy holidays?

Don't be surprised if you have a particularly rough
time during the holidays and on landmark days like
your old wedding anniversary. All divorced people
struggle at such memory-loaded times as Christmas,
Hanukkah, Valentine's Day, and Thanksgiving. The
list goes on and on. These were important days during your times together. You had traditions, routines, and activities that you shared and enjoyed.
Now that too is gone. It's not unusual for you to
have somewhat of a backslide into a little depression
or sadness, especially at the first such holiday without your spouse.

So how *do* you get through, say, the first
Christmas or Hanukkah after your divorce? In a
word, distraction. Fill your days with as much merri-
ment as you can, spending a lot of time with your
family and friends. Look for the portions of that

Unofficially . . .
The first year is
the hardest for
divorced people,
because every
annual event
that comes up is
the first one
they will have to
experience with-
out their partner.

holiday that don't change, even without your spouse there. You may enjoy writing and receiving holiday cards, getting the perfect gifts for the kids, enjoying that delicious but fattening holiday meal, and going to religious services. Above all, concentrate on the real reason for the season, not on the ways you *used* to celebrate it. Put the focus on *what* you're celebrating, and remember that you had many holidays before your ex came along in the first place. With a little effort on your part, you can make this first "solo" holiday a good one, and you'll lay the groundwork for many happy ones in the future as well. Yes, it's going to be hard. But it's not likely to be as hard as you expect.

But whether it's a holiday or just the day-to-day activities of normal life, you must allow the natural healing process to occur. Don't get in the way of your own adjustment to your new situation. You may need to experiment a bit before you learn how to recognize the things that upset you—like calls from your ex, hearing your wedding song on the radio—and avoid them for your own well-being. Get off the phone quickly if your ex calls. Stay polite, but don't chat. If your wedding song comes on the radio, switch to another station. If you know what pushes your hot button, you know what to avoid for now. Give yourself all of the conditions you need to heal, and it *will* happen.

Just the facts

- Not everything in your life will change with divorce.
- Your own basic sense of identity will change. You are no longer part of a "we." You are now an "I."

- You *will* get over it. It's just going to take time, positive perspective, and the thought processes which helped other divorced people before you.

- Don't prevent your own recovery. Allow the natural healing process to occur.

GET THE SCOOP ON...
The emotional aftermath ▪ Support groups ▪
Church and synagogue resources

Chapter 12

We All Need Help
Sometimes

Denial, anger, depression, grief, guilt, fear, anxiety, low self-esteem, loneliness—all these emotions are a regular part of the divorcing person's life. Expect them and accept them as natural healing mechanisms as you recover from the changes that divorce has introduced into your life. They will fade in time if you deal with them correctly. In this chapter you'll learn a little bit about how these emotions are normal in any situation of great change, and how to deal with them so that you can move on in your new life.

Accepting emotional support

While you're going through the divorce process, the first and best thing you can do is surround yourself with a strong support system. Your family, friends, co-workers, and neighbors are going to be there for you if you'll just give them a chance. They'll give you strength and understanding, a shoulder to cry on, or a sympathetic ear to listen to you as you unload

Bright Idea
Many recently divorced people report that talking about their feelings with their first level of support, their friends and family, allowed them to externalize their feelings. When you have the chance to voice your feelings and fears you can hear how ridiculous some of these torturing thoughts really are, and you will be able to erase them from your mind more quickly.

your thoughts, fears, and frustrations. They are all willing to understand that you're going through a big change, and they will not judge you because of it. They know this is quite possibly the roughest time of your life, and they will do all they can to see you through it. You should consider them your first level of support. Respect their willingness to be there for you and turn to them when you need their help.

The emotional support given by your friends and family can come in many different forms, from providing you with the chance to talk things out, to helping with the kids. And if any of your friends has already gone through a divorce, he or she can tell you all about what it takes to get through the process.

What about support groups?

Sometimes it helps to talk to relative strangers who've "been there"—or maybe are going through it right now just like you. You might recognize a bit of your own situation in theirs, and you might learn what worked for that person. At the very least, it's a place to go to vent, and you know the people there will understand.

Support groups are built on the dynamics of the members, so it's in your best interest to find one that not only appeals to you, but includes people who are either similar or sympathetic to you. Here are some things to consider as you shop for a good support group:

- Find a special interest group. It may be a divorce support group for women, for people in their 20s, or for a particular religious faith. Having a common interest serves to cement the members of the group, to start them off on common ground so that they can relate to each other better.

- Look for a workable size. A support group with five to eight members assures that everyone will get a chance to talk. It's not going to help you much to sit in a big circle with a few dozen other people if you don't get to say a word all night.

- Look at the group's dynamics. Does one person dominate the conversation? Does everyone speak? How is the feedback? Are people genuinely sympathetic, or are they just there to hear themselves talk?

- Is the location convenient for you? What about the meeting schedule? Why join a group if you're not likely to attend?

- Will the group be around for a while?

One of the best things about support groups is that while you're getting help for yourself, you're also helping others. You'll feel a particular rush at being able to say the right thing to someone who's having trouble in a stage of divorce that you've already passed. But there's also a possible down side to going to a support group—here are a few warnings to keep in mind:

- Don't continue to go to one in which the members never seem to talk about the issues at hand. If you're not getting anything out of it or if you feel uncomfortable find a new group that will help you.

- Watch out for people who attend meetings only to take advantage of other members. Certain professionals target divorce support groups. An insurance salesman, for example, may

Unofficially . . .
Experts say men are less likely than women to seek help through a support group. This may be because men tend to believe that they should be able to handle their feelings without outside help. However, the experts report that men who do go to support groups find immense benefit from the outlet and the bonding experience with other men in the group.

Timesaver
At your first support group meeting, if you think the meeting is unfocussed, unconstructive, or that the group dynamics don't suit your tastes, just leave. You don't need to sit there stewing for two hours. Just grab your coat, say you have to get home to the kids, that you're just checking out various groups for now, and go. You'll never see those people again.

attend the meetings just to cultivate new sales prospects.

- Don't date within your group.

- Think twice before you decide to attend a group that includes people you know—you don't get the benefit of talking things out with objective members who have not pre-judged you.

- *Never* attend the same support group as your spouse.

Church and synagogue resources

Many churches and synagogues run their own support groups. If you are a person of faith, it may serve you well to connect with a group that emphasizes the role of religion in your recovery. In fact, many recently divorced people find that their faith grows stronger through the trials and struggles of their divorces. Religion has given them a new sense of meaning, a sense of direction, and the insight to coping with hardship. That said, a return to faith can be seen as another benefit derived from your divorce.

Beyond support groups, your church or synagogue can provide another valuable asset: a new entry into social life. Through them, you may find study groups, singles social groups, charity groups, and other opportunities to connect with others in the outside world. You can become a volunteer, a counselor, a study group member or leader—and all can be enhancements to your new identity as a single person.

Church leaders may also give you helpful literature, books, tapes, even suggestions for spiritual retreats. They might join you with a peer within the church, a knowledgeable "buddy" who's been through this process before and can attest to the healing power of faith.

Many divorced people have found that talking to their priest, reverend, or rabbi is a great source of support. These spiritual leaders have counseled people countless times, and they've seen hundreds of people with the same struggles as yours. They're there to listen and to give you helpful spiritual counsel.

You may learn something from my own example: I went to my priest after my divorce because I was having trouble with the idea of forgiving my ex-husband. After all, forgiveness is a cornerstone of my faith. The priest took the weight of the world off my shoulders simply by telling me to relax. It was far too early in my healing process for me to pressure myself to forgive. I'd been victimized, he said, and it's entirely understandable that it could take me more time to move into forgiveness. I walked out of the church feeling wonderful. The pressure was gone.

Dealing with emotions

Maybe you've heard about the stages of grief: denial, anger, bargaining, depression, and acceptance. Elisabeth Kubler-Ross wrote about these stages in her book *On Death and Dying*. If you've ever lost a family member or friend, you undoubtedly know these stages well. Well, the stages of recovery from the upheaval of divorce are very similar to the stages of healing from a death in the family.

You can recognize which stage of grief you are in by the kinds of thoughts running through your mind:

Bright Idea
Supplement your religious guidance with regular visits to a Christian or Jewish bookstore. There you'll find a wealth of books, tapes, even magazines that can support your faith. Many recently divorced people have found at such places various mood-lifting items as refrigerator magnets, T-shirts, and plaques that inspire at each viewing.

- **Denial:** "This isn't happening," "He's just in a bad mood," "He doesn't mean what he's saying."

- **Anger:** "How can he do this to me after all I've done?" "I hope he gets hit by a truck," "Who does he think he is?"

- **Bargaining:** "Maybe if I tried to be nicer, he'll change his mind," "I haven't been considerate of his needs, so maybe if I took more of an interest in his life . . ."

- **Depression:** "I feel so alone," "I have no future now," "I don't even want to face the day without him."

- **Acceptance:** "We haven't been happy in a long time," "We'll both be happier apart," "Now I have a chance for the future I've always wanted."

You will no doubt experience all of these emotional responses—common to any situation of loss—and you will face others as well, such as grief and guilt. But if you understand what is going on with your emotions you have a chance to work through them all constructively and come out stronger for the experience.

Denial

When you first realize that your marriage is over, it all may seem like a bad dream. This is denial. Think of it as the starting point in your healing process—it's the universal first step to eventually moving on to a new life.

Your symptoms of denial may not be obvious. There are, after all, lots of the ways that denial can manifest itself. Maybe you're keeping your divorce a secret from your family. Maybe you're still counting on a reconciliation. Refusing to remove your wedding ring is often a sign of denial, as is keeping your wedding photos around.

None of these, obviously, are very healthy practices. They keep you emotionally numb, and they prevent you from accepting the realities of your life and taking the steps to move onward. Here, then, is what you need to do to get yourself through the denial phase:

- Let it out. Talk about your feelings with your support system.

- Remove all images of your married life—wedding pictures, rings, gifts.

- Get out into the world. Don't isolate yourself.

Finally, if you can't seem to move out of denial, if this stage just drags on and on, it's time to get some professional counseling.

Bargaining

As you move out of denial you may begin to feel that there has to be something you can do to remedy the situation. If you're in the "deciding to decide" stage of the divorce process (see Chapter 1) you may be tempted to vow to do anything to make your spouse happy. After awhile, though, this sort of behavior will become unsatisfying. You may even become disappointed in yourself for this behavior.

Anger

Anger is an understandable and normal part of the divorce process. In the initial phases, living with anger is difficult, even overwhelming.

Making decisions and acting out of anger will not only prolong your suffering, but it will negatively affect your divorce proceedings. If you do something for revenge, out of anger, it can very well

Timesaver
If you acknowledge that anger is normal and let your body's natural healing process move you through it, then the anger will fade. If you can be patient and not treat your anger as the motivating force behind your actions and thoughts, you will heal.

backfire and hurt your chances of winning in court. You must find a more constructive way to release your anger, for the benefit of yourself and your children.

So how do you handle this anger when it rears its ugly head? Your best course is to channel your negative energy elsewhere. Talk to someone, seek good counsel, pray, participate in group events. The energy it takes to maintain anger can be better directed toward positive activities: work to improve yourself or to help others. It is possible to turn anger into a positive drive, and if you concentrate on doing constructive things, everyone involved will be better off.

Depression

Unofficially . . .
There is a difference between depressive feelings and a depressive disorder. It's typical to feel some moderate symptoms of depression at this time of your life, but if the symptoms don't improve within a reasonable amount of time, you may have a depressive disorder.

Depression is another normal reaction to divorce. You feel empty, maybe cry a lot. It's hard to enjoy the things you used to like. There are physical symptoms of depression too—like significant weight loss or gain, or a disruption in your sleeping patterns. Maybe you're feeling fatigued, or finding it hard to concentrate. Maybe you're finding it hard to see the point in *trying* anymore. But what you might think of as just the blues could actually be the signs of a real medical problem.

The experts say that most depression linked to major life-changing events, such as divorce, is time-limited. That means that it normally fades out within a short period of time. In the most acute stages, the symptoms of depression can be completely disabling. That is why you've heard about recent divorcees who take to their beds for months.

If you do have symptoms of depression, and if they start to seriously affect your well-being or your ability to cope, it's very important for you to see your doctor. He or she will be able to tell you whether or not you actually have a depressive disorder. The major medical term for depression that requires treatment is "clinical depression." If you do, a course of treatment—possibly including psychotherapy and/or medication—can help.

There has been a lot on the news lately about herbal remedies for depression. But before you self-medicate with any herbal remedy, make sure that you check with your doctor. And never, never mix an herbal depression remedy with a prescription anti-depressant.

Medication, of course, is not for everyone. You may just need to get some counseling, to talk out your feelings and get them out of your system. Only your doctor can really tell you if medication is right for your situation.

Grief

When a marriage ends, grief is a natural human reaction. People are designed to experience loss this way, and although it may seem like a suffering that you've never known, this is probably not the only loss you've suffered in your life. This one just grabs you hard because of its size. Indeed, it may be one of the largest losses you've suffered in a long time, but it isn't the first one you've had to survive. Keep that in mind. If possible, remind yourself of other difficult experiences you've managed to overcome.

Guilt

There are many levels of guilt associated with divorce. The person who initiates the split may feel guilty over the pain that they are causing the other party. The person who's on the receiving end of the

❝

In the aftermath of my own divorce, I took all of the guilt on myself. Now that I look back on it, I'm shocked by how irrational that was! My counselor spelled out to me that I don't need to be protective of my ex anymore, that I am free to put the blame on him instead of on myself, as I'd been doing all along.
—Molly, recently divorced

❞

news may feel guilty over a past argument or mistreatment that may have contributed to the spouse's decision. You may be tempted to think back over your marriage, dwelling on all the things you should or shouldn't have done, but this is counterproductive. You can't change the past.

Why do we blame ourselves? Perhaps it's just too frightening to acknowledge the depth of a partner's wrong-doing. Perhaps it's just too frightening to admit how unhappy that person made you, and you may be angry with yourself for putting up with it for so long. But you're going to have to stop feeling guilty if you want to recover from this life change.

With the right perspective, you'll realize that a marriage is made up of *two* fallible human creatures. So the mistakes you've made in your life together—the miscommunications, the impatience, the nagging—are not unforgivable. And if you look at those errors as an opportunity to learn, then the experience was not a total loss.

Fear

Not all fears are unrealistic—especially in the case of abuse, where you may fear for your safety. Or you may have a very realistic fear of your spouse's retribution if you are the one who started the divorce process. These realistic fears should be handled through your lawyer and police department. Get a restraining order. Install safety measures in your home. Change your routine and the hours you keep.

We all, however, are prone to unrealistic fears, and these may be increased when going through a divorce. You may miss the sense of protection your spouse gave you, and you experience more fearfulness than before. But although you see yourself as more vulnerable now, that doesn't necessarily mean that you really *are*. And there are practical steps you can take to assuage this kind of fear. Make sure your home is adequately secure—good locks on the doors and windows, perhaps a light sensor outside your back door. If you're so inclined, you can take a course in self-defense.

Maybe your fears are of a different kind. Maybe your afraid of being unable to cope with the more practical matters of day-to-day life, like: What if the car breaks down? What if the dishwasher breaks? Hold to the thought that, if such things happen, you're not entirely helpless—you can learn how to solve the problem, or call on a trusted friend or relative who can help.

Another sort of fear has to do with facing the unknown—your post-divorce future. Will you be alone forever? Will no one ever love you again? You may have a fear of failure, of winding up homeless or jobless, or a fear of losing your kids. As one divorcee puts it, "If you couldn't predict that divorce would ever happen to you, you can't predict that you'll never love again."

Nearly everybody faces these fears of the unknown at the start of a divorce. Get a handle on these irrational thoughts by talking them out. Assuage your fears by knowing that your future has a great chance of being wonderful. Your new picture can be better.

The most logical way to cope with fears of the future is to start now to envision what you'd like your new future to hold. Think about what you'd like your career to be like. Imagine the home of your dreams—and start thinking about how to make it happen. Plan a future vacation. Think about new

> There is a difference between realistic guilt and unrealistic guilt. By all means, avoid unrealistic guilt—feeling badly about things you could not have controlled and may not have had anything to do with. Unrealistic guilt makes the whole process worse for you.
> —Dr. Paula Bortnichak, family therapist

talents or skills you'd like to develop. All these thoughts can get you thinking constructively about the future, and you just might find that your fear has been replaced with a sense of excitement about all the new experiences waiting for you around the corner. Write down all these thoughts, dreams, and plans—they give you something to aim for as you start building your new life.

Anxiety

Anxiety is an awful, nonspecific, yet persistent feeling of uneasiness. It manifests itself in many ways, including restlessness, fatigue, edginess, irritability, muscle tension, and sleep disturbances.

Like depression, anxiety can turn into a medical disorder. If so, talk to your doctor about your symptoms; he or she will evaluate the severity of your problem and advise the best course of treatment.

Anxiety is usually treated in the short term, meaning that it is expected to fade fully after the time and effort it takes to counteract it. Some actions to combat anxiety are: exercise, eating healthy, meditation, and relaxation. A deep, cleansing breath can make you feel better, too.

Don't be surprised if you experience a moderate level of anxiety, especially in the earliest stages of your divorce. Most people in your situation have experienced some level of suffering with this condition. Take the right steps to relieve your symptoms—don't panic over them—and they should lift over time.

Self-esteem

The whole idea of self-esteem is seeing the value within *yourself*. You may not have thought of yourself as an individual for quite some time now. Your identity in the past was tied to your spouse and formed, to some degree, by your relationship with that person. The sense of rejection or failure that comes as an integral part of divorce often attacks a person's feelings of self-worth. Feelings of not being good enough can erode anyone's self-esteem.

It may be that, in your marriage, your ex constantly harped on what he or she termed your "faults." Remember, self-esteem comes from within you. No one else can give it, no one else can take it away. So now's the time to get busy on building up your sense of self-esteem.

So how do you boost a deflated self-esteem? Simple. You start accentuating the positive. There are all sorts of ways to begin to build up a better sense of yourself. One way is to sit down and make a list of all of the good qualities you see in yourself. Don't be shy, and don't be modest. Your entries can be general and serious (I keep my promises, I'm kind to my family, the kids love me) and they can be trivial (I'm a really good tennis player, I completed my taxes on time last year, the dog loves me).

Now make another list: Think about the triumphs in your life, the things you're most proud of yourself for accomplishing. And think of what the people who love you say to you to remind you of your worth. Throughout this entire process, you are surrounded by people who love you and want to comfort you. They tell you that you don't deserve this kind of treatment, that you're very strong, that they admire you. They obviously see the value within you. If you're not ready to really believe in yourself just yet, keep in mind that they certainly do. If you remind yourself of their good opinions of you, you'll see that you really are a worthwhile person.

Bright Idea
Deep breathing delivers more oxygen into your bloodstream, automatically creating relaxation hormones in your body.

Loneliness

Being alone can be painful, especially in the earliest stages of your separation and divorce. You're not used to the house being so quiet. You're not used to sleeping alone. You miss having someone to hug. You miss hearing your partner's voice. If you remember that we marry for that sense of human connection, it's logical that losing that sense of human connection with a partner can leave us feeling lonely.

Make the effort to battle that loneliness. Spend more time with your family and friends. Fill up your days with the company of others. Being with others is a good distraction, and you're reminded that other people really do love your company. And remember, being alone doesn't have to mean being lonely. Learn to enjoy your own company.

Above all, don't let simple loneliness drive you immediately into a new relationship. Too many people, motivated by a fear of being alone, jump right into a new and serious relationship. Doing this may be unhealthy, perhaps dangerous, and certainly futile. After all, you need to heal and find peace within yourself before you can be part of a new, healthy union. You need to be strong as an individual, a complete person on your own, before you can be a functional part of any union again—otherwise, you risk repeating whatever mistakes existed in your old relationship. Taking one "broken" piece from an old machine and putting it on a new machine does not make that machine work very well. It's likely to not work at all.

Dealing with stress

We've already addressed the topic of stress and the negative health impact it brings. Besides your health, though, stress levels can impact your daily existence.

Managing your time

You're probably already used to stress as a common factor in your day. But during a divorce, and in the aftermath, the concept of time is going to give you some added stress in itself. As your daily routine changes, the amount of time on your hands will change quite dramatically.

Your concept and plans for time management are different now. You may have more time to yourself, depending on your arrangements for child custody, or you may have less time to yourself if you've had to get a new job to support yourself better or if you've now had to take over tasks that your spouse used to handle. You're going to have to rearrange your day to suit the new conditions of your life. Your entire schedule is subject to change.

Many divorced people find that their daily schedule changes in the following ways:

- They wake up later or earlier than they used to, due to the absence of their partner's alarm clock.

- They eat meals when they're hungry, not when their partner expects to be served.

- They find that they are actually a "morning person" or a "night person," getting more done according to their circadian rhythms than they ever knew they could when their spouse controlled the schedule.

- They have more control of their own free time.

In addition, as you deal with the issues and process of divorce, you may actually lose your sense of time. Time can stretch out endlessly during this

Bright Idea
Keep yourself organized by regularly using a calendar or datebook. Make sure you know when the bills are due, when special family events arise, and when holidays are coming around. You don't want to add to your stress by missing a payment, forgetting a birthday, or having to rush to a holiday party you forgot about.

very foggy, hazy portion of your life, and it is normal for a week to seem like a month. Often, you won't even know what day it is. Dealing with this altered perception of time is unsettling and can lead you to making annoying mistakes (like the oft-reported showing up for work on Saturday). You're going to have to work to keep on top of things.

Sustaining energy

You'll need to keep your energy up, not only for your health but for the big fight ahead of you. It's important that you remain in optimum shape, so that you're at your strongest during the divorce process. You need mental clarity and the ability to breathe away the anger and frustration that arise during the months of meetings, negotiations, and trial.

Your children also need you to maintain your energy, so that you can better care for them. If you're exhausted, they will not only become concerned about you, but they'll take on an unhealthy level of anxiety and assumed responsibility of their own. You need your kids to see you strong and alert, able to function in your daily life.

While you'll need the energy to care for yourself, your kids, and your home, you'll also need energy to do your job well. You'll need to be able to perform your duties on the job, and you need to be able to stay awake during those long and boring staff meetings. If a lack of energy detracts from your work, you could very well suffer a demotion or even lose your job.

So remember all that good advice your mother used to give you—get plenty of rest, eat right, and exercise. Take up meditation if that works for you. Take your vitamins. Get in touch with your natural

Watch Out!
Kids who worry about their parents experience frustration and fear. This compounds their own suffering, making the divorce far worse on them.

energy patterns and work with them. All this will help you stay on top of things.

Staying functional

There's a difference between being fine and being functional. All of the divorced people I spoke to said that a big key, especially in the beginning stages of your divorce, is getting through the day, taking care of all of the little things that have to be done. They, of course, had a variety of stories about their zombie-like first days and weeks: One made a telephone call and afterward threw the cordless phone in the trash. Others have forgotten appointments, almost missed paying bills on time, and accidentally put the milk in the pantry.

This foggy time can be quite frustrating. But it *is* pretty normal—and lots of people have come up with coping tips to help. Here are a few:

- Make lists, even if it's for the average everyday things that you normally would do. It sounds basic, but you'd be surprised at how easy it is— with a distracted mind and no sense of time—to forget to do the simplest of things. A list organizes your day for you, and you get the little jab of satisfaction whenever you can cross something off as accomplished.

- Use your calendar. Leave nothing to memory, even if you know you always have your chiropractor appointment at noon on Monday, Wednesday, and Friday. Write it down so you don't forget. Use color-coding. Remember to record your kids' activities as well. At this time in your life, you'll need easy-access information, spelled out clearly for you.

- Pay bills as soon as you get them. If you set them aside for the end of the month, you run the risk

Timesaver
You will experience strange bursts of energy from time to time, as your body rebounds from its stress-induced weakened state to a healthy level of normalcy. Use these times to catch up on everything you've let go over the past few weeks or months.

Bright Idea
Create an "in" box, into which you'll put all of your legal documents, forms, or anything important. You don't need to worry about filing by topic, but you know where everything is if you should need it.

of forgetting about them. If your home is a big mess, as it may be right now, they might get buried. Pay them now before you forget.

- Open your mail right away. Don't let it pile up. There may be something important under that packet from Ed McMahon.

- File important papers right away so that nothing gets lost.

- Keep a spiral notebook by the phone, and use that to record any phone messages, phone numbers, or appointments. The information will be handy, and you won't have to look for missing slips of paper.

- Make shopping lists. A simple list will prevent frustrating returns back to the store for the bread. Even if you've always had the shopping routine pretty well under control up to now, at this time, with your mind not completely focused, a list will save you trouble and keep you efficient in one shot.

In the end, this foggy period will pass. Until that day comes, all you can do is take steps to keep yourself on top of things, so that you don't feel trapped in the middle of a tornado, with all of your tasks and obligations swirling around you.

Just the facts

- The post-divorce period can be an emotional rollercoaster for anyone.

- A good support system will help you through your divorce.

- Professional counseling is a good idea if your emotional adjustment to divorce is particularly difficult.

- You need to sustain energy and get organized in order to fulfill the responsibilities of your daily life.

Get the Lowdown on Sticky Situations

PART V

GET THE SCOOP ON...
Conflict resolution ▪ Domestic violence ▪
Stalking ▪ Restraining orders ▪ Playing hardball

Chapter 13

Spouse and Family Discord

While some divorces can be classified as civil, friendly, mutual decisions to part ways, that is not always the case. The subject of divorce can bring about vindictive behavior from a scorned ex, and it can certainly escalate in ending marriages that have been marked all along by violent and abusive behavior. These problems are important enough to merit separate treatment, and in this part we will take up several "sticky situations" in some detail. This chapter takes up the issues of conflict, violence, and abuse—these are situations that must be handled with you and your children's ultimate safety as the primary consideration.

Conflict resolution

While your relationship with your spouse is likely to be strained at the time of your separation, any number of extenuating circumstances can intensify the depth of your problems. This might be the terms of your divorce. It could be struggles over child custody, financial agreements, even the division of your assets. When a conflict arises, it is best to avoid escalating the level of friction between the two of you, particularly if there is a danger that conflict may lead to actual confrontation. It may sound simplistic, but in the end you'll find that smart conflict resolution skills will make the entire process and its aftermath easier than it would be if you had allowed your emotions to rule your decisions.

The first step to diminishing conflict is the simple act of identifying the source of the conflict itself. In locating where the problem lies, you will be able to figure the smartest way to address it. Let's say, for instance, that you're angry with your spouse because he or she will not agree to a level of child support that you deem fair. But in addition to that anger, you may begin to "load on" other issues: Your spouse was always controlling your actions, for example, or monopolized access to the household finances. But letting your anger overcome your good sense, so that you can no longer keep straight in your mind the actual issue you're trying to resolve (in this case, setting the proper level of child support) you only intensify your emotional distress and—ultimately—set the stage for fierce fighting within your divorce process. If you strip away your own emotions from the facts of the conflict, you might see a way to address your spouse's point of view. Maybe he or she simply cannot afford to pay the level of child support you're demanding but doesn't want to admit to financial hardship. By identifying the source of the conflict, you may be able to defuse it.

Once the true source of conflict is identified, the next step is figuring out if there is a workable solution. This will require effort, particularly if you lacked communication within your marriage. It is not easy to remove your emotions from such loaded issues as child custody and dividing your assets. But the sooner you strip away your hurt feelings from the process and start to work on establishing open communication, the better your chance to resolve your conflicts fairly and civilly.

Unfortunately, conflict resolution techniques don't *always* work. If you cannot get cooperation from your spouse, but you think it's likely that a more impersonal forum might help, involve your lawyer. But if conflict threatens to escalate to dangerous levels, there are other steps you must take as well.

Domestic violence

Domestic violence is a sad fact of American society. It is, for the most part, a silent epidemic: Too many cases go unreported out of shame, guilt, or fear of reprisals. You might think that only men batter women, and you may have a picture in your mind of a particular class of people. If so, you are wrong. Domestic abuse is, in 5 percent of reported cases, also committed by women against men, and abusers exist in every racial and economic class there is.

Unofficially . . .
Three million women are beaten and 3,000 women are killed by their husbands or boyfriends each year.

Sadly, too many battered spouses endure hurtful treatment from their partners, partly out of fear of retribution, and partly due to financial dependence on that abusive spouse. A battered woman, for instance, may choose to put up with occasional outbursts because she doesn't have any financial resources of her own, or she doesn't have anywhere else to go. Another reason for staying is based on denial: The battered spouse may focus on the "good times," the months of happiness she and her spouse had in earlier days. She might try to convince herself that the abusive spouse was just having a bad day. Often, an abusive spouse expresses remorse for hurtful behavior, promising never to do it again. The battered spouse, unfortunately, gives the apologetic partner too much credit and agrees to stay.

In the case of the battered spouse who has had enough and threatens to leave, the abusive partner may use violence again to stop the exit, or promise retribution if the spouse does leave. In this case, the abused spouse may stay out of fear. Abusive partners use power and intimidation to control their spouses, and the result is a devastating relationship that's best left behind through divorce.

Are you being abused?

It is a mistake to think "Well, my spouse has never *hit* me, so I don't have a problem." Domestic violence reaches far beyond a punch, a slap, or a shove. Threats or intimidation are also abuse. Emotional abuse is marked by efforts to control or demean a spouse in order to keep that person in a position of dependence and inferiority. An abuser is simply doing everything possible to assert dominance over a partner. How can you tell if you're in an abusive relationship? Ask yourself—does your partner:

- Get angry when you disagree?
- Punch holes in the walls?
- Throw objects out of anger? Are they aimed at you?
- Destroy your belongings?
- Threaten you with objects (i.e., a kitchen knife, a bat, etc.)?
- Threaten to injure the children?
- Physically restrain your departure from the home?

- Insult or ridicule you?

- Get excessively jealous?

- Make you account for your exact whereabouts every minute that you are apart?

- Manipulate you with promises and lies?

- Isolate you from your friends and family?

- Make you ask permission to go out or make a career move?

- Abuse your pet to frighten you?

- Shove, kick, punch, or slap you?

All of these behaviors are abusive. The number of your "yes" answers indicates the degree of abuse prevalent in your marriage. At this point, you may be pretty shaken up—some people spend many years refusing to recognize the signs of abuse. Among the many difficult revelations brought about by the beginning of your divorce process might be the realization that, after years of denial, you *were* an abused spouse. But now is the time to face facts, to stop making excuses and finally admit to yourself the facts of your relationship with your spouse. And most importantly, you must keep in mind that you are not the only one potentially affected by your spouse's abusive behavior—what about the kids?

Domestic violence and children

Domestic violence affects children deeply. They may be directly affected if your spouse vents his or her anger toward them, intimidates them, or beats them. They may also be hurt by the *indirect* effects of abuse in the home if they observe domestic violence between the parents.

Even if they are not physically beaten, children absorb injury from the abuse they see. The experts

Unofficially . . .
An estimated 3.3 million children witness domestic violence in the home each year.

say that children who witness domestic violence exhibit clear signs of distress because of it. They may experience excessive fear, worry, confusion, and stress—the last of these most noticeable in the children's levels of stress-related health problems such as headaches, abdominal problems, ulcers, and bedwetting. Older children are clearly at a higher risk of drug or alcohol abuse, juvenile delinquency, and violence directed toward their peers or siblings.

Remember, these are your children's formative years. What they experience is likely to have a profound effect on their own self-esteem, and interpersonal skills later in life. Experts say that male children, if they witness domestic violence in the home, are more likely to repeat the same patterns when they get older. If you are abused, and you think that it's best to keep the marriage together "for the sake of the children," think about the abuse the children will witness if you stay. Think about the effects on your children's health, and think about what lessons they're learning from their environment and their experiences. And if you can't summon up the strength to leave for your own sake, do it for the kids.

Getting out

If you feel you are in *any* danger of retribution from your spouse, just *get out of the house*. Pack up the children and any special or necessary belongings, and just leave. There are domestic abuse hotlines in every state, so call information and get the number. Many hotlines are connected to or can refer you to various shelters and safe houses that will provide you and your children with a place to stay, meals, and protection from your spouse. These shelters are usually at unlisted locations—the hotlines will not give

66
What got me out of there for good was thinking about what lessons my son and daughter were learning. I don't want my son to be an abuser later on in life, and I don't want my daughter to get the message that she should stay in an abusive relationship.
—Carla, recently divorced
99

out the address to your abusive spouse. You will be safe there.

There are a few things to keep firmly in mind when you are getting ready to leave—first and foremost, do *not* confront your spouse and make a big production about leaving. If your spouse is prone to physical abuse, this statement is interpreted as your break from control, and he or she may increase the level of violence and intimidation as a reaction. Don't announce your intentions, just leave as quickly as possible.

Some experts say you shouldn't worry about taking the time to settle your financial affairs before you go, and in situations of immediate danger, that is definitely the best advice. However, if you have time to plan, calling a lawyer before you go can be a good idea. If nothing else, you may be able to protect yourself from financial retaliation from your spouse. Most important, however, is that you make sure you're out of the house before your ex finds out about what you've done. Nothing should be allowed to threaten your physical safety and that of your children.

Legal maneuvering

If you are in an abusive relationship, document the exact details of your spouse's mistreatment of you and the children. The court is going to require some proof of the abuse that you charge. A journal or daily log of abusive episodes will go a long way toward substantiating your claim should your spouse deny the charges.

Once you're safely out of the abusive situation, you must take some time to safeguard yourself and the children, and to think to the future. If you have had to go to the emergency room with injuries due

Moneysaver
Many shelters are non-profit establishments dedicated to helping people get out of abusive relationships. Some offer legal support, referrals, and access to free representation from attorneys. You'll also be provided with access to support groups, counseling, and medical care. Some will even help you secure transitional housing of your own.

Unofficially . . .
Most states have provisions for speeding along a divorce case arising from charges of domestic abuse. The courts want to protect you, and they'll help you finalize your divorce in the most expedient manner possible.

Watch Out!
Do not let your spouse know that you're recording his words or actions. He will only get angry and take it out on you. He may even destroy your record. Keep your journal or list in a safe, private place, one that only you know.

to physical abuse by your partner, or if your children have been injured by him, make sure you provide those medical records to your lawyer. The degree and specifics of such injuries on the medical record is viewed as an impartial source. In many cases, hospitals that suspect domestic abuse will call in a family crisis counselor to talk to you. If that has happened—even if you maintained at the time that you walked into a door—there are notes to that effect in your medical records. These notes should be made available to your lawyer and, if necessary, the court. In addition, testimony from any family members or friends who have witnessed first-hand any abuse you have suffered serves as proof to the court that your claims are true.

Stalking

One variant of abusive behavior is known as "stalking." An estimated 80 percent of stalking cases involved women stalked by ex-husbands and former boyfriends. Stalking is a frightening reality that reduces your world, making you live in constant fear. Perhaps your ex has made threats to you, or perhaps you have seen your ex lurking outside your home, intimidating you with his or her simple presence.

Most states have their own definitions of stalking, but all agree that a stalker is someone who willfully and repeatedly follows or harasses someone else with the promise to harm that person or members of their family. Stalking laws have been established in all states in the aftermath of the 1990 stalking and murder of *My Sister Sam* actress Rebecca Shaeffer. These laws serve to protect the victims of stalking and make it easier to punish convicted stalkers.

In most states, you can bring a civil suit against your stalker, and you can ask for monetary damages from that person. Most states impose a penalty of one year in prison and a fine of up to $1,000 for stalking. The courts do take stalking very seriously, often issuing restraining orders that prohibit the stalker from coming within a certain distance of the victim and the victim's family, and they do take a hard stand on the repeat offender. The penalties dramatically increase if the stalker continues to pursue a victim in violation of a court order—then the charge of stalking can be classified as a felony, with even stiffer penalties such as longer term incarceration.

Since many stalkers attempt to track down their prey by using driver's license records, you can request that your auto registration and driver's license records be released to no one other than law enforcement officials, insurers, and attorneys. To do this, you must submit court documentation of the circumstances of the stalking, and the Department of Motor Vehicles will most likely agree to withhold your documents for a period of one year. After that, you must again submit proof that you are still being stalked, and the records will be held for another year.

You may also be able to change your social security number, so that you cannot be found by the numbers that may be well-known to your ex. Your social security number is used, and easily traced, for a variety of transactions: health care, insurance, credit reports, banking, employee files. From these records, a stalker can easily gain access to your current address and other information about your life. Changing your social security number may, then, be a good idea. You will probably have to document the specifics of your case to get it changed. Call the resources below to find out what you'll have to do:

Unofficially . . .
Any conversations you have with a therapist or family doctor, while confidential between the two of you, can be called in as expert testimony and offered to the court as proof that there was an ongoing problem. So if abuse exists, discuss it openly with your therapist.

- Office of the Inspector General of the Social Security Administration: (800) 269-0271

- Your local Social Security Administration offices, listed in the government section of your phone book

Steps you can take

If your stalker remains a threat to your safety, you can protect yourself and your family until the authorities catch that person by doing the following:

- Keep all doors and windows locked at all times.

- Install motion light detectors at the front and back of your home, and at the location of your garage doors.

- Install deadbolts on all doors and locks on all screen doors.

- Install a quality home-security system, with automatic contact to law enforcement agencies.

- Raise the level of your porch door lights so that light bulbs can't be easily removed.

- Identify visitors before opening the door to your home. Teach your children to do the same.

- Keep lights and a radio on a timing mechanism for when you are away from home.

- Prepare an escape plan from your home, and drill children on the route.

- Install smoke detectors throughout your home, and keep a working fire extinguisher on each floor.

- Post emergency phone numbers by all phones, and enter them into speed dial.

Bright Idea
You can request that the Department of Corrections notify you before your accused stalker is scheduled to be released from prison. Make sure the department has your current phone number so that they can keep you informed of the situation. They will keep your contact information confidential so that your stalker cannot find you through them.

- Teach children how to dial 911 and give their location to the operator.

- Get a menacing-sounding dog as a deterrent to intruders, or investigate a security device that simulates the sound of a barking dog.

- Keep your garage door locked.

- Install a loud panic button alarm that can be activated from several locations within the home.

- Call the police if any unusual packages are left by your home.

- Accompany children to bus stops, and watch them closely outdoors while they play.

- Know the whereabouts of your family members at all times. Ask older children to call in if they will be changing their plans during the evening.

- Change your regular driving and walking/running routes often so the stalker will not learn your routine.

- Ask to see the identification of any service or repair people who need to enter your home.

- Inform your closest neighbor as to the situation, and provide him or her with a photo of your stalker for easier identification.

- While you are on vacation, have that neighbor pick up your mail or newspapers.

- While you are on vacation, have that neighbor park one of their cars in your driveway.

- Consider call-forwarding, so that phone calls placed to another location will be forwarded to your present location.

- Get a post office box and use it, rather than your street address, as your registered address.

This includes your creditors and the Department of Motor Vehicles.

- Remove your street address from your business cards and personal or business checks.

- Remove your name and address from any outside plaques, mailboxes, or doormats.

- Park only in well-lit areas.

- Lock your car doors while driving.

- Notice if another car seems to be following you, and if so, drive to the nearest police station, not your home.

- Install a phone system in your car, or carry a cell phone with you at all times.

- Have your name removed from any apartment or house mailboxes or visitor buzzer areas.

- At work, have your office assistant screen your phone calls.

- Alert everyone you know that your personal information and whereabouts are not to be given out.

- Get caller ID or call blocking features on your phone service.

- Put a message on your answering machine that warns callers that the conversation will be taped.

- Change your e-mail address.

- Carry a Polaroid camera or instant camera with you, so that you can catch your stalker in the act. Keep a camera in the glove compartment of your car for the same reason.

- Never verify your address over the phone, especially if using a cordless phone (the signal can be picked up at another location, and your conversations can be overheard).

Restraining orders

Stalkers, like any other abusive spouses, may be issued a restraining order requiring that they stay away from a partner or other family members. When a restraining order is issued, it becomes effective immediately and is served upon the stalker or abusive spouse by a local sheriff or qualified document server. In most states, the spouse upon whom the order is served *does* have the right to appeal the order—usually within 30 days of being served. Why would this be allowed? Consider the circumstances of Olivia and Darren. After Olivia filed for divorce, Darren continued to see his children on their agreed-upon times. Olivia was not happy with the way the divorce settlement was shaping up, so she trumped up charges of abuse against Darren. The court, in assessing her charges, served Darren with a restraining order. Darren filed for the appeals hearing and was able to convince the judge that he not only had never abused Olivia or the children, but that Olivia was using this tactic to punish him for having an edge on her in their divorce case. Without the opportunity to appeal, Darren would have been unfairly shut out from his children's lives.

The court takes all requests for restraining orders—and their appeals—very seriously. Every effort is made to assess the facts of the situation, and if it is found that one partner attempted to use a restraining order as a bargaining chip or punishment against a partner, that move could be damaging against his or her case.

A restraining order is simply a court-ordered mandate that one partner stop abusing or threatening the other partner or the children. It may specify that the partner in question stay a certain distance away from the other partner's home, place of

Unofficially . . .
Depending upon the state in which you live and the circumstances of your complaint, the judge might also issue a "peace bond." A peace bond is a bond that the abuser posts and is held by the court. If the abuser repeats any abuse against you, the bond is forfeited. Many states consider the idea of lost money to be a good deterrent to the idea of abusive behavior.

business, relatives' homes, or the children's school. Depending upon the circumstances, it can effectively remove the abusive partner from the home or provide police protection for any family member who wishes to pack up and leave the home. It can also form the basis for a temporary custody arrangement for the children.

A restraining order is not just for the abusive spouse who stands outside your home waiting for an opportunity to injure you. Look at the example of Marti. Marti's husband left her for another woman, a longtime friend of Marti's. Stung by their betrayal, Marti repeatedly called up her ex at the old friend's apartment and yelled at him, calling him and the new girlfriend a string of names. Adding insult to injury, Marti's husband got a restraining order which forbade Marti to call him at his girlfriend's home or at work. This incident became an issue within their divorce proceedings, quite ironically giving Marti's husband an edge in the settlement.

Watch Out!
A restraining order cannot protect you fully. Unless you have police presence outside your home and around your person 24 hours a day, you can never be fully protected from an abusive or vindictive person. Use the restraining order in conjunction with the self-protection tips listed above.

Family discord

There are other disruptive situations that may arise in conjunction with your divorce that need careful handling. While not as immediately dangerous as spousal violence or abuse, they can have a strong impact on the well-being of you or your children. Family discord is one such difficult situation that calls for "kid glove" handling at times. We've already established that friends and family may react in a variety of ways to the news of your impending divorce. But what happens if their reactions result in serious difficulty for you and for your children? Family discord can only add to your anger, stress, and depression, and it can make it difficult for your children to maintain normal relations with some of their relatives, so it is important to handle family disapproval in a constructive way.

Dealing with disapproval

Just as there will be people who support you, there will be others who turn up their noses and walk away. When these people are members of your family, that is difficult to take. A friend of mine tells me that certain members of her family practically disowned her when she reported her plans to divorce her husband. There had been no divorce in her family for three generations, and her decision meant that her family's "streak" had been broken. Her relatives snapped back at her, unbelievably, with "How could you do this to us?" It seems unbelievable, but this is how some families react. Understanding where they're coming from can make their disapproval a little easier to take.

But some forms of disapproval cut closer to the heart. Your family may have a sense of loyalty to your ex that is so strong, it seems like their love for your ex surpasses their love for you. If you kept your displeasure regarding your ex to yourself for years, your family may only see that person in the positive light that you created. Now, your uninformed family will be surprised that your spouse is not that ideal partner.

Because they are working with what may be a false idea of what your spouse was *really* like, your family may be surprised and shocked at your announcement of plans to divorce. This is not the time, however, to indulge in a crash course of spouse-bashing for their benefit. Instead, understand the reasons for their reactions, but don't let their disapproval sway you from the course you know to be best for you.

Watch Out!
Don't attempt to suddenly change your family's impressions by spouting off about your ex's faults now. Acknowledge to yourself that your family's false positive image of your spouse is partly of your own creation. There is nothing to be gained by trying to tear your spouse down at this late date.

Remember that just as you needed time to handled the decision to divorce, so may your family. Understanding this may help you realize that your family may not be in a position to help you right away; they have to deal with their own "stages of grief" first. This is a difficult time for everybody, and you're going to have to give people time to come to grips with the changes. Do not take it personally.

Dealing with in-laws

Your in-laws too will have their own reactions, and these are likely to be complicated by the fact of family loyalty—to your soon-to-be ex. While some people are lucky enough to be able to maintain a relationship with their in-laws even after a divorce, just as often this is not possible, at least, not right away. And the loss of loved ones on your spouse's side of the family can hurt tremendously, especially if you considered yourself to be very close to your in-laws. The disappearance of this group of loved ones, confidantes, and friends can be very painful, especially if you didn't cause the end of the marriage. And complicating matters further is the fact that they are still your children's grandparents, aunts, uncles, and cousins. They may have shut you out, but they still are likely to maintain contact with your kids.

If there is a risk of problems arising with family and in-laws regarding ongoing contact with your children, it would be wise to establish some ground rules:

- Encourage regular visits between your children and your spouse's family. Doing so removes any suspicion that you are trying to separate your children from the other side of the family.

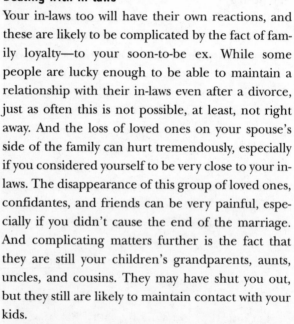

Watch Out!
Some in-laws may be so angry that they will shut out the children to some degree. If this becomes the case, do your best to maintain communication with the children, but if that doesn't work *do* try to shelter them from disappointments. Support them through any feelings of abandonment that they express. And consider counseling to help them deal with their feelings.

- Invite your in-laws to such family parties as your child's birthday, graduation, other celebrations. They then have the option of deciding whether or not to attend, but at least you've made the effort to include them.

- Keep your in-laws informed of your child's accomplishments. Send out announcements of such triumphs as making the honor roll, winning a sporting championship, or being elected school president.

- Establish beforehand that your in-laws are not to discuss the divorce with the children. Under no circumstances are the in-laws to discuss the mechanics of the case or any tensions that exist between you and your spouse.

The reactions of most in-laws are likely to fall somewhere between complete rejection to total acceptance of you, post-divorce. There may be a chill in the air, but you generally can create a new relationship with your in-laws that reflects your new position in their lives. Here are some points to keep in mind:

- Make contact with your in-laws right away.

- Explain the basic reasons for the end of the marriage, and tell them that it in no way reflects on how you feel about them.

- Express a wish, if applicable, for you all to remain close.

- Let them know that you will fully accommodate their wishes to see the kids.

- Do not try to sway them to your "side." Acknowledge that this is not a competition. It is a family sorting through issues.

Bright Idea
Encourage your children to stay in contact with your spouse's family on their own. Many children of divorce exchange e-mail messages with their grandparents, keeping the bond strong and sharing stories of their lives with people who care about them.

Unofficially . . .
The biggest issue
among in-laws is
how the split
will affect their
relationship with
your kids. Your
spouse's family
will fear being
separated from
the children if
you should move
away with them,
and they may
fear that the
children will
grow apart from
them.

- Do not discuss the divorce process with them. The business end of your split is not their business, and you never know what news will get back to your ex.

- Maintain a normal relationship as best as possible, continuing to send holiday cards or gifts as you so choose.

If you and your spouse do not have children, the issue of maintaining a relationship with your in-laws becomes a wholly individual issue. While the absence of a bond through your children might mean that you have no real reason to maintain a relationship, you might choose to keep these people within your circle of loved ones, if on a different level. The formation of a continuing relationship is dictated by your wishes and theirs. Whether or not you have children, it is going to take some time for your new relationship with your in-laws to form. It will take a concerted effort from you to maintain the kind of close relationship with your in-laws that you might desire.

Handling the holidays

In Chapter 11 we discussed how you might best be able to cope with your reactions to the holiday season and other emotionally fraught dates and events. As we noted, the holidays are likely to be hard for you within the first year after the end of your marriage. They are also a time when most people are heavily involved with family—and now, ex-family. Not only will you have to deal with the loaded issue of the absence of your ex and the changing of your own personal holiday routines and traditions, you will have to find a way to fit that entire issue into your family's holiday plans. And this is the first time you'll have to face the effects of your visitation agreement—naturally, both you and your spouse will want to share this special family time with the children.

Forming your arrangements can be quite a headache, so consider these ground rules for dealing with your kids' custody during the holidays:

- Plan to share the holiday by splitting up the weekend. This is the best and most fair arrangement.

- Consider having an "early" Christmas or Hanukkah with the kids if you don't have them this year.

- Consider alternating the kids' birthdays as well. This way both parents get a chance to enjoy the "big day."

- Make sure everybody involved knows the schedule—the kids need to know where they'll be spending the holidays, and grandparents want to know where to call the kids.

It's not just holidays that can be altered by your divorce—other big events can be similarly affected. In the case of your child's wedding, for instance, there is a whole collection of etiquette issues regarding invitation wording, seating, and other hot topics related to children of divorced parents. If you do have marriage-aged children, remember that your divorce is not the issue of the day. Deal with your happy bride or groom on an individual level, and work as hard as possible to reduce divorce-related stress on them.

Your child's wedding is not the place for theatrics. Try to be one of those divorced parents who puts the bride and groom first. Some wedding rules to help you:

Bright Idea!
Most couples arrange to alternate their custody of the kids during the holidays: You get them for Thanksgiving, your ex gets them for Christmas or Hanukkah, and you switch next year. For the first year, at least, think about sharing the holiday (i.e., you get Christmas Eve, and your ex gets Christmas Day). This arrangement will make things easier for everyone concerned.

Bright Idea
Many non-custodial parents get the kids during the summers as part of their custody arrangements. This could mean that the custodial parent never gets to take the kids on a vacation. Arrange with your spouse to "get" a week during the summer, or take the kids away during winter break.

- Agree to be cordial to your ex and his or her new partner, if there is one throughout all of the wedding events.

- Be agreeable about posing for photos as parents of the bride or groom.

- Agree to work *with* your spouse on the plans of the wedding. Do not use the wedding as just one more opportunity to fight about who is paying the bill, who raised the child all these years, or who should be seen as the top parent.

- Agree to sit together in the front row or pew. Your child will want both parents given this seat of honor, and he or she will appreciate not having to choose a parent to sit in the second row. As a rule, you should consider the bride and groom's wishes if second wives or husbands are not truly welcome in the front row.

- Accept the bride's wishes about who should give her away. Your child has had to deal with the rift between you long enough. She may have strong feelings about which parent, if any, should be given this honor, and her decision should stand with no argument.

- Inform relatives that the divorce issue, if it occurred close to the date of the wedding, is to be ignored during the wedding day.

- Reinforce the fact that you are both still parents by offering as a gesture of love a toast from the both of you to the bride and groom.

When you must attend big family events, go as the new individual you are, not as the former spouse of your ex. In many ways, your persona has changed. Allow the self-sufficient person you have become to shine through. Displaying your newfound happiness will not only be true to your image, it will reinforce to your family that your divorce was indeed a good decision for you. They will be reassured that you are fine on your own, and they will be pleased to see you so content.

Just the facts

- Conflict resolution techniques can reduce the amount of confrontation you face in your divorce.

- Your state, the police, and the courts can provide protection from the threat of violence, abuse, or harassment by your ex.

- If you or your children face immediate physical threat, get out of the house and work out the details later, once the situation has been secured.

- Family disapproval can be difficult but must be overcome—especially when there are children involved in the divorce.

- Children should be encouraged to maintain a relationship with your in-laws.

66

I didn't know how to ask my Dad to come to the wedding without his new girlfriend. I didn't want my Mom upset, so I wrote him a letter. He was so insulted, he didn't bother coming to my wedding at all.
—Richard, groom

99

GET THE SCOOP ON...
Divorcing a business partner ▪
Long-distance divorce ▪
Prenuptial agreements ▪ Lawyer troubles

Special Circumstances

Chapter 14

I n any divorce, special circumstances can arise. Your own divorce situation may stipulate certain needs: Perhaps you signed an ill-considered prenuptial agreement back in the early days of your relationship when you were young and in love. Perhaps your spouse has fled the state, and you now need to track that person down in order to continue the divorce process. Or what about discovering that the lawyer you felt so good about hiring has turned into something of a lemon? In this chapter we'll give these special circumstances some special consideration.

Divorcing your business partner

Nothing could be worse for business than a messy divorce between the partners. If you and your ex own a business, you're going to have to find a way to work together during, and probably after, the divorce. Unless one of you buys the other out, maintaining a working relationship after you part ways is going to take some effort on both of your parts.

Now, with hurt feelings and possibly some bitterness swirling around the two of you, you may find it hard to put your emotions aside when it is time to sit down and work on the new account or draw up that proposal for a business loan—but that's precisely the kind of cooperation you're going to have to manage.

Obviously, the best post-divorce working relationships are achieved when the couple has mutually agreed to divorce and can stay on friendly terms with one another. That, however, is not always the case. To keep the effects of your divorce on your business to a minimum, you're going to have to establish some new ground rules for working together.

First and most important, keep all divorce talk out of the office. This is not the place to discuss your child custody agreement or the division of household property. Tempers might flare, and your employees (or customers) simply do not need to participate in this with you. Save your discussions for the lawyer's office. Put your workers at ease. If they hear the bosses are splitting, they are going to be on edge. Some of them may even feel the need to "choose sides" between you, with potentially devastating consequences for your business.

A friend of mine worked in an office in which the former husband-wife owners were divorcing. Apparently, the husband had been secretly carrying on an affair with another worker, and the wife discovered them after hours. The "other woman" quit her job, and the rest of the workers—all female—were disgusted by the sight of the offending husband. They all sided with the wife, becoming outright hostile to the male owner. The resulting clashes ultimately hurt the functioning of the business, and the female owner had to tell the workers to cease their warfare. She explained that it was hard enough to come into the office everyday during this time—she did not need the business to go under, too.

One way to avoid allowing your divorce to harm your shared business is to think consciously of your partner's business strengths. Your new business relationship should be kept separate from the negatives that have ended your marriage. For this partnership to work, you will somehow have to stop thinking of this person as your ex, and start thinking of them *only* as your partner.

If you haven't yet reached the point where you can look past the fact of your divorce and see your ex purely as a good business partner, it is going to be difficult, if not impossible, to establish a working relationship together. If this is true for you, maybe you should begin to consider the possibility of one partner buying the other out. If it comes to that, bring your lawyers into it. This can be made a part of your divorce settlement agreement. Legal counsel is a must for this type of problem—do *not* attempt to handle the division of the business on your own. Lawyers will have to negotiate figures, terms, any stock options, or profit sharing, and the termination of a business partnership is far too complex to attempt to handle without professional help.

Long-distance legal battles

Another "special circumstance" arises when one party to a divorce flees the state prior to the settlement of the action. This can happen for several reasons—perhaps your spouse believes that this will keep the divorce from going through, or perhaps he

Bright Idea
Your workers should be informed of the impending divorce, but keep the details to yourself. Make it clear that you and your spouse will still be working together as professionals, and you expect no less of your employees.

or she is hoping to avoid having to comply with one or more of the terms of your divorce settlement. If your partner flees the state, it may have a strong impact on your ability to enforce your divorce agreement. You will undoubtedly wish to pursue your ex for payment of alimony or child support, but you should know that this is a very involved process, and can become quite costly.

Watch Out!
Since all states' laws regarding divorce, alimony, and child support may differ from one another, you may at this point be forced to deal with state laws that are different from the ones that formed your original agreement.

Let's say, for instance, that you and your ex lived and were divorced in New Jersey. You have your original divorce papers, mandated by a New Jersey court, stipulated by the terms of New Jersey law. If your ex packs up and moves to California, he or she may hope to become exempt from the terms of the agreement, but this is not necessarily so.

To begin the process of securing enforcement for your court orders for settlement, your first step is to notify your lawyer that your ex has left the state, and you are not receiving checks from him. Your lawyer will file a motion with the state court, informing it that your ex has fled. After that, your lawyer will help you bring action against your ex in the state to which your spouse has gone.

This latter action—filing a legal action in a state other than your own—is a very involved procedure, often requiring that you hire another lawyer in the state where your ex now resides. It is this new lawyer who will file suit against your spouse. In our example above you would need to hire a lawyer in California who would file the papers with the California court, and then have your ex served with papers from that court.

Adding further red-tape to all of this is the fact that not all states will cooperate fully with inter-state motions. "Sister states"—states that share a border

or are part of a single region—tend to be more willing to cooperate with one another in situations like
this. Several lawyers and divorced people we spoke
to said that the southern states, particularly Florida
and Georgia, are less likely to cooperate fully. When
the state to which your spouse has fled is uncooper-
ative, you may have to personally travel to that state
to pursue a new divorce case. This, as you might
imagine, can become very expensive. Sometimes,
however, it is your only recourse.

Prenuptial agreements

Another potential source of trouble when you find
yourself in the position of trying to work out a fair
and equitable divorce settlement is the "prenuptial
agreement." A common misconception is that the
only people who have prenuptial agreements are
the very, very rich. The premarital agreements of
people like Donald Trump always make the front
page, and we're always hearing about what the latest
divorcing celebrity couple's pre-nup stipulated. But
prenuptial agreements, also known as premarital
agreements, are no longer just for the jet-setting
crowd. More and more "regular" couples are drawing up such documents. In today's society—after all,
men and women are waiting until later in life to
marry, and in the meantime have amassed sizable
assets and career trajectories of their own. And second and third marriages are more common now
than ever before—and the hard lessons learned in
the first go-around are not likely to be repeated.

    If more and more couples are signing prenuptial
agreements, you can be assured that more and more
couples are also dealing with pre-nup jitters. The
presentation of a prenuptial agreement is not exactly the greatest and most symbolic gift in the world.

Unofficially . . .
Just because you
signed a pre-
nuptial agree-
ment does not
necessarily mean
that you can be
legally bound by
its terms.

Some people interpret such a document as a sign of doubt, a very un-romantic "What If?" expressed at what is supposed to be the most romantic time in a couple's life.

There may be significant pressure put upon the intended signer of a prenuptial agreement, especially if the fiancee's family is wealthy and fear that the new addition to the family is seeking a cut of the family fortune. But some people reluctantly sign a pre-nup out of love and loyalty to their intended, or out of fear that if they don't the marriage will be called off. And they tell themselves that this love will last forever, so the pre-nup will never be needed.

Well, if this sounds familiar to you—if you signed a prenuptial agreement before you were married—you may be worried now about the consequences of signing that agreement back in the golden days of your relationship. Perhaps you did not read the document fully. Perhaps you signed an extremely limiting pre-nup in the love-is-blind belief that your marriage would last forever. No need to panic. Although consenting adults may generally contract for anything that is legal and consistent with public policy, a prenuptial agreement may be found to be invalid for a number of reasons.

It is not that prenuptial agreements are worthless documents. Some may be binding. But there are circumstances that may make it possible for you to bypass their stipulations For example, your judge may have a personal distaste for prenuptial agreements—many do. Many judges may cut away at the validity of pre-nups if the following findings are evident:

- The terms of the pre-nup are not fair.
- One partner was pressured to sign.

- The agreement was signed very close to the wedding date.

- One or both partners did not have a lawyer.

- There was incomplete disclosure of the assets belonging to one or both partners. This is, in fact, the best grounds for discarding a prenuptial agreement.

- There is a significant difference in the partners' ages, status, and/or sophistication regarding the issues. However, if both parties are represented by legal counsel, it may be assumed that each fully understood the terms of the agreement.

If it sounds to you as if judges are trying to protect the "have nots" from being pressured by the "haves" into signing away their financial rights, you've heard it right. What especially displeases judges is any pre-nup stipulation that one partner will receive full custody of any children born to the marriage, or that one partner will not have to pay child support in the event of a divorce. Whereas you (or your spouse) may legally sign away your own rights, you generally cannot enter into any legal stipulation that adversely affects the welfare of your children. And any obvious attempt to manipulate the other spouse is frowned upon by most judges, and any points that do so may be eliminated from the agreement. On the other hand, as long as it can be demonstrated that you fully understood the rights you were giving up, and that you voluntarily signed the agreement, the court is likely to hold the pre-nup to be valid.

If you signed a pre-nup that says up front that your ex gets the kids, the house, the cars, all of your

Unofficially . . .
Many judges believe that prenuptial agreements are by nature just tools of manipulation. They hold that any valid concerns that might be spelled out in a pre-nup are more appropriately addressed in other legal documents such as wills and deeds.

belongings, and anything you brought into the marriage, take heart. If you can prove that you were pressured to sign, or if you were made to sign the day before your wedding, you do have grounds to nullify your pre-nup.

The rules for nullifying a prenuptial agreement are based on the Uniform Premarital Agreement Act. This act controls the legality of the arrangements made by persons who are planning to marry. It generally stipulates which claims are allowed to be made in premarital agreements, usually involving issues of alimony, property division, and insurance. What is universally disallowed under this act is any statement regarding child custody or support. The states that, at this time, adhere to the Uniform Premarital Agreement Act are as follows:

- Arizona
- Arkansas
- California
- Hawaii
- Illinois
- Iowa
- Kansas
- Maine
- Montana
- Nebraska
- Nevada
- New Jersey
- North Carolina
- North Dakota
- Oregon
- Rhode Island

- South Dakota

- Texas

- Utah

- Virginia

Your lawyer should look into the possibility that your pre-nup, or portions of it, may be invalid. If it turns out that this is the case, he or she will be able to take legal action to protect your rights and financial interests.

Dissention in the ranks: problems with your attorney

Experiencing problems with your ex, your family, or your in-laws is an expected part of the divorce process. Experiencing trouble with your attorney is not. Your attorney, after all, is supposed to be the captain of your team. If he or she fails to "play" well, then you're going to have to find someone who will. But finding a way to deal with a problem attorney can be a little tricky.

Some people do have fundamental, threatening problems with the attorney they have hired. Perhaps they failed to invest enough time in researching their attorney's credentials and strengths. Perhaps the attorney has taken on too many additional cases since being hired to handle this particular divorce, so that now he or she is no longer giving 100 percent to their case. Whatever the reason, the problem must be addressed, since keeping an inferior attorney is one of the best way to hurt your chances of getting what you want from your settlement.

Common complaints

By far, the number one complaint about divorce lawyers is a lack of communication. When an attorney commits this offense, the case can drag on for months and, without contact from the attorney, the client is left wondering what's going on.

We mentioned in Chapter 4 that a good lawyer will keep in regular touch with his or her clients, updating them as to the proceedings. Even if no action has been taken, or if your attorney has yet to receive responses and documents vital to the progress of the case, he or she should regularly inform you about where things stand. Your attorney should respect your right to know, and understand your interest in keeping abreast of the developments of your case.

A related, and frequently heard, complaint is that the attorney is never in when you call. While it is true that your attorney does have other cases and may be in court some of the times that you try to contact him or her, your case is as important as any other that he or she is handling. You have a right to expect that your lawyer return your calls in a timely manner.

Another common complaint against an attorney has to do with billing practices. While the receipt of a large bill is never a pleasure and may be cause for complaint in itself, the thing that most frustrates clients is the format and delivery of legal bills. If, say, your case is handled on a retainer basis, chances are that your attorney's accountant will send you a monthly account statement, listing deduction from the retainer amount. The problem is that the codes used for individual entries may be less than informative. One commonly encountered code is "memo." This code does not accurately explain the charge, which may represent hours of research, writing, editing, and strategic planning that went into

Bright Idea
If you're not getting call-backs, let the receptionist know your displeasure. After the second unreturned phone call, tell your lawyer's office that you will consider terminating the relationship. You deserve timely and efficient service, and you should take your case elsewhere if their office can't provide it.

making a good legal brief for presentation to the court.

In addition to these common complaints, you may have more particular problems with your lawyer. You may find that he or she has failed to fully research the laws of your case, for instance. This can, and does, actually happen: A friend of mine went into her lawyer's office with material she found on the Internet. Apparently, her state had a law regarding child support that her attorney had never told her about. It turned out that the lawyer did not even know about it. He floundered, saying that it was a new law, and that he simply had not found time yet to incorporate it into her case. Sensing the dodge, she fired her lawyer and found a better one.

How to complain

Once you've identified any problems you have with your attorney, you will need to take the correct steps to remedy the situation, if possible. Your first step should always be to talk to your attorney. Be direct. Explain exactly what it is that displeases you in a diplomatic and respectful way. This is not the time to be demanding or condescending. That approach will only put your attorney on the defensive, and that is not the way to open up a good dialogue to resolve the problem.

Very often, you may find that the problem you have with your attorney is really the fault of a receptionist or legal assistant. Your attorney may simply not have been aware of the problem. How is your lawyer to know that letters to you are taking a week to get out of the office? By bringing your concerns directly to your attorney's attention, you may have hit upon the simplest way to resolve all your problems.

Timesaver
Avoid a lengthy and potentially convoluted discussion with your attorney by spelling out your complaints in writing and sending the letter to your attorney's office. Of course, you must be careful to be diplomatic and direct about the issue at hand, and request that these matters be cleared up immediately.

When you *do* go to your attorney with a complaint, be specific. Avoid resorting to generalized statements about problems in your divorce. If your problem is with billing, say so and offer examples of the bills you find to be unclear. If you have a problem with accessibility, provide the dates and times you called. The more specific you can be, the better your attorney is able to solve the problem.

Unofficially . . .
To your lawyer, you represent not only your case, but future referrals and future income for him. So your lawyer does have yet another motive for serving you well, and with this in mind he is likely to accommodate your professional wishes.

- **Be honest.** If you are displeased with some action or inaction on your lawyer's part, do not ignore the problem or deny the problem out of a sense of intimidation or shyness. Remember, you are paying your lawyer to serve your best interests. He or she has an obligation to give you the kind of service you expect. It is counterproductive to your goals to accept inferior service in deference to your attorney.

- **Be realistic.** Are you expecting too much from your attorney? You must remember that your attorney does have other cases, and you cannot expect his attention to be focused only on you. So make allowances for normal time spans, and remember that your attorney is only human. It is unrealistic to expect results overnight, especially if you have a very involved case.

- **Be assertive.** A lawyer appreciates a client who will state his needs, since that is the only way to maintain true communication. Just the same, it can only be detrimental to your working relationship if you become a nuisance to him. You do not want to create a situation in which your lawyer starts to dislike you.

Taking it higher up

If your attorney does not fix any problems you have with his office or with him, take your complaints higher up. If you're working with a junior lawyer in a big firm, talk to their direct supervisor or a senior partner in the firm. Objectively, your lawyer represents the whole firm, and any complaints you have with your lawyer direct reflects on the firm that employs him. Just as your lawyer depends on your satisfaction with his handling of your case for future referrals and future income, so too does the firm.

If you must, make an appointment to see the supervisor or senior partner, and spell out your complaint in a clear and diplomatic way. Be professional. Be direct. Be honest and avoid exaggeration. The senior lawyers in the firm will consider whether or not your expectations are realistic, and they will weigh the elements of your concerns. If they agree that you have a problem on your hands, most likely they will promise to talk to your lawyer.

If your problem with the lawyer is one that involves a breach of ethics, you should definitely terminate your relationship. In addition, contact the State Bar Ethics Committee. You may have fired your lawyer and lost hundreds of dollars in wasted time, but it should not end there. If you report the breach to the Ethics Committee, an investigation will get underway, and at the very least they will no longer be listed as a recommended attorney from the Bar Association. This could spare some future divorcing person from having the same ethical difficulties you had to face.

Complaint categories

Your problems with your lawyer are likely to fall under certain categories: simple dissatisfaction with performance, ethics violations, and malpractice. When speaking to your attorney or his or her higher-ups, you should know which category your complaints fall under.

Watch Out!
Everyone handles constructive criticism differently, and lawyers are no exception. While it might be that your lawyer will accept that you've gone "upstairs" with your problems, you could find yourself facing a vindictive attorney who is angry that you went over his or her head. If that is the case, get a new lawyer. This is not the person you want to represent you.

■ **Simple dissatisfaction.** You are not getting progress reports on time, your billing is confusing, the case is taking too long. These are simple issues that can usually be cleared up with clear communication between you and your attorney.

■ **Ethics violations.** If your attorney has lied to you or misrepresented himself or the case to you, then your attorney's behavior has been unethical.

In most cases, though, if an attorney engages in unethical behavior, it is directed toward the other side. He may lie to your ex's attorney. He may not disclose facts properly or honestly, in a sneaky effort to protect your assets or win the case. For example, your attorney may tell your ex's attorney that you have $2,000 in a savings account, when you really have $10,000. This is an ethics breach. Your attorney, in this case, is not handling your case in the right way, but there is no intended or unintended damage to you.

■ Malpractice goes beyond ethics violations in that the client is damaged. Henry, recently divorced, shares this story: Henry's lawyer served divorce papers on his wife, and his wife's lawyer never responded. When the time limit for responding passed, Henry's lawyer filed for a judgment of default, and Henry won his divorce case, getting everything. Who knows what his wife's lawyer was thinking? But in not responding to the divorce papers filed by Henry's lawyer, he hurt his client and lost the case. That is malpractice. If your lawyer has already done something to blow your case, or if you could prove after a judgment against you that you would have won the case if not for your attorney's actions, you have a malpractice situation.

Documenting problems

It is vital to document the details of your divorce case throughout the process by taking notes of your meetings and progress. But if you are becoming dissatisfied with your attorney's handling of your case, it is especially important that you keep careful records of your observations and complaints. In the event that your case is damaged by your lawyer, and you do have to pursue malpractice against him, you will need detailed records of the attorney's actions and inactions.

Here is a sample record:

12/4—Met with lawyer for initial consultation. Discussed facts of case, presented list of assets, made next appointment. 1½ hours.

12/9—Met with lawyers from both sides to form property settlement agreement. My lawyer presented my list of assets; his side presented his list. Discrepancies over investment accounts. 2 hours.

12/12—Got letter that my lawyer discovered hidden assets of my husband's.

12/17—My lawyer canceled our meeting.

12/19—Rescheduled meeting via phone contact.

12/22—No answer at the lawyer's office. Tried four times.

12/28—Meeting at the lawyer's office. Went over child support agreement. 1 hour.

12/30—Ex's lawyer contacted my lawyer for a meeting. My lawyer put it off until after his ski trip (!!!).

Moneysaver
Keeping a written record of your attorney's activity is a handy way to keep track of the hours he or she spends with you. When you receive billing statements, you can check your accurate records for discrepancies in your attorney's billing totals. In addition, it provides the proof that you may need should you have reason to file charges of malpractice against your lawyer.

1/5—In meeting with ex's lawyer, my lawyer said that I had $4,000 in my new bank account, when I really have $12,000. He lied! All they have to do is check and I'm busted.

1/8—Lawyer canceled meeting due to family emergency.

1/12—Met with both sides to finalize shared custody and alimony. I was kicking my lawyer under the table when he forgot about settling up for holidays and birthdays. What's wrong with this guy? 1½ hours.

1/16—Lawyer forgot to file something with the court!!! His secretary called me today, asking if I had a copy.

This list is, naturally, essential should you need to sue for malpractice, for it documents how your attorney may have damaged your case. It is also a good item to present to your lawyer's supervisor or senior partner if you should decide to fire him and go to another firm. You may even send a copy to the State Bar for their records. In any case, it is always a good idea to keep a running journal on your divorce process. Your memory, at this time of upheaval, may not be sharp enough to maintain all details.

How to fire your attorney

You have every right to fire your attorney if you feel that he or she is not serving you well, or is damaging your case. Many people, intimidated by their lawyer's authority or afraid of "making waves," are hesitant to walk into their lawyer's office and proclaim, "You're fired." But remember—your best interests are the most important factor here, and you may need to take this step for your own protection. Here's one way to go about firing your counsel—send a formal termination letter similar to the one we provide here:

Dear _____:

It is with regret that I must inform you of my plans to terminate our working relationship. I feel that it is in my best interests to seek other counsel.

Sincerely,

_____

You may choose to go into more detail, but a simple statement like the sample we provide will suffice. Do *not* use this letter as an opportunity to launch a personal attack on the lawyer, no matter what your feelings are. It will do you no good and may cause you harm should you take malpractice action later. Just state your intentions, and move on.

Another option if you are uneasy about firing your attorney personally is to hire a new attorney and have that person contact your former lawyer about the change. Your lawyer, remember, has years of experience. He has probably dealt with this situation before, especially if he is by nature unethical or unprofessional in the manner shown to you. Your new lawyer will handle the details of terminating your old relationship with your former lawyer, and your former lawyer is ethically obligated to cooperate in the conversion.

Of course, it is best to make such a change early in your divorce proceedings. Waiting until the final hours wastes a lot of money and time. Another issue to think about regarding the timing of your termination of your lawyer is this: What will the judge think if you are switching lawyers now? Whether rightful or not, the judge may think that the problem is *yours*, rather than the lawyer's, especially if the

Watch Out!
When you fire your attorney, you may still be responsible for paying any fees incurred up to that point. If your lawyer is on retainer, you should remember to get the unused balance of that back.

case is not going your way. And the judge would really frown on you if you seem to be switching lawyers every other week.

In any case, you must remember the roles and expectations of a good attorney. This person has been hired to protect your best interests and those of your children. That is a great responsibility, and in acknowledging this you have placed great trust in your attorney's hands. If your attorney betrays that trust, you have every right to terminate your relationship.

Just the facts

- Maintaining a business partnership with your ex will require setting ground rules to govern your new working relationship.

- If your ex flees the state, you and your lawyer will have to pursue him or her through the courts of the state to which he or she has fled.

- Prenuptial agreements can be challenged if they appear to have been coerced or are manifestly unfair.

- If you have serious difficulties with your lawyer, do not hesitate to replace him or her with counsel that is more capable of seeing to your needs.

Get the Lowdown on the Post-Divorce Financial Issues

PART VI

GET THE SCOOP ON...
Wills ▪ Probate ▪ Estate and tax
planning ▪ Other estate planning documents

Chapter 15

The Paper Chase . . . Legal Documents

Throughout the divorce process, you will see the need to either create or change various legal documents to reflect your new circumstances. In addition, you may find that you have to rethink, or re-negotiate certain practical matters, involving taxes and insurance, for example. In many cases, you'll need the assistance of an attorney or financial planner to help you draw up these forms. Don't underestimate the importance of these concerns and legal documents. As a newly single person you will need to protect your assets and provide for your family wisely.

Wills

As part of your divorce, you will most likely devise very specific terms for the division of your assets and liabilities and further for the care and support of your children, while you are alive. In addition to planning for these issues during your and your spouse's life, it is a good idea to adequately plan for the unlikely event that you and/or your spouse passes away. One important aspect of planning for such a case deals with your Last Will and Testament.

When you file a divorce action or when you and your spouse separate with an eye toward divorce, you may want to write a new will. Very often, married couples have wills in which each leaves most, if not all, of their property to their spouse. While married, this of course makes sense, but upon divorce or separation, you will want to make other provisions for your assets. Now that you're getting divorced, if you died, do you want your spouse to get all your money?

Considering the many emotional issues involved when your divorce or separation begins, it is quite understandable that you're not thinking about what would happen if you died before you were actually divorced. If you had a will that left all your property to your spouse and you died before you were divorced, your spouse would most likely inherit all your property. Considering you would have been in the process of obtaining a divorce, other relatives or friends may have an opportunity to contest the terms of the will, but, generally, a will speaks for itself, and it is often extremely difficult, if not impossible, to overturn it.

To avoid this problem, you may simply wish to write a new will. Until you actually settle your divorce, you may not be able to address all the issues that you would ultimately like to resolve in your will, but, at the very least, you can write a very basic one that explains your present marital situation and makes arrangements to leave your assets to someone other than your spouse. Once your divorce is completed, you can of course go back and draft a more complete will.

Although you cannot always legally write your spouse out of your will while you are still technically married, in the case of a pending divorce, you may have more leeway in leaving your assets to someone other than your spouse. At the very least, by writing a new will, you will protect your assets to the fullest extent allowed by law.

Very often, married couples do not have wills. When this is the case, the laws of intestacy would divide their property, and most often the surviving spouse would receive most, if not all, of the property. For example, if you and your spouse do not have children, under the laws of intestacy, your spouse will generally inherit your assets. If you do not have a will, divorce or separation is a very practical time to write one. In the event you should die while a divorce is pending, you do not want the laws of your state to determine whether or not your spouse is entitled to your assets.

Guardianship

If you have children, you most certainly will want to address the issue of guardianship and support within a will. A will typically not only makes provisions as to how you would like to leave your assets, but may also nominate guardians to care for your children in the case of your death. For example, if you had sole physical custody of your children and passed away before they were old enough to care for themselves, your spouse would in all likelihood assume custody. This makes both practical and legal sense.

But if you believe there are very good reasons why your spouse should not be granted custody, a will is a good place to address those issues. However, you should be aware that a natural parent's right to custody generally supersedes all others' rights.

Unofficially . . .
Many states have laws which prohibit you from completely writing your spouse out of your will. Remember, you cannot financially abandon your spouse, either during life or upon death.

Nevertheless, in your will, you could specify who you would like to see get custody of your children, and further you could state specific reasons why your spouse should not take custody. At the very least, you may be able to have some input, in essence, from your grave.

Creating a trust

While, as we've just noted, your spouse would most likely assume custody of your children in the event of your death, you may still want to ensure that your assets are used for the support and welfare of your children. If you do not believe that your ex-spouse would use your assets solely for the childrens' benefit, you may want to leave the assets in *trust*.

When you leave assets to an unemancipated minor in a will, you do not leave the assets outright to the minor, but rather, you leave the assets "in trust" for their benefit. In other words, you create a type of guardianship for the money. A trust is an entity unto itself in which the children's money is held. This may take the form of an investment or a bank account.

In your will, you may wish to name a trustee—the person who is in charge of managing the money. In your will or related document, you can typically direct the trustee how to use the money and specify when he or she can spend the funds or invade the trust. For example, you may wish to give the trustee very broad discretionary authority by allowing him or her to use the money, unlimited, for any purpose, so long as it benefits the health, education, or welfare of the children. Or, you can narrow the trustee's ability to use the money, for example, for college or medical care. You can limit the amount of money the trustee can spend in total, or on a yearly basis. Even though you may have passed away, a trust allows you to continue to direct how your money should be spent.

When you leave money in trust to your children, you should also decide when the children will be entitled to actually control the money for themselves. For example, you may decide that upon turning age 18, your son or daughter should get his or share of any funds that may remain in the trust. Or you may wish to give him or her the money over a period of time, maybe 25% at age 18, 25% at age 25, 25% at age 30, and the remainder at age 35. Your decisions may be influenced by how much money you believe will be left in the trust and what other provisions may have been made for the children's support.

Typically, any competent person or entity can be the trustee of the trust. For example, if you believe that your ex-spouse will utilize all money in a proper manner for the benefit of the children, you can name him or her as trustee. However, you may wish to name your sister, or father, or friend as trustee, which may help ensure that the children, and not your ex-spouse or his or her new spouse, winds up with the money. You should name someone who you trust will carry out your directives and use the money in accordance with your wishes for the full benefit of your children.

Living trust
Instead of a will, you may have, or may wish to write, a living trust. A living trust is an alternative method of passing assets to your children and is popular in states in which the will probate procedure is either very costly or time-consuming. A living trust exists while you are alive and typically leaves assets by

Bright Idea
If you have children that require special care due to a disability or for any other reason, a trust is often a good way of addressing the issue and ensuring that his or her needs are adequately met.

designating a beneficiary who, while you are married, may be your spouse. As a result, like a will, upon separation or divorce, it is important to speak with an expert in estate planning so as to avoid unwanted circumstances.

You may also wish to consider the unlikely event that both you and your ex-spouse pass away before the children are fully grown. Who will take care of the children? You and your spouse may wish to agree upon a guardian for the children.

Estate and tax planning

Depending upon the amount of assets you and your spouse own, you may have had sophisticated estate planning documents drafted that, as a result of your divorce, may no longer be meaningful. For example, some very common and effective estate planning techniques, such as a marital by-pass trust, are dependent upon the fact that you are married and lose their relevance upon your divorce. Or, for example, you and your spouse may own life insurance or certain annuities as a way of planning for the future. Upon your divorce, the need for these retirement plans may change or you may wish to modify their terms. As a result, you should consult with your attorney and your estate planning advisor with regard to your estate plan and the consequences of your divorce. He or she may also have important advice regarding the division of your assets and liabilities.

Probate

As part of writing a new will, you should be aware of which assets actually pass by way of the terms of your will, that is through probate, and which do not. An asset that is solely titled to you, such as a bank

Watch Out!
As a practical matter, the fact that you are getting divorced does not change prior decisions regarding guardianship. If you need to alter that decision, both you and your spouse will need to discuss the issue. This would be a good topic to cover during your mediation or during negotiations with your lawyers.

account, titled "Jane Doe" does pass under the terms of your will. As you are the sole owner of the account, your will has the authority to direct how the asset should be distributed. However, if you have a joint bank account titled "Jane and/or John Doe, with rights of survivorship," this account would not pass under the terms of your will, but would instead pass directly to the surviving owner, John. In this case, you and John are co-owners of the account, and the joint ownership, which carries rights of survivorship, rather than the terms of your will, directs who gets the money. It is extremely important to understand how your assets are titled when writing a new will as a result of a separation or divorce.

Let's say you and your spouse own a bank account and a house, both of which are titled "Jane and John Doe, with rights of survivorship." This is very common, especially in the case of real estate, which, when married couples purchase a house, is automatically titled jointly. If you write a new will that leaves nothing to your spouse, but die leaving these jointly owned assets, the entire house will most likely pass to your spouse. These types of issues can often be addressed by re-titling your assets prior to the final resolution of your divorce. For example, it is very easy to divide the bank account and place your share in an account that is solely titled to you or jointly owned by someone else. The house may be more difficult to divide, but with the appropriate procedures, you may be able to adequately plan. It is important to address these issues with your attorney at the beginning of your divorce proceeding.

Other estate-planning documents

A power of attorney is simply a document that gives a person broad discretionary powers over your

Watch Out!
While the divorce is pending, you and your spouse have not yet divided your assets. This means that you remain co-owners, so you won't yet be able to make certain decisions regarding their disposal in your will.

finances. Before your divorce, you may have granted power of attorney to your spouse. In light of a divorce or separation, you may wish to revoke this type of document and execute new ones.

Watch Out!
If you fail to change your power of attorney at your bank or other financial institution, your spouse will continue to have access to all of your assets.

There are generally two types of power of attorney, one which takes effect as soon as the agreement is drafted, that is upon execution, and one which only takes effect if you are disabled. If you executed a power of attorney that took effect upon execution, you may wish to immediately address this situation by revoking it and naming a new attorney in fact. Even if your power of attorney takes effect only upon disability, you may wish to make alternative arrangements for your financial security. Although chances are that you will not become disabled prior to your divorce, you are better off safe than sorry.

For example, you may have filed a power of attorney with your bank. You may easily be able to write to the bank and revoke the power of attorney. Further, you should notify the attorney that drafted the document and discuss with him or her your available options specific to your circumstances.

Another document you may wish to have drawn up is a "living will," which is typically used to speak for you in the event that you are unable to do so as a result of an injury. It typically informs a hospital, doctor, or other medical professional as to the type of medical treatment you would request if you were able to do so. For example, if you sustained an extremely serious injury and required feeding tubes and other artificial means to keep you alive, a living will may direct that if two doctors agreed as to the seriousness of your injury and the necessity for permanent artificial life-sustaining equipment, the hospital may remove you from the equipment. Or, a living will may direct that the hospital or medical professional do everything in his or her power, regardless of cost, to keep you alive. It is a directive for your health care.

Typically, a living will not only states your intentions with regard to health care, but also names a health care guardian, or someone who may speak for you if you are unable to do so due to disability or illness. Most often, if you are married, your spouse is named as your health care guardian and as a result, upon divorce or separation, you may wish to change your health care guardian to someone else.

These are issues that you and your spouse may wish to discuss, but are typically not issues that the court will resolve. Generally, the court is not interested in your will or other estate planning documents unless it is forced to address the issues under the terms of your divorce agreement. For example, your divorce agreement may state that you and your spouse will write new wills within 30 days after your divorce and name your sister as guardian of your children. If your spouse fails to write a new will according to the terms of the agreement, you may be able to bring a motion or similar application before the court and seek the enforcement of the terms of your divorce agreement. However, if you and your spouse cannot agree upon a guardian for the children and do not agree to write new wills, the divorce court will typically not involve itself. Although it often makes great sense to resolve these type of issues, the court typically does not consider them to be paramount in getting you divorced.

Divorce issues with health insurance

As you and your spouse divide your marital assets, you should demand that health insurance be listed as a marital asset. Of course, your ex may scoff, but you have a weapon here. Just tell your spouse and your spouse's lawyer that since the Financial Accounting Standards Board requires all employers to figure in the value of their employee's future benefits (including health insurance) and record those figures as a liability for their own financial records, it stands to reason that a liability for the company is an asset to the worker who receives the benefits package. That is the very definition of an asset, so it should count that way for you too.

Because of the often exorbitant costs of insurance, you and your spouse will need to negotiate during your settlement meetings who will be responsible for these payments. For example, you or your spouse may require alimony payments to help subsidize the cost. Or, you and your spouse may agree that you will pay your spouse's insurance premiums for two years, giving your spouse a chance to ease into the expense. Most typically though, you and your spouse will each be required to pay for your own health insurance and further be required to pay all deductibles and unreimbursed expenses.

If, while you were married, both you and your spouse had medical benefits through your individual jobs, then you won't have much of a battle on your hands when it comes to the issue of health insurance. In the traditional household, however, the standard is that the husband is the main wage-earner and the wife is covered on his health insurance plan. In the event of their divorce, the wife is no longer covered. As an individual, she must find health insurance for herself.

For many women, this is a problem. Take the case of Jean. Jean is in her late 40s, and she

Bright Idea
In cases where there is a great discrepancy between you and your spouse's ability to afford health coverage, you will need to include these costs in your requested total support package. If you do not, you may forget the cost of insurance and as a result, grossly underestimate your monthly financial requirments.

suffers from heart problems. Dropped from her ex-husband's health insurance plan, she is having trouble finding affordable health insurance for herself. After all, she isn't in prime health, and her age and other risk categories put her at rather unfavorable rates on the insurance companies' charts. If she does qualify for health insurance coverage, she would have to pay a higher amount of money for that plan. Being a 20-year stay-at-home homemaker, Jean doesn't have much income to spare now, and the prospects of being able to afford a good health care plan do not look good for her.

Fortunately for her, and perhaps for you, the Consolidated Omnibus Reconciliation Act (COBRA) states that the ex-wife can be covered by the ex-husband's company's health insurance plan (if that company has at least 20 employees) for up to three years after the divorce. At the three-year mark, the coverage ends. During the time of coverage, the ex-wife must pay her own premiums, as the ex-husband is not responsible for that expense.

Getting insurance under COBRA is a good option for someone like Jean. You might think that Jean is only biding her time until the inevitable. Indeed, that may be true. But during those three years, Jean may be able to go back to school and get a degree or a better job that might offer her health coverage. Or, she can get a well-paying job with no coverage that allows her enough income to afford a quality health care plan. COBRA has just these goals in mind.

Unlike the situation of the ex-wife, if your entire family was covered under your spouse's health insurance plan, the children can still be covered, even though you are no longer on your spouse's

Watch Out!
If you're using the COBRA plan, you must pay your premiums on time. If you miss a payment, your ex-spouse's company can drop your coverage automatically.

policy. So it usually makes sense for the children to continue to be covered by whatever health insurance plan existed during the marriage. If the plan is provided to you or your spouse at no cost, you and your spouse will only need to address payment of deductibles and unreimbursed expenses. However, if you or your spouse must pay for the insurance, you will have to decide who is going to pay the premium. As a general rule, like child support, parents are required to pay for the expenses of their children in the ratio of their individual earnings to the total earnings of both spouses. This rule of thumb is often used to resolve disputes of child-related costs because it is equitable and ensures that the children are properly supported.

Taxes on alimony and child support

As you figure out your income and expenses, you might wonder how alimony and child support payments fit in. Is it taxable income? Can you write it off? In a nutshell, alimony payments are taxable income to the recipient, and they are tax deductions to the person who pays the alimony. It seems unfair, in essence, to punish the person who is on the receiving end of alimony payments and give an additional tax break to the person paying. But until thousands of people write to Congress for a change on that bill, those are the rules for now. Child support payments, on the other hand, are not taxable income to the recipient, and they're not a tax deduction to the payer.

Taxes on assets

You may have heard of the term capital gains tax. That, quite simply, is the tax you would have to pay on the appreciated value of any asset if you were to sell that asset. Since the main asset that most people have is a house, let's use that as an example. Let's say the value of your house, when you originally bought it, was $100,000. Now that you're divorcing, you've decided to sell the house. Its value now, you find out, is $200,000. That $100,000 profit you make is your capital gains. If you do not buy another home within two years, you have to pay capital gains tax on that amount as part of your taxable income. That can be a hefty price tag.

If you do buy a new home within two years, the capital gains tax from your original home can be rolled over into your new home. There are specific requirements for this option, however. If you move out of the house before it's sold, you lose the benefit of this option. Specific language in this situation states that the house must be your "principal residence."

But what happens if you and your spouse have separated, and you've moved into an apartment across town. You didn't know at the time that the house would be sold, so how could you know that moving out of it would cost you so dearly in capital gains tax burdens? You can avoid this by establishing what is called "intent to return." This, basically, keeps your house as your principal residence, even if you're currently living in your new apartment. You are stating that, although you live elsewhere right now, you claim the option of returning to your principal residence. These are the specific steps you can take to show your "intent to return" to your principal residence:

■ Rent, don't buy, another place to live. If you buy a new house, then that rules out your original house as your principal residence.

Unofficially . . .
You can reduce your capital gains taxes with regard to your house. Look at the equity that you've built up in your home (the value of the house minus the mortgage that remains is your equity). Your capital gains tax would be applied to your net equity, and your net equity is the actual equity minus any accrued tax.

- Leave some of your belongings in the original residence.

- Continue to have your mail delivered to your original residence.

- Continue to perform any maintenance work on the house.

Of course, if you and your spouse have put the house up for sale before you move out, documented evidence to this effect prevents you from having to take these steps. And taxes related to your house will vary depending upon what state you live in. So check with your financial advisor or the IRS for any specific laws and statutes that apply to you.

You do have other assets that are touched by this tax issue. Think back to your list of assets. You might have included your retirement plans. If you have a tax-deferred retirement plan such as an IRA or a mutual fund, you know that if you cash it in, you'll have to pay taxes on the dollar value, plus a penalty for cashing in early. For this reason, you should always look at the tax situation when you're considering cashing in your funds to split with your spouse. Assess the tax value, and make your decision.

Tax protection in your divorce settlement

You should speak to your lawyer about the tax issue when you're working to form your divorce settlement. Not only do you want to make sure that you and your spouse are clear on who pays what taxes and who gets what deductions, you'll also need to take some steps to protect your future interests with regard to your tax standing.

Take the case of Kelly and James. For years, James had always prepared their joint tax returns, and at the end of the process he had Kelly sign the papers. Now, in the event of their divorce, Kelly fears that James has been a little "creative" with some deductions and the reporting of his income. Knowing now what other kinds of deceit James is capable of, Kelly is very nervous that he cheated on their taxes. Now, with her name signed on the dotted line, she fears that she might be held liable if their past tax returns should ever get audited.

Kelly was so frantic about this situation, she talked to her lawyer, who was able to calm her fears. Together, they put in a request to James, asking him to provide a written statement that would indemnify Kelly for any tax liability and penalty. James, scoffing as usual at Kelly's irrational fears, gladly signed a paper of indemnification, and Kelly felt much better with it in hand.

This type of release form does calm nerves in a great many divorced people. As their marriage ends, there is a lot of mistrust between partners, and there are a lot of irrational and rational fears flying around in their heads. Most people are aware that the IRS will seek collection from both spouses on a joint return if the information provided is not accurate, and they do seek a way to absolve themselves of responsibility for their spouse's actions on this front. A written indemnification will qualify you for full reimbursement from your spouse in the event of any audit or tax penalties levied on you.

Filing tips

The following are smart tax filing tips to help save you time and money:

- If you know that you will just not be able to pay your taxes on time, apply for an automatic four-month extension by filing Form 4868

"Application for Automatic Extension of Time to File U.S. Individual Income Tax Return." You can request this form from the IRS on their phone line or download over the Internet. Make sure this form is postmarked by April 15.

- Even if you can't pay your tax bill, be sure to file on time. If you're late filing, the IRS will impose a penalty of 5 percent of the overdue amount every month you're late until the amount reaches 25 percent of your original amount due. In this case, you should fill out Form 9465, "Installment Agreement Request Form." The IRS will assess your request to submit your payment in installments; they'll discuss a payment plan for you, at a fee of over $40.

- Avoid simple errors, such as a mistake in your address, forgetting to sign your form, or making addition mistakes. These little hiccups attract the attention of the IRS and may improve your chances of getting audited.

- Don't attempt to hide a portion of your income in an effort to avoid paying taxes. This is illegal, and you could be punished severely.

- Don't get creative with deductions. The IRS knows which categories attract false itemizations, and they're looking for entries that do not fit.

- Make sure to use the correct filing status for your return. Using the Head of Household status, if you qualify, will save you substantial money at tax time.

- See if the change in your financial status, post-divorce, qualifies you for claiming the Earned Income Credit. If you work, but your income falls below the maximum limit to qualify, you may get a tax credit.

Transferring assets

As you and your spouse divide all of your financial assets, your lawyers may help to transfer these assets through their channels—at their hourly wages—or you could arrange to divide these assets yourself. You might start with dividing your bank accounts, savings accounts, and credit card accounts. You and your spouse, after all, will not be sharing these joint accounts anymore, and it's best if you separate these by either closing down your accounts and opening new ones or by changing the names on your accounts.

This is going to be a hectic time, and the task of dividing your accounts is not the most joyous one of your life. Don't trust that you'll remember what you've accomplished. Keep a written record of who you contacted, what accounts are closed, what accounts are new, who you spoke to at the bank, the date, and the time. Always ask for a confirmation letter.

If all goes well, you'll both be pleased with the division of your assets, and the process will go smoothly. Of course, it's wishful thinking for anything to go smoothly during a divorce, but the best way to improve your odds of a smooth transition is to be as organized and on top of this task as possible. Do not let financial issues wait.

Credit issues

Too many recently divorced people find themselves with little or no credit. Perhaps the accounts were all in one spouse's name with the other spouse as the cosigner. When the accounts are divided, all the

Timesaver
Don't expect to be able to divide your accounts with a simple phone call. The bank or credit card company is going to ask you for a request in writing that your account be closed and separate accounts be opened in your names. Write out a detailed letter giving your circumstances, your account number, and your request to open a new account. Follow up on the letter with a phone call in a few days.

Watch Out!
A more calculat-
ing ex-spouse
may attempt to
transfer some of
his or her assets
to a third party,
blocking your
rightful access to
them. If you sus-
pect that this is
happening, tell
your attorney.
Your attorney
then can try to
block the trans-
fer. This might
involve hiring a
private investi-
gator to prove
your spouse's
deceitful actions,
and it almost
certainly will
involve a judge's
order to block or
reverse the
transfer.

credit may be in that one spouse's name. Having
no credit means that it could be hard for you to get
a credit card of your own, or even a mortgage of
your own. When you go to a bank and ask them for
credit, they assess you according to several criteria:

- What is your income?

- What is your credit history?

- What collateral do you have?

You'll need to prove to them that you have
income of your own, that you're not a bad credit
risk, and that you have collateral in your own name.
This often means showing them proof of your
employment and allowing them to take a look at the
joint credit you had with your spouse.

What happens if you have a hard time getting
credit? First, understand the problem. It may be that
you were always just a cosigner on your spouse's
credit accounts. All of the good credit rating that
the two of you built is now assigned to your spouse.
You're essentially left out in the cold. Your only
recourse now is to start building good credit in your
own name, and you can do that by taking the following steps:

- Open a bank account if you do not already have
  one. Banks and creditors like to see that you
  have some money set aside, that you're responsible with it, and perhaps that it can be used as
  some collateral in the event of collection.

- Open up an account with stores that give instant
  credit, such as department stores or gas stations.
  These accounts, once you get them, are good
  opportunities to show that you can handle a
  credit account responsibly. They give you something to work with in order to establish your new
  credit track record.

- Pay your bills off in full and on time. This usually means that you keep your charges low and that you pay off your full balance each month. This too shows that you're responsible with your credit accounts, that you're not a risk for maxing out your card and defaulting on payments. Over time, if you keep your accounts in good standing, the creditors will raise your credit limit. It is this show of faith and opportunity, earned by your responsible payments, that adds positive marks to your credit record.

Of course, you probably won't earn a Gold Card overnight. It takes time to build a solid credit rating, but soon you'll be on your feet with good credit backing you up. In any case, it's always a good idea to get a copy of your credit report and inspect it for accuracy and mistakes. You can get a copy of your credit report from the following reporting agencies:

- **TRW:** (800) 392-1122
- **Equifax:** (800) 685-1111
- **Experian:** (800) 682-7654
- **Trans Union:** (800) 916-8800

If you do find a mistake in your credit report, call the reporting bureau that delivered it. Upon learning of any discrepancy, they have 30 days to investigate the error. In doing so, they will contact the creditor that reported the supposed mistake in your report, giving them any evidence that you can provide to support your version of the facts. The creditor then will review your file and afterward report their findings to the credit bureau. You will get a written report of this complete investigation and, if any changes are made as a result, an updated and corrected copy of your credit rating. If the

Unofficially . . . Under the Equal Credit Opportunity Act, all people have the right be fairly considered for credit, with no discrimination against their gender or marital status. This law is built to protect your eligibility, but it does not protect you against any credit flaws caused by your spouse or the circumstance of your divorce. For this reason, some people have a hard time getting credit in their own names after divorce.

discrepancy remains, you will have to take further action to resolve the issue, perhaps writing letters to the company president, the Better Business Bureau, and so on. It's *your* credit rating, and it's very important to your future financial health. Remember, it will take time to build a solid credit record.

Do-it-yourself options

Of course, while it is advisable to get a professional's help when deciding what to do with your finances, it is possible for you to take matters into your own hands and research your options on your own. Look to the following resources when analyzing your financial picture:

- Books on personal financial planning that you'll find in bookstores and libraries
- Computer software
- Financial planning clinics offered at adult education centers or community centers
- Online financial centers
- Literature provided by the IRS

You may find that as an additional benefit to handling your own financial outlook, you get a fresh education in the issues that tremendously affect your life. Now you have a better idea, for instance, of what your investments are really doing for you, how to make your own money perform better for you, and what your options are for the future. Divorce, you'll find, doesn't have to destroy your financial well-being. By forcing you to take charge of your money, it might help you to reach a better financial standing than you would have had otherwise.

Just the facts

- Throughout the divorce process, you will see the need to either create or change various legal documents to reflect your new status and the conditions and circumstances of your life.

- When you and your spouse separate with an eye toward divorce, you may want to write a new will.

- A living will is typically used to speak for you in the event that you are unable to do so as a result of an injury.

- Divorce will have an impact on your taxes. Make certain that you use the appropriate filing status.

- While child support is non-taxable, taxes must be paid on alimony received.

- Post-divorce, you may find yourself suddenly with no credit. Take steps early to make certain you have established credit in your own name.

Glossary

Alimony (or separate maintenance payments) Support paid from one spouse to the other to satisfy their legal obligation. The paying spouse may deduct these payments, and the receiving spouse must declare them as income if they are "periodic" (payable over a definite period—usually more than 10 years). It may be altered as circumstances change. If a spouse fails to pay, the court may issue a contempt citation, punishable by fines and/or jail time. Keep in mind, under equal protection, either spouse may owe the obligation, depending on financial factors.

Annulment Serves to dissolve the marriage from the very beginning, as if there were no marriage; a divorce simply dissolves the marriage at the end.

Arbitration Parties meet with the arbitrator (person acting as a judge) and perform a "mini-trial" and subsequently, the judge issues an opinion or ruling in favor of one party after hearing the evidence. The decision may be binding or non-binding on the parties, depending on whether the parties agreed to it or whether the judge in the case ordered it. *Arbitration differs greatly from mediation.*

Child support   A separate award may be granted for the financial support of the children of the marriage, with or without an award of alimony. It may be altered as circumstances change. If a spouse fails to pay, the court may issue a contempt citation, punishable by fines and/or jail time until the arrears (past due amounts) are paid.

COBRA   Allows you to continue your insurance coverage up to six months after you leave your employment.

Community property   A method of division of marital property, followed by about eight Western states. Basically, property accumulated by a spouse prior to or following a marriage belongs solely to that spouse. Property accumulated by the spouses during a marriage are to be evenly split upon dissolution of the marriage. *Contrast this with most states that follow the rule of Equitable Division, where property accumulated during the marriage is to be divided on principles of equity, or fairness, i.e., contribution (%) to the marriage, ability to independently generate income after the marriage, adultery, or abandonment, etc.*

Credit   The measure of trustworthiness of repayment, based on income, past credit history, assets and liabilities. Your credit record may be affected by your spouse's past credit history too.

Custodial parent   The parent who has physical custody of the child(ren). In other words, the children will reside primarily with this particular parent. *A distinction should be made between a legal guardian (who has the ability to make legal decisions on behalf of the child) and the custodial parent: Technically, a legal guardian may have no custody rights at all.*

Custody The care, control, or direct supervision of the child. The court awards custody to one parent (*sole custody*) or grants *joint custody,* allowing both parents the right to physical care, control, or direct physical supervision of the children.

Debt Services, money, or goods owed by one party to another.

Decree Nisi/Rule Nisi An order by the court stating that a conditional divorce will become absolute by a certain date, unless a party contends it.

Defendant One against whom a complaint is made. Defendant must answer the complaint within a certain time specified by law and must make any counterclaims at that time or risk losing those claims.

Deposition Testimony taken by a party or witness in a legal setting, though usually out of court, where a person takes an oath and relates testimony in response to questions posed by a party's attorney.

Direct examination The process by which a person is questioned under oath by the attorney of the party on whose behalf the person is testifying.

Discovery 1) A process by which parties learn of each other's evidence. Parties may ask for admissions, ask questions (*interrogatories*), and request documents/evidence; the opponent must respond within a period of time, set by statute, or face sanctions: having the answer admitted, having evidence suppressed by the court, and/or fines. 2) The period of time in which this is done.

Discrimination Refers to unfair treatment on the basis of race, creed, color, religion, or sex.

Dismissal Occurs when a party voluntarily drops the case (in some states) or when a judge finds that a case totally lacks merit.

Divorce The legal proceeding by which a marriage is legally terminated. It may be contested (where one party denied the allegation and/or wants to keep the marriage in place) or uncontested.

Domestic violence The physical abuse of one family member by another.

Emancipation The age at which a child is no longer considered under a parent's support; child support payments stop, for instance, when a child turns 18 or 21, depending on the state.

Equitable distribution The act of dividing property among the parties in a fair and equal way.

File/filing Every case brought to court must be filed with the court clerk in order for the court to take action upon the case. A case is filed when a party (plaintiff) writes a written complaint and brings it to the clerk, who files it. The plaintiff must also serve the opposing party with a copy of the complaint. Filing is important because it usually tolls the statute of limitations, or the time limit in which you must bring your case or have it dismissed because too much time has passed.

Foundation In order for a piece of evidence to be admitted and considered, a proper foundation must be laid; the attorney must elicit the facts upon which the report, diagram, or piece of evidence was made, by whom, when, and under what circumstances so that it accurately and fairly represents what the maker remembers. If a piece of evidence lacks foundation it will not be admitted or considered as evidence.

Garnishing The act by which support money is obtained from the non-paying spouse's employer; the non-paying spouse's employer then draws that amount from his or her paycheck.

Grounds   The legal reasons for the divorce.

Hearing   The opportunity for a party's motion to be heard. Often, the parties must request oral argument, or else the judge will decide a motion on the parties' written submissions.

Immunity   The protection afforded to certain individuals according to their status (i.e., diplomats) preventing their prosecution.

Incompatibility   The inability of persons to get along; a ground for divorce.

Joint custody   *See* Custody.

Judgment   The court renders an award or judgment to one party on the merits of a motion or case. It allows the winner of the judgment to satisfy its terms, as the judge has ordered, to be executed by the sheriff directly, or to be followed by the loser of the judgment under penalty of contempt.

Lis pendens   A piece of property cannot be transferred during a pending lawsuit that may change the disposition of it, once a notice has been filed in the public record.

Litigation   The process by which a civil case settles parties' rights.

Malpractice   The improper or immoral conduct on the part of a professional done by intentionally or carelessly ignoring a party's best interest. Generally, a malpractice action is hard to win because the plaintiff also has to prove that the outcome of their case would have been more favorable.

Mediation   The process by which the parties try to settle their differences with the assistance of a mediator who facilitates communication between them, but does not issue a judgment or opinion. *Arbitration differs greatly from mediation.*

Mitigation Circumstances where a party who has lost an argument and faces a penalty can try to have the penalty reduced by factors showing the court reasons why the penalty should be lighter (i.e., good moral character, community work, etc.).

Motion A request by a party for the court to rule in its favor on a particular issue for a particular reason or set of reasons, supported by fact and law.

No contest/nolo contendere When a defendant in a criminal case neither admits guilt nor claims innocence, but instead refuses to fight. It must be entered voluntarily and intelligently and then accepted by the court.

No-fault A divorce which is granted without regard to the fault of one party, i.e., a period of time of separation has passed.

Notary A person approved by the state to verify the person's identity who signs a legal document; a notary impresses the document with a stamp and signature indicating that the signature is authentic; usually for a small fee.

Order A decision made by the judge, giving direction or forbidding actions.

Paralegal A legal assistant to an attorney, usually certified by the state, who is trained in legal research.

Perjury The act of lying while under oath.

Petition A formal written request for the court to take action, usually referred to in an equity (fairness, not money damage) proceeding.

Plaintiff One who brings a lawsuit by filing a complaint.

Plea bargain When the defendant and the prosecution negotiate a plea of guilty in exchange for a reduced sentence to be recommended to the judge, which may or may not be followed.

Pleadings The documents used in the lawsuit to establish the parties' positions (i.e., the plaintiff's complaint, the defendant's answer).

Precedent Decisions found in other pre-existing cases which factor into the case at hand.

Prenuptial agreement Prior to a marriage, partners contractually agree how assets and liabilities will be divided in the event of divorce. Prenuptial agreements are usually upheld, absent fraud, coercion duress, or severe misrepresentation.

Pretrial motion *See* Motion.

Primary caretaker A factor in consideration of who should be the custodial parent; the person who usually takes care of the children.

Pro se When a person appears without an attorney and is not represented by an attorney.

Reconciliation When parties decide to get back together. They may sign a reconciliation agreement, which is enforceable by the court.

Restraining order An order by the court requiring a person to stay away from another person by a certain distance, or from a certain place, for a certain time. Temporary restraining orders usually last 10 days until such time as a full hearing for a restraining order can take place.

Retainer The amount of money an attorney requires to be paid up front for services rendered. The money is put into an escrow account, and amounts are deducted as decided by the client and attorney.

Separation A legal separation is granted by the court granting the parties a partial divorce: They must live apart, but the marriage is not dissolved until the divorce is granted.

Separation agreement An agreement by spouses who want to divorce, which discusses how property will be divided, how children will be supported, and the amount of alimony to be paid. It is a legally enforceable agreement that is not generally subject to modification, with a few exceptions. Because child support payments are not deductible by the payer and periodic alimony payments are, the separation agreement may impact the tax consequences of the parties.

Sole custody   *See* Custody.

Standard of living   A factor when settling alimony, allowing the recipient an adequate amount to maintain their current lifestyle.

Standing mute   When a criminal defendant refuses to plead guilty, not guilty, or nolo contendere. Usually held to be a not-guilty plea.

Statutory guidelines   Legislation setting minimum and maximum sentences and/or fines as a guide for the judge and jury.

Transcripts   The written record of the divorce proceedings, testimony, or depositions.

Uncontested divorce   *See* Divorce.

Visitation   A court will grant this right to see the children, usually limited in time, place, and manner. Increasingly, states are granting this right to grandparents and close relatives.

Warrant   An order compelling the proper authority to do a certain act, most commonly for the arrest of a person.

Resource Guide

Associations

American Association of Law Libraries:
www.aallnet.org

American Civil Liberties Union: www.aclu.org

Association of Trial Lawyers of America:
www.atlanet.org

National Association of Legal Assistants:
www.nala.org

National Federation of Paralegals Association:
www.paralegals.org

National Organization for Women: www.now.org

Small Business Association: www.sba.gov

Career

Bureau of Labor statistics, Department of Labor:
http://stats.bls.gov

Charts on average earnings for various careers, job outlooks, job descriptions, and relocation resources.

Child custody

ACJ net: www.acjnet.ord/docs/custody.html
Child custody information and frequently asked questions.
DivorceNet: www.divorcenet.com
Child custody information.
Divorce Source: www.divorcesource.com
Child custody information.

Credit

Equifax: www.equifax.com
Provides you with a copy of your credit report ($8).
Get Smart: www.getsmart.com
List of credit card rates.

Divorce web sites

Divorce Care: www.divorcecare.com/HOME.html
Provides information and support-group locators.
Divorce Central: www.divorcecentral.com
Provides a wealth of information and online support.
Divorce Home Page: www.hughson.com
Provides information on divorce topics.
Divorce Helpline: www.divorcehelp.com/index.html
Provides information on divorce topics, plus readings on family law and worksheets.
DivorceNet: www.divorcenet.com
Provides articles and information on the main topics of divorce, plus a highly useful state-by-state resource guide, chat rooms, and family law resources.
Divorce Online: www.divorce_online.com
Provides articles and information on legal, financial, and emotional aspects of divorce, as well as a professional referral service.

Divorce Services Online: www.dsol.com
Provides information on divorce topics.
Divorce Source: www.divorcesource.com/
wwboard/bulletin.html
Provides information and forums on all divorce
subjects.

Financial

Brokers

Discover Brokerage: www.discoverbrokerage.com
DLJ Direct: www.dljdirect
e.Schwab: www.eschwab
E*Trade: www.etrade.com
National Discount Brokers: www.ndb.com
Quick & Reilly: www.quick-reilly.com
Wall Street Exlectronica: www.wallstreet.com
Waterhouse: www.waterhouse.com
Web Street Securities: www.webstreetsecurities.com

Financial Planning

Deloitte and Touche: www.dtonline.com
Financial and retirement advice.
FinancCenter/SmartCalc: www.financenter.com
Retirement advice.
Intuit: www.intuit.com
Examples of financial planning software.

Investment companies

Alliance Capital: www.alliancecapital.com
American Express Financial Advisors:
www.americanexpress.com/advisors
Charles Schwab & Co., Inc.: www.schwab.com
Dreyfus Service Corporation: www.dreyfus.com
E*Trade Securities, Inc.: www.etrade.com
Fidelity Investments: www.fidelity.com
INVESCO Funds Group, Inc: www.invesco.com

Merrill Lynch: www.plan.ml.com/zine/tax/
National Discount Brokers: www.ndb.com
OppenheimerFunds, Inc.: www.oppenheimer-funds.com
The Principal Financial Group: www.principal.com
Scudder No-Load Funds: funds.scudder.com
Stein Roe Mutual Funds: www.steinroe.com
T. Rowe Price: www.troweprice.com
The Vanguard Group: www.vanguard.com

Investment sites
IBC Financial Data: www.ibcdata.com
ICI Mutual Fund Connection: www.ici.org
Invest-o-rama: www.investorama.com
Microsoft Investor: www.investor.msn.com
Morningstar, Inc.: www.morningstar.net
The Motley Fool: www.motleyfool.com
Mutual Funds Interactive: www.fundsinteractive.com
Nest Egg: www.nestegg.com
Net Results: www.isnetwork.com
PC Financial Network: www.pcfn.com
PR Newswire: www.prnewswire.com
The Street.com: www.thestreet.com
The Vault: www.scott-burns.com

Mortgages
Bank Rate Monitor: www.bankrate.com

Health issues
American Dietetic Association: www.eatright.org
Food and nutrition information.
American Heart Association: www.amhrt.org
Heart health care, breakdowns of heart attack and
stroke risk, and stress information.

Articles
American Housecall Network: www.housecall.com
Encyclopedia of health information.

Centers for Disease Control and Prevention:
www.cdc.gov
Info on health issues and sexually transmitted diseases.

CNN Health site: www.cnn.com/HEALTH
CNN's health articles.

Food and Drug Administration: www.fda.gov
Health, food, and vitamins.

Holistic: www.holistic.com/essays/index.html
Information on holistic practices.

Mind Tools: www.mindtools.com
Information on stress release, meditation, and resources to create a stress diary.

Pritikin Longevity Center: www.pritikin.com
Expert answers to your health questions and nutrition information.

Stress Free: www.stressfree.com
Therapist referrals, stress tests, and infomation on beating stress.

Stress Less:
www.stress-less.com/Products/SRskills/
SRskills.html
Video, audio, and other items for stress reduction.

Stress Release: www.stressrelease.com/index.html
Anxiety management program.

Women's Wire Body Channel:
www.women.com/body
Stress release tips and analysis of your eating habits.

Yoga Class: www.yogaclass.com
Introduction to basic yoga methods.

Insurance

Insurance Corner: www.insurance-corner.com
Prudential Insurance: www.prudential.com
State Farm Insurance Companies:
www.statefarm.com

Legal web sites

American Bar Association: www.aba.net
Legal information, resources, and additional web sites.

Cornell University Law Department:
www.law.cornell.edu
Legal information and resources.

Family World: www.family.com
Legal information and family law issues.

Federal Bar Association: www.fedbar.org
Legal information and referrals.

Internet Lawyer: www.internetlawyer.com
Legal information and resources.

Law Info Legal Links: www.lawinfo.com
Legal information and related web sites.

Martindale Hubbell Lawyer Locator: lawyers.
martidale.com
Legal resources and references and lawyer locator.

U.S. Department of Justice: justice2.usdoj.gov
Department of Justice legal information, explanations, and web sites.

U.S. House of Representatives Law Library:
law.house.gov
Legal information and state law library.

Men's issues

Men's Defense Association: www.mensdefense.org
Men's Rights Agency: www.ecn.net.au
National Organization for Men: www.tnom.com

State bar associations

Alaska: www.alaska.net
Arkansas: www.arkbar.com
California: www.calbar.org
Canadian: www.algonquinc.on.ca

Colorado: www.usa.net
District of Columbia: www.dcbar.org
Florida: www.pwr.com
Georgia: www.kuesterlaw.com
Illinois: www.illinoisbar.org
Indiana: www.iquest.net
Kansas: www.ink.org
Maryland: www.msba.org
Michigan: www.sbmnet.org
Missouri: www.mobar.org
Nebraska: www.nol.org
New Hampshire: www.nh.com
New Jersey: www.njsba.com
New York: www.nysba.com
North Carolina: www.barlinc.org
Pennsylvania: www.pbi.com
South Carolina: www.scbar.org
Tennessee: www.tba.org
Utah: www.utahbar.org
Washington: www.wsba.org
Wisconsin: www.wisbar.org

Taxes
Internal Revenue Service: www.irs.ustreas.gov

Women's issues
National Organization for Women: www.now.org

Recommended Reading List

Child custody

Child Custody: Building Agreements That Work, by Mimi E. Lyster. Nolo Press, 1996.

My Kids Don't Live With Me Anymore: Coping With The Custody Crisis, by Doreen Virtue. Compcare, 1988.

Sharing the Children: How to Resolve Custody Problems and Get On With Your Life, by Robert E. Adler. Adler & Adler Publishing, 1988.

Children

Adolescents After Divorce, by Christy M. Buchana, Eleanor E. MacCoby, and Sanford M. Dornbusch. Harvard University Press, 1996.

At Daddy's on Saturdays, by Linda Walvoord Girard and Judith Friedman. Albert Whitman and Co., 1991.

The Boys and Girls Book About Divorce, with an Introduction for Parents, by Richard A. Gardner. Bantam Books, 1992.

Caught in the Middle: Protecting the Children of High-Conflict Divorce, by Carla B. Garrity and Mitchell A. Barris. Jossey-Bass Publishers, 1997.

Daddy Day, Daughter Day, by Larry and Chaia King. Dove Kids.

Difficult Questions Kids Ask and Are Too Afraid to Ask About Divorce, by Meg F. Schneider, Joan Zuckerberg, and Joan Offerman-Zuckerberg. Fireside, 1996.

The Dinousaurs Divorce, by Laurene and Mark Brown. Little, Brown and Co.

Divorce is Not the End of the World, by Zoe, Evan, and Ellen Sue Stern. Tricycle Press.

The Divorce Workbook: A Guide for Kids and Families, by Sally B. Ives. Talman Company.

The Divorce Workbook: A Guide for Kids and Their Families, by S. B. Ives and M. Lash. Waterfront Books, 1985.

D-I-V-O-R-C-E-S Spell Discover: A Kit to Help Children Express Their Feelings About Divorce, by Bonnie Crown. Courageous Kids, 1992.

Growing Up Divorced: How to Help Your Children Cope with Every Stage From Infancy Through Teens, by Linda Bird Francke. Fawcette Crest, 1983.

Helping Children Cope with Divorce, by Edward Teyber. Lexington Books, 1992.

Helping Your Child Succeed After Divorce, by Florence Bienenfield. Hunterhouse, 1987.

How It Feels When Parents Divorce, by Jill Krementz. Knopf.

My Parents Still Love Me Even Though They're Getting Divorced, by Lois V. Nightengale, Nightengale Rose Publications.

Why Are We Getting a Divorce?, by Peter Mayle. Crown.

Child support

Child Support Survival Guide: How to Get Results Through Child Support Enforcement Agencies, by Bonnie M. White and Douglas Pipe. Career Press, 1997.

How to Collect Child Support, by Geraldine Jensen and K. Jones. Longmeadow Press, 1991.

Coping with divorce

The Best is Yet to Come, by Ivana Trump. Pocket Books, 1995.

Coming Apart: Why Relationships End and How to Live Through the Ending of Yours, by Daphne Rose Kingman. Fawcette Ballantine, 1987.

Divorce Hangover: A Step-by-Step Prescription for Creating a Bright Future After Your Marriage Ends, by Anne N. Walther. Pocket Books, 1991.

How to Forgive Your Ex-Husband and Get On With Your Life, by Marcia Hootman and Patt Perkins. Warner, 1985.

How to Survive the Loss of a Love, by M. Colgrove, W. Bloomfield and P. McWilliams. St. Martin's Press, 1988.

Life After Divorce: Create a New Beginning, by Sharon Wegscheider-Cruse. Health Communications Inc., 1994.

The Newly Divorced Book of Protocol: How to be Civil When You Hate Their Guts, by Gloria Lintermans. Barricade Books.

Post-Divorce Reconstruction, by Christine Smith. PDR Publications.

Rebuilding When Your Relationship Ends, by Dr. Bruce Fisher. Impact Publishers.

Financial

Bankruptcy and Divorce: Support and Property Division (Family Law Library), by Judith K. Fitzgerald and Ramona M. Arena. Wiley Law Publications, 1994.

The Dollars and Sense of Divorce: Take Control of Your Financial Life Before, During and After Divorce, by Judith Briles. Ballantine, 1991.

Financial Fitness Through Divorce, by Elizabeth S. Lewin. Facts on Files, 1988.

The Financial Guide to Divorce, by Frances Johansen. United Resources Press, 1991.

The Handbook of Financial Planning for Divorce and Separation, by D. Larry Crumbley and Nicholas G. Apostolou. John Wiley and Sons, 1990.

Health

Survival Manual for Men In Divorce, by Edwin Schilling and Carol Ann Wilson. Quantum Press, 1992.

The Ultimate Stress Handbook for Women, by Ursula Markham. Element Books.

Thriving: The Complete Mind/Body Guide for Optimal Health and Fitness for Men, by Dr. Robert Ivker and Edward Zorensky. Crown.

Transforming Pain into Power: Making the Most of Your Emotions, by Dor. Leving, MD. Basic Books/HarperCollins.

Law

Family Law Dictionary, by Robin Leonard and Steve Elias. Nolo Press, 1990.

Mediation

Choosing a Divorce Mediator: A Guide to Help Divorcing Couples Find a Competent Mediator, by Diane Neumann. Owlet, 1997.

Divorce Mediation: How to Cut the Cost and Stress of Divorce, by Diane Neumann. Henry Holt, 1989.

Men

Divorced Fathers: Coping with Problems, Creating Solutions, by Gerald Hill. Betterway Publications, 1989.

Parenting

The Divorced Parent: Success Strageies for Raising Your Children After Separation. William Morrow, 1994.

Divorcing Book for Parents, by Vicki Lansky. New American Library, 1989.

Growing Up with Divorce: Helping your Child Avoid Immediate and Later Problems. Free Press, 1990.

Healing Hearts: Helping Children and Adults Recover From Divorce, by Elizabeth Hickey and Elizabeth Dalton. Gold Leaf Press.

Helping Your Children Cope with Divorce and Its Aftermath, by Vicki Lansky. Signet.

Joint Custody and Shared Parenting: Sharing your Child Equally, by Mirium Galper. Running Press, 1990.

Long Distance Parenting: A Guide for Divorced Parents, by Mirum Galper Cohen. Signet, 1989.

On Our Own: A Single Parent's Survival Guide, by John Defrain, Judy Fricke, and Julie Elmen. D.C. Heath, 1987.

Putting Kids First: Walking Away From a Marriage Without Walking Over the Kids, by Michael Oddenino. Family Connections Publishing.

Personal growth

The Adult Years: Mastering the Art of Self-Renewal, by Frederic Hudson. Jossey-Bass, 1991.

Everyday Soul: Awakening the Spirit in Daily Life, by Bradford Keeney. Riverhead, 1996.

Finding the Hat That Fits: How to Turn Your Heart's Desire into Your Life's Work, by John Caple. Dutton, 1993.

How to Find Your Mission in Life, by Richard Bolles. Ten Speed Press, 1991.

Life Skills, by Richard Leider. Pfeiffer and Company, 1994.

A Passionate Guide to the Rest of Your Life, by Frederic Hudson and Pamela McLean. The Hudson Institute Press, 1995.

What Color is Your Parachute?, by Richard Bolles. Ten Speed Press, 1997.

Wherever You Go, There You Are: Mindful Meditations in Everyday Life, by Jon Kabat-Zinn. Hyperion, 1994.

Your Money or Your Life: Transforming Your Relationship with Money to Achieving Financial Independence, by Vickie Robin and Joe Dominguez. Viking, 1992.

Religious

Catholics Experiencing Divorce: Grieving, Healing and Learning to Live Again, by William E. Rabior. Liguori Publications, 1991.

Dear God, I'm Divorced!: Dialogues with God, by Sara Thrash. Baker Book House, 1991.

Divorce and Remarriage in the Catholic Church, by Gerald D. Coleman. Paulist Press, 1988.

Remarriage

And Marries Another: Divorce and Remarriage in the Teaching of the New Testament, by Craig S. Keener. Hedrickson Publishers, Inc, 1993.

Single life

Are You the One for Me?: Knowing Who's Right and Avoiding Who's Wrong, by Barbara DeAngelis. Dell Publishing.

Keeping the Love You Find: A Personal Guide, by
    Harville Hendrix, PhD. Harper Perennial.
The Single Again Handbook, by Thomas F. Jones.
    Oliver Nelson Books, 1993.
*Suddenly Single: A Lifeline for Anyone Who Has Lost a
    Love,* by Hal Larson and Susan Larson. Halo
    Books, 1990.

Stepparenting

*Cinderella Revisited: How to Survive Your Stepfamily
    Without a Fairy Godmother,* by Dr. Peter Marshall.
    Whitecap Books.
The Good Step-Mother: A Practical Guide, by Karen
    Savage and Patricia Adams. Crown, 1988.
How to Win as a Stepfamily, by Emily and John
    Vishner. Dembner Books, 1982.
Making it as a Step-Parent: New Roles, New Rules, by
    Clare Berman. Harper and Row, 1986.
Step-father's Advice on Creating a New Family, by Mark
    B. Rosin. Ballantine, 1987.
*Yours, Mine, and Ours: How Families Change When
    Remarried Parents Have a Child Together,* by Anne
    C. Berstein. Norton, 1989.

Women

Divorce: A Woman's Guide to Getting a Fair Share, by
    Patricia Phillips and George Mair.
*The Dollars and Cents of Divorce: The Financial Guide
    for Women,* by Judith Briles. Master Media, 1988.
*Cutting Loose: Why Women Who End Their Marriages Do
    So Well,* by Ashton Applewhite. HarperCollins,
    1997.
*Money Smart Divorce: What Women Need to Know About
    Money and Divorce,* by Esther Berger, CFP. Simon
    & Schuster.

Sharing the Children: How to Resolve Custody Problems and Get On With Your Life, by Robert E. Adler.

The Survival Manual for Women in Divorce, by Carol Ann Wilson and Edwin Schilling III, Esq. Quantum Press, 1990.

A Woman's Guide to Divorce and Decision Making: A Supportive Workbook for Women Facing the Process of Divorce, by Christina Robertson. Fireside/Simon & Schuster, 1989.

Important Documents

Preparing to see your attorney

Before your first meeting with your attorney, collect the following information for full disclosure of the conditions of your marriage and divorce:

PERSONAL DATA

_____ Your full name
_____ Your spouse's full name
_____ The date of your wedding
_____ The location of your wedding
_____ Your birth date
_____ Your spouse's birthdate
_____ Your religion
_____ Your spouse's religion
_____ Your address and phone number
_____ Your spouse's address and phone number
_____ Your personal health profile
_____ Your spouse's personal health profile
_____ Information on any prior marriages (you or your spouse)
_____ Whether or not you plan to keep or change your married name
_____ Your plans to relocate

MARITAL CONDITIONS

_____ Length of the marriage

_____ Length of any separations between you and your spouse

_____ Details of your discussions about separation or divorce

_____ Length of any marital counseling attempted

_____ Previous filings for divorce between you and your spouse

_____ Your spouse's contributions to the end of the marriage

_____ Your own contributions to the end of the marriage

_____ Any infidelities on your spouse's part

_____ Any infidelities on your part

_____ Details of any spousal abuse

_____ Details of any restraining orders or physical protection needed

_____ The grounds for your divorce (i.e., extreme cruelty, non-communication, abuse, etc.)

FINANCIAL STANDING AND PERSONAL ASSETS

_____ Your occupation

_____ Your spouse's occupation

_____ Any future job changes for either of you

_____ Your income (take-home pay plus income from any other source)

_____ Your spouse's income (take-home pay plus income from any other source)

_____ Any changes expected in income for either of you (raises, promotions, better-paying job, etc.)

_____ Income-tax return history (filing jointly, etc.)

_____ Current value of your home

_____ List of your personal and jointly owned personal belongings, with current values of each item

_____ Amounts of money in your personal and joint financial accounts

_____ Amounts of money in stocks and bonds

_____ Current value and details of your insurance policies

_____ Current value and details of your spouse's insurance policies

_____ Current debts held by you

_____ Current debts held by your spouse

_____ Expected inheritances or large financial gifts

_____ Any alimony you receive from or pay to a former spouse

_____ Your expected household budget

_____ Your "wish list" for division of property

_____ Your financial support needs

DATA ON CHILDREN

_____ The names of your children

_____ Your children's birthdates

_____ Whether or not you (or your wife) are pregnant at the time

_____ Addresses of the children, if not living with you

_____ The name of the legal guardian

_____ The names of any person or persons who might claim legal custody of the children (grandparents, etc.)

_____ Children's special needs or disabilities

_____ Children's health conditions

_____ Children's school year and grade average

_____ Current visitation schedule of the children by your ex

_____ Any knowledge of abuse of the children by your ex

_____ Any conditions specific to the children's well-being while in your ex's custody

Discovery preparations

The following is a list of the items you should seek out through the discovery portion of your divorce process.

_____ Personal checking account statements

_____ Joint checking account statements

_____ Children's savings account statements

_____ Business checking account statements

_____ Business savings account statements
_____ Partnership statements
_____ Personal loan statements
_____ Educational loan statements
_____ Loans from family members
_____ Personal credit card account statements
_____ Joint credit card account statements
_____ Business income tax returns
_____ Joint income tax returns
_____ Canceled checks from personal checking account
_____ Canceled checks from joint checking account
_____ Canceled checks from business checking account
_____ Canceled checks from children's checking account
_____ Investment statements: IRAs, mutual funds, money market funds, etc.
_____ Stock certificates
_____ Bond certificates
_____ Expense account statements
_____ Frequent flier mile statements
_____ Statements of bonuses, commissions, deferred salary increases
_____ List of safe-deposit box activity/sign-in sheet
_____ List of contents of safe-deposit box
_____ Phone bill statements
_____ Business phone bill statements
_____ Cell phone bill statements
_____ Journals or diaries
_____ Written record of spouse's personal or financial behavior
_____ Medical records
_____ Photographs or surveillance evidence

Deposition preparations

During the deposition phase of your divorce, you or your spouse may be asked any of the following questions:

Grounds for divorce

1. What were your spouse's specific actions that caused you to file for mental cruelty?

2. Did your spouse call you names?

3. Did your spouse belittle you in front of other people?

4. What are the names of those people who witnessed this behavior?

5. Did your spouse restrict your personal freedoms? In what ways?

6. Did your spouse intimidate you in order to exert control over your actions? In what ways?

7. Did your spouse sabotage any of your personal achievements? In what ways?

8. Did you hit your spouse on January 12, 1991?

9. Did you use a closed fist or an open hand when you struck your spouse?

10. Did that physical contact leave any bruises on your spouse?

11. Did anyone witness this event?

12. What are those people's names?

13. What was your spouse's reaction to this event?

14. What actions were taken after this event?

15. Have there been any other incidents in which you also struck your spouse?

16. Name the dates and circumstances.

17. Did anyone witness these events?

18. What are those witnesses' names?

19. Has your spouse filed a restraining order on you?

20. Have you adhered to the restraining order?

21. Do you drive a blue Toyota Camry?

22. Is the license plate number XXXX?

23. Did you own this car in 1991?

24. Did you ever park this car in the overnight garage connected to the Lincoln Towers apartment complex?

25. Do you reside at the Lincoln Towers apartment complex?

26. For what reasons did you park your blue Toyota Camry, license plate number XXXX in that overnight garage connected to the Lincoln Towers apartment complex?

27. Did you ever spend the night at any apartment in the Lincoln Towers apartment complex?

28. What apartment number?

29. Who resides in that apartment?

30. Did anyone else witness your presence at that apartment?

31. What are the names of those people?

32. Is your home telephone number 555-0810?

33. Is this a copy of your home telephone bill?

34. You see highlighted on this bill 20 calls made to the number 555-0704, correct?

35. Did you make those telephone calls to that number?

36. Whose number is that?

37. What was the nature of those telephone calls?

38. For what purpose would you make a business call at 3am on a Saturday night?

39. Was there a business crisis at 3am on the night of the 17th on January?

40. Does your company have any record of the business crisis occurring on that date?

Financial information and assets

1. What is your current occupation?

2. What is your place of employment?

3. How long have you been employed there?

4. What is your current income?

5. Has your current income increased or decreased since the start of your divorce proceedings?

6. Why has your income decreased so substantially since the start of your divorce proceedings?

7. Do you receive any bonuses or commissions from your work?

8. What other sources of income do you have?

9. What are the details of your employee benefit package?

10. Is your spouse currently covered under your employee benefit plan?

11. Are your children currently covered under your employee benefit plan?

12. What deductions are taken from your paycheck?

13. What exemptions are you taking from your paycheck withholding?

14. Do you have any outstanding personal debts?

15. What are the amounts and details of those debts?

16. Have you claimed bankruptcy in the past year?

17. Have you transferred any of your assets to a third party?

18. Did you withdraw any money from the checking accounts of your children?

19. What did you do with that money?

20. In what ways did your spouse contribute to your business success?

21. Did your spouse help pay for your law school tuition?

22. Did your spouse help you apply to law school?

23. Did your spouse help you study for the bar exam?

24. Did your spouse put off her own education until you received your law degree?

25. Do you and your spouse own a home?

26. What is the current value of the home?

27. What additions have been made to the home?

28. How would you divide up between yourself and your spouse the responsibilities for the maintenance of that home? 50-50? 60-40? 80-20?

29. Do you own a vacation home in Florida?

30. What is the current value of that home?

Support

1. What was your pre-separation average household monthly income?

2. What were your fixed household monthly expenses?

3. What is your spouse's monthly income?

4. What are the precise figures of your children's monthly expenses?

5. Can your spouse meet the household monthly expenses in your absence?

Custody

1. Who spends more hours a day with the children?

2. Did your spouse stay home with the children as they were growing up, rather than take a job?

3. What is the average daily routine of the parent who stays home with the children?

4. Who cooks for the children?

5. Who bathes the children?

6. Who does the majority of the diaper changes?

7. Who attends the children's school events?

8. Who attends parent-teacher conferences?

9. Who takes the children to the doctor?

10. Who disciplines the children?

11. Describe your disciplinary measures?

12. Did you hit your daughter on the evening of April 14, 1997?

13. What were the circumstances of that event?

14. Did you leave any bruises on your daughter?

15. What pat of your daughter's body did you hit?

16. Did you encourage your daughter to lie to her teacher about the bruises?

17. Did you ever threaten to take your children far away and never let your spouse see them again?

18. On what date did you make this threat?

19. Were there any witnesses to this threat?

20. What are those witnesses' names?

21. Did you ever report your spouse to the police for child abuse?

22. What actions were taken after that event?

23. What is your work schedule?

24. Do you often go away on business trips?

25. Who would watch the children while you were out of town?

26. Is there anything that you can provide to the children that your spouse cannot?

27. What emotional trauma has your child undergone during your marriage and separation?

28. Has the child been taken for counseling?

29. Which spouse initiated the counseling for the child?

30. Why didn't you take action to help your child?

31. Does your child have a preference as to which parent he or she would like to live with?

32. Do you have room in your current place or residence for your child to stay?

33. What are the names of your children's friends?

34. What are the names of your children's teachers?

35. What is the name of your child's Little League team?

Flow of events

The following is a sample of the average trial outline and flow of events:

1. Opening statements

2. Introduction of client

3. Basic information on length and circumstances of the marriage

4. Establishment of spouses' income from all sources

5. Presentations and deliberation over list of personal and shared marital assets

6. Discussion of equitable division, community, or marital property

7. Discussion of values of assets

8. Decision on distribution

9. Deliberation over support

10. Discussion of intact family's standard of living

11. Discussion of family budget and expenses

12. Disclosure of future financial needs

13. Disclosure of other spouse's spending habits

14. Disclosure of expenses and financial needs related to children

15. Deliberation over child custody

16. Disclosure of children's personal data

17. Discussion of children's mental health, school activities, and physical health

18. Discussion about child's former home

19. Discussion about child's future living situation

20. Discussion about each parent's strengths and weaknesses as potential custodial parent

21. Discussion of any past parenting incidents

22. Discussion of any problems in the home

23. Discussion of spouse's past parenting performance

24. Discussion of any new elements that factor in to the child's environment (father lives with new girlfriend, etc.)

25. Expert witnesses' testimony

26. Other witnesses' testimony

27. Additional unique circumstances or issues

Lawyer's tips on advantageous court performance

1. Dress professionally. Don't be afraid to check with your lawyer on wardrobe choice. You want to give off an image of being a stable, professional person who respects the court by dressing appropriately.

2. Show up on time.

3. Do not exhibit anger or vindictiveness toward your ex.

4. Do not exhibit anger or vindictiveness toward your ex's lawyer.

5. Keep your temper in check.

6. Do not make obvious dramatic facial expressions while anyone is speaking in court.

7. Answer questions succinctly. Going into great detail, with too much flourish, provides too much information, and makes you come off as dishonest.

8. Answer questions with an air of helpfulness and innocence, not defensiveness.

9. Do not put out a "poor me" impression.

10. Do not kiss up to the judge.

11. Do not be overly nervous. You need to think clearly to answer questions correctly.

12. Do not memorize answers. Judges can tell if you've been "prepared" by your lawyer, so answer naturally.

13. Listen carefully to everything that is said.

14. Whisper any questions into your lawyer's ear or quickly jot them down and slide them to your lawyer.

15. If you do not understand a question, ask to have it clarified.

16. Take a second to think before you answer a question. Your ex's lawyer may attempt to speed things up and fluster you.

17. Speak clearly.

18. Speak confidently.

19. Don't attempt to be funny or charming. Just answer the questions.

20. Keep calm. Your ex's lawyer may up the tension by shouting at you, but you should never allow yourself to lose your composure. Answer calmly, and your ex's lawyer will come back down to a normal volume when he sees he isn't getting to you.

21. Do not cry. Try to keep your emotions in check. The judge will not be as swayed by waterworks as you think he might be. Your emotions will register in your voice, and you may be respected more for remaining strong.

22. Look the lawyer or judge directly in the eye as you answer. This connotes a sense of strength and belief in what you're saying.

23. Be honest, no matter what the question. Your ex's attorney could have evidence that refutes what you're saying, and it's best to be upfront than to come off as a liar on the stand.

24. Create no surprises for your lawyer. You should have fully disclosed all the facts of your case beforehand. Your lawyer cannot perform damage control if you've kept something from him.

25. Use exact words. If your spouse called you every name in the book, tell the court exactly what was said. It comes off as more powerful than "He called me names."

26. Don't answer a question with another question. This comes off as flippant.

27. Respect your ex's attorney as you respect your own. His job during cross-examination is to get you to undermine your own evidence, and that can bring out a tough side in this person. Just speak to him as a person and answer calmly and honestly.

28. Never refuse to answer a question. The judge can find you guilty of contempt, and that doesn't help your case.

29. Watch out for trick questioning. Think very clearly about what you're being asked. You won't get a change to say, "What I meant was . . ."

30. Allow your attorney to control the questioning. If your ex's attorney over-steps his boundaries, your lawyer will object.

Questions to ask your attorney

When hiring

1. Have you handled cases that are similar to mine, dealing with the same issues involved (child custody, spousal support, abuse, etc.)?

2. How many cases have you handled?

3. How many of those cases have gone to trial?

4. Will you be willing to take my case to court if we cannot reach a good settlement?

5. Do you have time right now to take on my case, or do you have any big trials coming up?

6. Will you handle my case personally, or do you hand off to an assistant? What are your assistant's credentials?

7. Can I interview that assistant?

8. What are your hourly rates?

9. Do you charge a retainer?

10. Is the retainer refundable for unused portions?

11. What is your billing schedule?

12. Do you charge for outside help (accountants, secretary, private investigators service, etc.)?

13. What are those fees?

14. Do you charge extra for court time, or is that included in your regular hourly rate?

15. Do you charge for copies of paperwork, or do I get those for free?

16. Will I get regular bills in writing?

17. Will I be billed for phone charges?

18. Do you bill by the full hour or by hour portions (half-hour, quarter-hour)?

19. What extra fees do you charge?

20. What are court costs?

21. What are your office hours?

22. Can you be reached at home? By beeper? By answering service?

23. What laws apply to my case?

24. What is expected of me as far as discovery and attendance at meetings, hearings?

25. Do you know my ex?

26. Do you know my ex's attorney?

27. How much input will I have in the case?

28. Will you contact me regularly regarding the status of my case?

29. What do you foresee as the outcome of my case? What are my chances of winning?

30. How long do you think this type of case will take?

About the settlement

1. Do you feel that the settlement, as it stands now, is fair?

2. What are our chances of getting our changes made in negotiations?

3. Which elements of the settlement are likely to go our way in negotiations?

4. Which elements of their settlement wishes are unfair?

5. What is the other side trying to get us to change?

6. What changes should I make to the settlement to be fair?

7. Would you accept this offer if you were in my shoes?

8. Should we try to negotiate with the other side, or should we take it to trial?

9. How long will the trial take?

10. Would going to trial actually hurt my settlement wishes in the long run? What are the risks?

About the trial

1. What is the general course of the trial going to be?

2. What is involved?

3. Will I be called to testify?

4. Will I be prepared ahead of time for my answers on the stand?

5. Will my spouse have to testify?

6. Will anyone else have to testify on my behalf or against my spouse?

7. What if I get nervous and answer something wrong?

8. Will you be able to help me out while I'm on the stand?

9. What should I say if I'm asked about . . . ?

10. Can I look at any of my notes or evidence while I'm on the stand?

11. Will there be evidence used in my case? Exhibit A, etc.?

12. Will you contact my witnesses and tell them where to go and what to do?

13. Can I talk to my witnesses before the trial?

14. Can I talk to my witnesses during breaks?

15. How can I let you know my questions as the trial is taking place?

16. How should I address the judge?

17. How should I address my ex's attorney?

18. How should I refer to my ex?

19. Can I bring other members of my family to court to watch?

20. Should I bring the children to court during the custody phase of the hearing?

About the final judgment

1. When will the divorce be final?

2. What has to be accomplished before the divorce is final?

3. When will alimony and child support start?

4. When will the visitation schedule begin?

5. How will support and visitation be enforced if my ex does not cooperate with the final judgment?

6. Can my ex appeal the judgment?

7. What documents will I receive for the final judgment?

8. Do I have to have those documents notarized?

9. When will our division of assets take place?

10. Who oversees the division of assets?

11. Can I openly date another person now?

12. What elements will be grounds for changing the final judgment? If I remarry, etc.?

13. When is your balance due?

Questions to ask your therapist

When hiring

1. How much experience do you have working on issues like mine?

2. What kind of session schedule do you have in mind for me? Weekly appointments? Twice-weekly?

3. How do you organize your therapy? Do you employ medicine and psychotherapy, or do you just attempt to solve the problem with medicine?

4. Do you assign "homework"?

5. How accessible are you? Can I contact you via voicemail or cell phone if necessary?

6. What is your billing schedule?

7. What kind of payment do you accept?

8. How long do sessions last?

9. Do you have group therapy options as well?

10. What is your policy on canceled appointments?

11. Do you accept my insurance?

12. Do you belong to any professional associations or boards?

13. Do you offer individual, child, and family counseling as well?

About medications

1. What kind of drug is it? Anti-depressant? Anti-anxiety? A combination of both?

2. What is the name of the drug?

3. How long will it take to kick in and start giving me relief?

4. How long should I wait to call you if I'm not experiencing any relief from my symptoms through this drug?

5. How does the medicine work? (Your doctor should explain to you about the various chemicals in the brain (serotonin, norepinephrine, etc.) and how they work to carry messages through the brain's receptors. Some medicines are clued in to the various chemicals in the brain, and that's how they alleviate your symptoms.

6. What is the exact dosage?

7. How many pills can I take a day?

8. Are there any interactions with medications I'm already on?

9. Are there any interactions with certain foods?

10. Can I drink alcohol while on this medication?

11. Can I take over-the-counter drugs, such as cold medicine, while on this medication?

12. Do I have to take this medication with food?

13. How long can I expect to be on this medication?

14. Is my prescription re-fillable, or is this a one-shot deal?

15. What side effects are common with this drug?

16. What side effects are a sign that something is wrong, and at what point do I report them to you?

17. How should I store this medication?

18. For how long is the medicine good? Does it lose its potency over time?

19. What should I do if I forget to take a dose? Double up? Skip it?

20. Is there a generic, less-expensive form of this medication?

Within therapy

1. Are my feelings normal?

2. How can I raise my self-esteem?

3. What parts did I play in the end of my marriage?

4. Can you help me understand my spouse's point of view?

5. How long will these emotions last?

6. Do you have any recommended reading that I can do for new perspectives?

7. How can I learn to trust again?

8. How can I help my children cope?

9. How can I form a workable relationship with my ex?

10. How can I start to create a new identity for myself?

LEGAL ASSISTANCE CHECKLIST

_____ Get referral from the State Bar Association

_____ Get referrals from people you respect

_____ Call around to prospective lawyers' offices for basic information

_____ Set up preliminary interviews

_____ Disclose basic information about your case

_____ Discuss legal details of the handling of your case

_____ Hire the best candidate

_____ Begin discovery process

_____ Begin filings

_____ Deliberate on alimony

_____ Deliberate on child support

_____ Deliberate on child custody

_____ Deliberate on division of assets

_____ Begin negotiations

_____ Consider the help of expert witnesses

_____ Consider mediation

_____ Consider arbitration

_____ Prepare for the trial

_____ Prepare for the final court hearing

_____ Settle up loose strings

_____ Rewrite wills

_____ Establish credit in own name

_____ Change awarded assets into your own name

FINANCIAL ASSISTANCE CHECKLIST

_____ Freeze assets (credit cards, accounts, etc.)

_____ Determine values of assets

_____ Determine values of debts

_____ Divide debts

_____ Divide investments

_____ Divide pensions

_____ Determine future social security benefits

_____ Transfer assets

_____ Block your spouse's illegal asset transfers

_____ Form new individual accounts

_____ Sell assets for capital

_____ Decide whether or not to sell the house

_____ Form household budget

_____ Form income/expense list

_____ Cut household expenses as much as possible

_____ Get out of debt

_____ Evaluate financial experts

_____ Interview financial experts

_____ Hire a financial expert

_____ Research financial management on your own

_____ Set financial goals

_____ Evaluate investment goals

_____ Research individual investments

_____ Procure investment policies

_____ Evaluate income tax standing

_____ Collect past tax returns

_____ Collect present tax returns

_____ Hire an accountant, or . . .

_____ Prepare to file your own taxes

_____ Call the IRS with your tax questions

_____ File your federal taxes

_____ File your state taxes

_____ Apply for credit in your own name

_____ Get a copy of your credit report

_____ Correct credit report problems

_____ Build good credit

_____ Evaluate bankruptcy pros and cons

_____ Get a bankruptcy lawyer

_____ Evaluate do-it-yourself options

_____ Purchase financial or tax-planning software

_____ Take tax or financial planning seminars or classes

COUNSELING CHECKLIST

_____ Evaluate counselors
_____ Get referrals from professional associations
_____ Get referrals from your local hospital
_____ Get referrals from another doctor you trust
_____ Look into free counseling options
_____ Call individual therapists for details
_____ Conduct preliminary interviews
_____ Hire a counselor
_____ Arrange a payment plan
_____ Arrange session scheduling
_____ Determine what kind of therapy you need
_____ Determine the length of the therapy
_____ Determine whether or not to go on medication
_____ Complete therapist's detailed questionnaires
_____ Outline your biggest issues and questions to be tackled in therapy
_____ Consider group therapy as well
_____ Evaluate counselors for your children
_____ Get referrals from professional associations
_____ Get referrals from your local hospital
_____ Get referrals from another doctor you trust
_____ Look into free counseling options
_____ Call individual therapists for details
_____ Conduct preliminary interviews
_____ Get your child's input on which counselor to hire
_____ Hire a counselor
_____ Arrange a payment plan
_____ Arrange session scheduling
_____ Determine what kind of therapy your child need
_____ Determine the length of the therapy
_____ Determine whether or not your child needs to go on medication
_____ Have child complete therapist's detailed questionnaires

_____ Outline your child's biggest issues and questions to be tackled in therapy

_____ Consider group or tandem therapy for your child as well

DOCUMENT CHECKLIST

_____ Prenuptial agreements

_____ Separation agreements

_____ Alimony agreement

_____ Child support agreement

_____ Visitation schedule

_____ Assets list

_____ Appraisals

_____ Transfer of assets

_____ Illegal transfer block

_____ Motions

_____ Settlement agreement

_____ Final divorce decree

_____ Retainer agreement

_____ Billing agreement

_____ Hiring agreement

_____ Mediator's report

_____ Therapist's report

_____ Expert witness' reports

_____ Restraining order

_____ Criminal charges

_____ Peace bond

_____ Will

_____ Legal guardian statement

_____ Living will

_____ Power of attorney

_____ Medical power of attorney

_____ Trusts

_____ Credit report

_____ Budget

_____ Income/expense summary

_____ Net worth statement

_____ Pension plan

_____ Mortgage
_____ Tax statements
_____ Tax forms
_____ Canceled checks
_____ Receipts
_____ Phone bills
_____ Safe-deposit box activity list
_____ Bank account statements
_____ Stock certificates
_____ Investment certificates
_____ Life insurance policy
_____ Health insurance policy
_____ Homeowner's insurance policy
_____ Disability insurance policy
_____ Auto insurance policy
_____ Medical records
_____ Medical record release forms
_____ Mutual release forms
_____ Social security benefits statement
_____ Change of name documents
_____ Passports
_____ Marriage certificate

Tax forms you may need

Contact the IRS at (800) TAX-FORM for copies of the tax forms you need as a result of your new filing status. Some of the forms you may need are as follows:

W-2 Wage and Tax Statement

Form 1040 U.S. Individual Income Tax Return

Form 1040 A U.S. Individual Income Tax Return

Form 1040 A&B Itemized Deductions and
Interest/Dividends

Form 1040 C Profit or Loss from Business

Form 1040 ES Estimated Tax for Individuals

Form 1040 EZ Income Tax Return for Single and
    Joint Filers

Form 1040 E Supplemental Income and Loss

Form 1040 SE Self Employment Tax

Form 1040 SS U.S. Self Employment Tax Return

Form 1041 Capital Gains and Losses

Form 1098 Mortgage Interest Statement

Form 1099 C Cancellation of Debt

Form 1099 DIV Dividends and Distributions

Form 1099 INT Interest Income

Form 1099 MISC Miscellaneous Income

Form 1099S Proceeds from Real Estate
    Transactions

Form 2119 Sale of Your Home

Form 2350 Application for Extension of Time to
    File U.S. Individual Tax Return

Form 2441 Child and Dependent Care Expenses

Form 2848 Power of Attorney and Declaration of
    Representative

Form 3903 Moving Expenses

Form 4506 Request for Copy or Transaction of
    Tax Form

Form 4562 Depreciation and Amortization

Form 4972 Tax on Lump Sum Distributions

Form 5500 A Insurance Information

Form 6118 Claim of Income Tax Preparers

Form 8283 Noncash Charitable Donations

Form 8332 Release of Claim to Exemption for
    Child of Divorced Parents

Form 8396 Mortgage Interest Credit

Form 8822 Change of Address

Form 8829 Expenses for Business Use of Your
Home

Form 9452 Filing Assistance Program

Form 9465 Installment Agreement Requests

Important Statistics

NATIONAL DIVORCE STATISTICS, 1994

Rank	State	Number	Rate per 1,000 Population
1 (lowest)	Massachusetts	14,530	2.4
2	Connecticut	9,095	2.8
3	New Jersey	23,889	3.0
4	Rhode Island	3,231	3.2
5	New York	59,195	3.3
	Pennsylvania	40,040	3.3
7	Wisconsin	17,478	3.4
	North Dakota	2,201	3.4
9	Maryland	17,439	3.5
10	Minnesota	16,217	3.6
	Louisiana	***	3.6
12	Illinois	43,498	3.7
13	District of Columbia	2,244	3.9
	Iowa	10,930	3.9
15	Nebraska	6,547	4.0
	Vermont	2,316	4.0
17	Michigan	38,727	4.1
18	South Dakota	3,022	4.2

continues

Rank	State	Number	Rate per 1,000 Population
	South Carolina	15,301	4.2
	Hawaii	4,979	4.2
21	California	***	4.3
22	Maine	5,433	4.4
	New Hampshire	5,041	4.4
24	Ohio	49,968	4.5
25	Virginia	30,016	4.6
26	Kansas	12,093	4.7
	Utah	8,999	4.7
28	Delaware	3,385	4.8
29	Montana	4,153	4.9
30	Missouri	26,324	5.0
	West Virginia	9,179	5.0
32	North Carolina	36,292	5.1
	Colorado	18,795	5.1
34	Georgia	37,001	5.2
35	Oregon	16,307	5.3
36	Texas	99,073	5.4
37	Alaska	3,354	5.5
38	Washington	29,976	5.6
39	Mississippi	15,212	5.7
40	Kentucky	22,211	5.8
	Arizona	23,725	5.8
42	Florida	82,963	5.9
43	New Mexico	9,882	5.9
44	Idaho	7,075	6.2
	Alabama	26,116	6.2
46	Indiana	***	6.4
47	Wyoming	3,071	6.5
48	Tennessee	34,167	6.5
49	Oklahoma	21,855	6.7
50	Arkansas	17,458	7.1
51 (highest)	Nevada	13,061	9.0

Source: *Monthy Vital Statistics Report,* Volume 43, No. 13, Centers for Disease Control and Prevention/National Center for Health Statistics.

Time Period	Number of Divorces	Rate per 1,000 Population
April 1996	95,000	4.4
May 1996	103,000	4.6
June 1996	103,000	4.8
July 1996	96,000	4.3
August 1996	101,000	4.5
September 1996	92,000	4.2
October 1996	99,000	4.4
November 1996	94,000	4.3
December 1996	94,000	4.2
January 1996	93,000	4.1
February 1996	87,000	4.2
March 1996	94,000	4.1
April 1997	106,000	4.8

Source: "Births, marriages, divorces and deaths for April 1997." *Monthy Vital Stastics Report,* Volume 46, No. 4. National Center for Health Statistics.

A

R

respondent, 93
reactions to divorce, 277-246
  children, 29–32
  co-workers, 241
  family members, 283–284
  in-laws, 284–286
  married friends, 235
  parents, 32-34
  siblings, 35
real estate, appraisal, 125–126
reasons for divorce, 3
receipts, 54
reconciliation, 339
record keeping
  alimony payments, 47–48
  attorney problems, 305–306
  child support payments, 47–48
  children's activities, 46–48
  domestic violence, 275–276
  expenses, 47–48
  income, 47–48
  pre-planning, 46–48
  visitation, 47
rehabilitative support, 212–214
reimbursement alimony, 214–215
release statements regarding finances, 51
responsibilities of attorney, 64–67
restraining orders, 45–46, 339
  stalkers, 281–282
resolution, 135–156
  arbitration or mediation, 140–141
  court trial, 141–150
  hearings, 148–150
  telephone negotiation, 136
retainer fee for attorney, 72, 339
retirement plans
  401(K) accounts, 178
  in pro se divorce, 60
  QDRO (qualified domestic relations order), 178
role changes after divorce, 234
rule nisi, 335

S

safety issues, 44
savings account, 54
school tuition, agreement planning, 26
school work, grades change with each parent, 47
self-esteem issues, 236, 258–260
sense of loss, 229–230
separation, 11–15, 339
  agreement, 13–14, 339
  child visitation during, 14
  contact during, 15
  insurance during, 14
  legal, 11–15
    finances during, 14
  personal belongings, 14
  preparing for, 14–15
  time limits of, 14
service of papers, 92–93
  ignoring, 96–100
settlement, 372
  discussions, 136
  proposal, 137
  tax protection, 324–325
  written agreement, 150–152
  vs. retribution, 37
sex after divorce, 236–237
shared custody of children, 161
shelters from domestic violence, 274–275
siblings
  announcing divorce, 34–36
  reactions toward spouse, 35
  as support system, 35
sleep pattern changes in your children, 31
social life, 234–236
  activities for the newly divorced, 232–233
  church resources, 250
  new relationships, 236–237
  sex, 237
social security, 178
software kits for do-it-yourself divorce, 59

The *Unofficial Guide*™ Reader Questionnaire

If you would like to express your opinion about divorce or this guide, please complete this questionnaire and mail it to:

The Unofficial Guide™ Reader Questionnaire
Lifestyle Guides
Wiley Publishing, Inc.
111 River Street
Hoboken, NJ 07030

Gender: ___ M ___ F

Age: ___ Under 30 ___ 31–40
___ 41–50 ___ Over 50

Education: ___ High school ___ College
___ Graduate/Professional

What is your occupation?

_____

How did you hear about this guide?
___ Friend or relative
___ Newspaper, magazine, or Internet
___ Radio or TV
___ Recommended at bookstore
___ Recommended by librarian
___ Picked it up on my own
___ Familiar with the *Unofficial Guide*™ travel series

Did you go to the bookstore specifically for a book on divorce? Yes ___ No ___

Have you used any other *Unofficial Guides*™?
Yes ___ No ___

If "Yes," which ones?

_____
_____
_____

What other book(s) on divorce have you purchased?

_____
_____
_____

Was this book:
___ more helpful than other(s)
___ less helpful than other(s)

Do you think this book was worth its price?
Yes ___   No ___

**Did this book cover all topics related divorce
adequately?**   Yes ___   No ___

Please explain your answer:

_____
_____
_____

**Were there any specific sections in this book that
were of particular help to you?**   Yes ___   No ___

Please explain your answer:

_____
_____
_____

**On a scale of 1 to 10, with 10 being the best rating,
how would you rate this guide?** ___

**What other titles would you like to see published in
the _Unofficial Guide_™ series?**

_____
_____
_____

**Are _Unofficial Guides_™ readily available in your
area?**   Yes ___   No ___

Other comments:

_____
_____
_____

Get the inside scoop...
with the *Unofficial Guides*™!

Health and Fitness

The Unofficial Guide to Alternative Medicine
ISBN: 0-02-862526-9

The Unofficial Guide to Coping with Menopause
ISBN: 0-02-862694-X

The Unofficial Guide to Dieting Safely
ISBN: 0-02-862521-8

The Unofficial Guide to Having a Baby
ISBN: 0-02-862695-8

The Unofficial Guide to Living with Diabetes
ISBN: 0-02-862919-1

The Unofficial Guide to Smart Nutrition
ISBN: 0-02-863589-2

The Unofficial Guide to Surviving Breast Cancer
ISBN: 0-02-863491-8

Career Planning

The Unofficial Guide to Acing the Interview
ISBN: 0-02-862924-8

The Unofficial Guide to Earning What You Deserve
ISBN: 0-02-862716-4

The Unofficial Guide to Hiring and Firing People
ISBN: 0-02-862523-4

Business and Personal Finance

The Unofficial Guide to Beating Debt
ISBN: 0-02-863337-7

The Unofficial Guide to Investing
ISBN: 0-02-862458-0

The Unofficial Guide to Investing in Mutual Funds
ISBN: 0-02-862920-5

The Unofficial Guide to Managing Your Personal Finances
ISBN: 0-02-862921-3

The Unofficial Guide to Marketing Your Business Online
ISBN: 0-7645-6268-1

All books in the *Unofficial Guide*™ series are available
at your local bookseller.

About the Author

Sharon Naylor can tell you everything you need to know about divorce. Sharon is the author of *100 Reasons to Keep Him . . . 100 Reasons to Dump Him* (Harmony, 1998); *Create the Wedding of Your Dreams* (CD-ROM Softsource, Inc., 1998); *Learning the Ropes* (Ferguson, 1998); and *1001 Ways to Save Money and Still Have a Dazzling Wedding* (Contemporary Books, 1994). Her articles have appeared in various women's magazines, including *Woman's Day, Brides,* and *Good Housekeeping.* Recently divorced, Sharon describes her decision to work on this project as "making lemonade out of fresh lemons." She lives in East Hanover, New Jersey.